WALES TODAY

WALES TODAY

Edited by David Dunkerley and Andrew Thompson

UNIVERSITY OF WALES PRESS • CARDIFF • 1999

© The Contributors, 1999

British Library Cataloguing-in-Publication Data.
A catalogue record for this book is available from the British Library.

ISBN 0–7083–1544–5 (paperback)
    0–7083–1521–6 (hardback)

Cover illustration: Kevin Atherton, *A Private View*, steel, bronze and optical elements. Installed 1995, Cardiff Bay. Commissioned by South Glamorgan County Council through Cardiff Bay Arts Trust.
Photograph by Patricia Aithie.

Cover design: Jane Parry

Typeset at University of Wales Press
Printed in Great Britain by Dinefwr Press, Llandybïe

Contents

All photographs in this volume are by Charles and Patricia Aithie, except for p. 74 by Glenn Edwards, p. 110 by Brian Tarr and p. 164 by permission of the Llanelli Star.

List of Figures

List of Tables

Foreword

Devolution within the United Kingdom is a journey embarked upon, in earnest, as recently as the early 1990s and leading us all, with increasing rapidity, to a totally unknown destination. Is devolution a mere staging post to the break-up of the UK into autonomous nation states, or to a federal UK? Is it the final end-product in itself? Will it mean radically different things for different parts of the UK?

The fact that these questions can be asked at all reveals the scale and, in a typically British fashion, the international uncertainty that surrounds the constitutional changes that have given rise to the Scottish Parliament and the Assemblies in Wales and Northern Ireland. Despite being of profound importance, these changes are not part of a grand constitutional plan. They are, to a considerable extent, open-ended, a political and constitutional leap into the dark. This is certainly true for the Welsh Assembly itself and its impact on Wales. The Assembly's powers are limited in that it cannot pass primary legislation, or raise taxes, and must therefore operate within a framework that will continue to be determined in Whitehall and Westminster. Yet the Assembly will control the allocation of billions of pounds and will affect deeply most aspects of life for all who live and work in Wales. To what extent and how far for good, or ill, remains a mystery that will only gradually unfold over five years, ten years, a generation.

Faced with such change, many emotions begin to crowd the stage. They range from the pessimistic and sceptical, through hope and elation, to outright utopian fervour. But if opportunities are to be seized and important battles are to be won in the coming years, there is great merit in tempering emotion with solid analysis: analysis of where we are now; of what Wales really looks like as we embark on our new political journey; of the problems to be solved and the tasks to be undertaken. This book is a unique guide and contribution to this process of national stocktaking.

The editors' objective was to gather the best available expertise on a wide range of issues facing Wales and to provide an analytical-descriptive overview of interest not only to A-level and undergraduate students, but also to the many members of the general public for whom policy and politics in Wales have become a newly invigorated topic of discussion and debate. The editors succeeded magnificently in drawing in the most well-informed specialists from a variety of institutions across Wales. They also – the nightmare task of any editor – managed to obtain contributions (even my own) on time. The contributors, as readers will readily recognize, have taken the time and effort needed to translate expert knowledge into accessible, understandable but not overly simplified, 'maps' of the issues, ills, conundrums and opportunities for beneficial change which lie before us.

Perhaps one of the biggest tasks which faces us as we take a much fuller responsibility for the standard of living and quality of life in Wales into our own hands is the absence in Wales of a well developed policy infrastructure. Much as the difficult decisions and final accountability rest with them, wise and effective government never springs unbidden from the minds of politicians. It is the product of lively interaction within a network of well informed 'policy-brokers': politicians and party apparatuses, of course; also civil servants, local government members and officers; but necessarily embracing people and institutions beyond the formal boundaries of the political process, such as universities, academics, think-tanks – even not excluding lobbyists. Vested interests and powerful opinion-formers must inevitably be heeded in any political process, but truly effective government depends on innovative thinking and on constantly challenging dominant ways of defining problems, seeing issues and evaluating proposed solutions.

The policy infrastructure needs to be well developed, to represent a plurality of interests and views of the world, and to extend well beyond – as well as deeply into – the government machine if innovation and challenge are to help shape sound policy. The policy infrastructure also needs to be deeply committed to vigorous evaluation of success and failure if policy is to be a learning, and not merely a visceral, process. Political life in the UK has underplayed the importance of the policy infrastructure throughout the past two decades of 'conviction politics'. And in Wales there has been limited need for good policy analysis in the absence of real political power.

That all of that must – and can – now change is also revealed by this book. Not all of the institutions needed in a good policy infrastructure are present in Wales (we are sadly bereft of think-tanks). We also need rapidly to expand the policy networks linking the Welsh Office, local government, the WDA, universities, business and industry. But that Wales has the people and much of the knowledge needed to make good progress is evidenced by this book.

As the contributors to this book variously demonstrate, the story of our future must begin here – with an understanding of our problems (as well as our strengths) and with a mobilization of the significant talent available to devise and evaluate the policies needed to take Wales forward.

Adrian Webb
Vice-Chancellor, University of Glamorgan

Contributors

David Adamson Associate Head of the School of Humanities and Social Sciences at the University of Glamorgan. He has written on issues of Welsh identity as well as researching patterns of social change in Welsh working-class communities. Recent work has focused specifically on issues of poverty and social exclusion and the development of anti-poverty strategies based on community development methods. He writes on these and related issues for *Contemporary Wales*, *Planet* and the *Western Mail* and is a frequent broadcaster on Welsh social and current affairs.

John Aitchison Gregynog Professor of Geography at the Institute of Geography and Earth Sciences, University of Wales, Aberystwyth. He is also a Director of the International Centre for Protected Landscapes. In addition to numerous studies of language change in Wales, he has written extensively on rural and environmental issues.

Stuart Allan Senior Lecturer in Media and Cultural Studies at the University of the West of England. His publications have been primarily in media sociology, cultural theory and nuclear issues, and include *Theorizing Culture: An Interdisciplinary Critique after Post-modernism* (UCL Press/NYU Press 1995), and *News, Gender and Power* (Routledge, 1998). He is currently writing a book on the news culture, and co-editing one on journalism and environmental risks.

Adrian Barton Lecturer in Criminology in the University of Glamorgan. He has researched into neighbourhood watch schemes, crime prevention and social exclusion, initiatives designed to break the drug/crime cycle and the structure and work of an Area Child Protection Committee.

Steve Blandford Principal Lecturer in Theatre and Media Drama at the University of Glamorgan. He has research interests in British film and television drama and is currently working on an edited collection on recent Welsh film and television together with a new dictionary of film studies. He is a published playwright and commissioned screenwriter. He has directed and performed in numerous theatre productions on the fringes of Edinburgh and elsewhere.

Teri Brewer Principal Lecturer in Anthropology at the University of Glamorgan. She was educated at the University of California and at the University of Chicago. She has undertaken field-work in the United States, England, Wales, Eire and Austria and is currently involved in field-work projects in Wales and in Egypt. She has written on aspects of native Americans, cultural representation, cultural landscape mapping in Wales and edits *The Marketing of Tradition* (Hisarlik).

Harold Carter Professor Emeritus. He held the Gregynog Chair of Human Geography at University of Wales, Aberystwyth until his retirement in 1988. He has published widely on culture and language in Wales, and has written major texts in the field of human geography.

Graham Day Sociologist and head of the School of Sociology and Social Policy at University of Wales, Bangor. He was co-editor of *Contemporary Wales* and has written widely on the sociology of Wales, and on rural and community sociology. He was convenor of the BSA Sociology of Wales Study Group, and has compiled reports on social change in rural Wales for training agencies, for Wales Rural Forum and for the Countryside Council for Wales.

Sara Delamont Reader in Sociology at University of Wales, Cardiff. Her interests are the micro-sociology of education and gender, expressed in her books *Interaction in the Classroom* and *Sex Roles and the School*. She was the first woman to be President of the British Educational Research Association, in 1984.

David Dunkerley Professor of Sociology at the University of Glamorgan. He has written extensively in the area of the sociology of organizations and on employment matters. He is currently working on an ESRC-funded study relating to the changing role of middle managers and an EU-funded comparative project on youth opportunities in south Wales, Marseilles and Lisbon. His most recent book, *The Globalisation Reader* (Athlone, 1999) is co-edited with John Beynon.

Ralph Fevre Professor of Social Research at the University of Wales, Cardiff. His most recently published works include the *Sociology of Labour Markets* (1992) and several studies of the theoretical significance of various aspects of Welsh nationalism. He is perhaps best known within Wales for his study of the effects of industrial restructuring in south Wales in the 1980s, *Wales is Closed* (1989).

Susan Hutson Senior Lecturer in Sociology at the University of Glamorgan. She was previously a Research Fellow at University of Wales, Swansea, where she undertook research into young people and policy issues including homelessness, young people leaving care, housing and support, and sport. She is author, with Mark Liddiard, of *Youth Homelessness: The Social Construction of a Problem* (1994); also of *Supported Housing: The Experience of Young Care Leavers* (1997) and, with David Clapham, *Homelessness: Public Policies and Private Issues* (1999).

R. Merfyn Jones Professor of History and Dean of the Faculty of Arts and Social Sciences at the University of Wales, Bangor. He is currently working on a book, *Wales in the Twentieth Century*, and is the author of the landmark volume on north Wales quarrymen published by University of Wales Press.

Marcus Longley Associate Director of the Welsh Institute for Health and Social Care. Marcus joined the NHS in 1981 as a National Administrative Trainee, and subsequently held a variety of managerial and planning posts in the NHS in England and Wales. Current research interests are the impact of 'substitution' on health care, and the development of the health professions in the future.

Tom O'Malley Senior Lecturer in Media Studies at the University of Glamorgan. He has published widely on media history and policy. His recent publications include the books *Closedown? The BBC and Government Broadcasting Policy 1979–92* (Pluto, 1994) and, co-edited with Michael Bromley, *A Journalism Reader* (Routledge, 1997). He is also co-editor of the journal *Media History*.

Gareth Rees Professor of Education Policy at University of Wales, Cardiff. His interests are in the macro-sociology of industrial and post-industrial Wales with particular reference to labour markets, education and training, and urban-rural contrasts. He is editor of *Poverty: The Facts in Wales* (with T. L. Rees), and the first seven volumes of *Contemporary Wales* (with Graham Day).

Teresa Rees Professor of Labour Market Studies at the School for Policy Studies at the University of Bristol. She is also the Equal Opportunities Commissioner for Wales. She has been a consultant to the European Union on equality issues for many years and is the author of *Women and the Labour Market* (1992, Routledge), co-editor of *Our Sisters' Land: Changing Identities of Women in Wales* (1995, University of Wales Press) and author of *Mainstreaming Equality in the European Union* (1998, Routledge).

David Smith Associate Head of the School of Humanities and Social Sciences at the University of Glamorgan. He has undertaken research into public satisfaction with policing, detective expertise, zero-tolerance policing and community safety in Merthyr Tydfil.

Alys Thomas Lecturer in Comparative Politics in the University of Glamorgan Business School. She has previously held research posts with the Assembly of Welsh Counties and the University of Exeter Institute of Cornish Studies and has published on the subjects of Welsh devolution, the politics of language and the regional dimension in Europe.

Andrew Thompson Principal Lecturer in Sociology at the University of Glamorgan. Graduating with a Ph.D. in Sociology from the University of Wales, Bangor, in 1995, he has since published studies on nationalism, European integration and the mass media. He is the co-editor (with Ralph Fevre) of *Nation, Identity and Social Theory: Perspectives from Wales* (University of Wales Press, 1999).

Morton Warner Director of the Welsh Institute for Health and Social Care and Director of the WHO Collaboration Centre for Health Strategy and Management Development in Europe. He joined the NHS in 1987 and from 1989 to 1995 he was Executive Director of the Welsh Health Planning Forum.

Charlotte Williams Lecturer at the Centre for Applied Community Studies, University of Wales, Bangor. She has been active in anti-racism in Wales for many years and has written widely on this topic. She also has a particular interest in minority issues in Europe. She is of Welsh-Guyanese parentage.

Introduction

DAVID DUNKERLEY and ANDREW THOMPSON

Four principal concerns shaped our considerations as the rationale for *Wales Today*. First, we wanted to highlight the manner in which various processes of change, while evident in other parts of the United Kingdom and elsewhere, nevertheless manifest themselves in Wales in particular ways. As many of the contributions to this volume illustrate, this is the case whether we are considering economic restructuring, government policy or patterns of social change, as in the instance of the position of women or black and ethnic-minority populations in Wales. To this end, then, each of the contributors to *Wales Today* stresses the need to be alert to the particularities of social change in Wales and the importance of being sufficiently flexible in our use of the devices that social scientists employ in explaining these instances of change.

We were, second, also mindful of the need to demonstrate the breadth of social scientific research currently being conducted in Wales and to demonstrate the value of social science research for conceptualizing social change in Wales. *Wales Today* is not unique in fulfilling this brief, but it does serve to act as an update of social science research in Wales. Since the late 1970s a number of stimulating and innovative volumes on social change in Wales have been published (Williams 1978, 1983; Rees and Rees, 1980; Hume and Pryce, 1986). Moreover, since 1987 those interested in understanding contemporary processes of change have been aided by the annual journal *Contemporary Wales*. Introducing the first volume of *Contemporary Wales*, in 1987, Graham Day and Gareth Rees (1987, 1) explained that 'social and economic research has a key role to play in tempering the excesses of some of the wilder images of present-day Wales, thereby facilitating a better informed debate on the problems currently confronting us'. It is our hope that *Wales Today*, by virtue of the range of subjects which it explores, can lend a helping hand in furthering that objective.

This task is, perhaps, of even more importance given the developments that have been witnessed in Wales in recent years. Since September 1997, when the idea of a Welsh National Assembly was transformed from a possiblity into a political reality by the result of the devolution referendum, there has emerged a sense, audible in some quarters, that the National Assembly will serve to remedy the ills that presently affect Wales. Against this backdrop, a third concern for us has been to impress the importance of casting a critical eye over the differing forms of social change in Wales in order that we may be more sensitive to the kinds of intervention and stimulated change that may be necessary in future.

Finally, throughout each of the stages that have seen this volume evolve from initial discussion to the final product, we were concerned to create a text that would act as an accessible and interesting guide to the changing tides of change in contemporary Wales. Each of the contributors, we know, has taken great care to combine the basic ingredients of social science: factual information, theoretical analysis and, of course, a healthy drop of informed cynicism!

In the opening chapter, one of the foremost contemporary commentators on the history of Wales, Merfyn Jones, documents some of the many social changes that have been experienced in Wales in the post-war period. The major conclusion from Jones's survey is that Wales has shared in and experienced social changes common to many other countries, but that in Wales these changes have expressed themselves in a particular form and with some distinctive features. Although optimistic about the direction in which the currents of change are carrying Wales, his discussion is nevertheless laced with some notes of despair as he explores the seismic impact of industrial decline in Wales for workers and the communities which grew up around these industries.

Jones's wide-ranging discussion provides the appropriate historical backdrop for the chapters that follow. In Chapter 2 David Dunkerley examines more closely one of the issues touched on by Jones, namely how social change relates to the population of Wales. In presenting his account of this particular, but central, dimension of social change, Dunkerley surveys changes at both the national and county level. A picture emerges of overall population growth in Wales but with certain areas experiencing decline in recent years. The reasons for such change are largely twofold: inward/outward migration and differences between birth rates and death rates. Dunkerley also examines the social structure of Wales and exposes the very significant differences in deprivation and prosperity to be found in the principality. All of this is discussed through the use of official statistics. The 'coldness' of such a quantitative analysis is overcome by David Adamson's contribution in Chapter 3 where he looks at the specific phenomena of poverty and social exclusion in Wales. He notes the significant rise in the incidence of poverty over the last two decades, with over a quarter of the Welsh population now defined officially as living in poverty compared with less than 10 per cent twenty-five years ago. Global, national and local causes of this poverty are discussed along with the socio-economic consequences of these for family and community structures. The case of the south Wales Valleys is given particular emphasis and through this an explanation of social exclusion is provided that also enables the Welsh experience to be placed in wider European debates.

Ralph Fevre's discussion of processes of economic change in Wales, and his concentration on the labour market in Wales in particular, suggests that the recovery necessary to alleviate the kinds of problems described by Adamson will be difficult to bring about. Fevre broadly evaluates the changes in patterns of employment that have arisen as a consequence of economic restructuring in Wales and assesses the significance of these developments for levels of prosperity in Wales. The focus on inward investment in this discussion highlights an issue that has become the subject of increasing debate in Wales in recent years, most notably with the turmoil that surrounded the LG plant in Newport, and Fevre provides some critical reflections on the social and economic consequences of inward investment. In general, Fevre opposes claims that Wales is experiencing an 'economic miracle' and instead argues that dependency on imported jobs and government subsidies in Wales does not represent a healthy economic foundation.

In Chapter 5 Graham Day continues to shed light on the human consequences of economic change in Wales, although the theme shifts from the emphasis on industrial change to rural social and economic change. One of the founding editors (along with Gareth Rees) of the journal *Contemporary Wales*, and still one of its co-editors, Day has long been a prominent figure in social-scientific debates on Wales and in his contribution to this volume he offers some insights into the changing situation in rural Wales. Day's chapter uses the now classic studies of Welsh rural communities conducted in the 1950s and 1960s as the starting point for his review of the changing nature of rural Wales and its communities, and of the ways in which sociologists, anthropologists and human geographers have interpreted it. Throughout his discussion Day demonstrates the diversity of social and economic life in rural Wales, and points to the varied social experiences of different social groups. As with a number of the other chapters in *Wales Today*, Day's discussion of the evolving meaning of 'rurality' highlights how processes of social and economic change are serving to cast some of the most fundamental aspects of life in Wales.

To this point the chapters have largely been concerned with mapping the broader features of social and economic change in contemporary Wales. In the following chapters, however, the discussion moves to analyses of more particular aspects of change throughout contemporary Wales. In Chapter 6 John Aitchison and Harold Carter explore an issue that has been the subject of increasing public debate over the last thirty years: the changing fortunes of the Welsh language. Aitchison and Carter have spent many years undertaking a detailed analysis of the numbers and distribution of Welsh-speakers and in their contribution they summarize this analysis and examine the position of the language in the traditional Welsh-speaking areas and in the more anglicized areas of north-east and south-east Wales. The debates about numbers and quality of language are also highlighted alongside the increasing status of Welsh in public life.

The matter of the changing status of the Welsh language is also raised by Steve Blandford in the course of his discussion of Welsh film, pop music and theatre. In the past couple of years the role of these art forms has become the focus of growing media attention throughout Britain and, indeed, further abroad in Europe and North America. In his chapter, however, Blandford moves beyond media clichés to explore the extraordinary diversity in the recent history of Welsh theatre, film, television drama and popular music. In doing so, he makes connections across these art forms to consider whether we are witnessing a new-found Welsh cultural confidence. As Blandford argues, there is much to praise in relation to these art forms in Wales, but as he explains this is still very much a 'fragile culture' for which the next decade will be an important test of its foundations.

In Chapter 8 Stuart Allan and Tom O'Malley also draw attention to changes in the media in Wales, although here the emphasis is on developing a sociological analysis of the newspaper press, radio and television. In the course of their discussion they direct attention to each medium's respective historical, economic, political, cultural and technological development. A key question asked by Allan and O'Malley is how the media in Wales contribute to the creation of a public sphere for the articulation of popular discussion, debate and dissent about political issues. With an eye on the current emergence of digital television, Allan and O'Malley also raise some timely questions about the implications of developments in media technologies for public representations of Wales and Welsh identities.

Teri Brewer's discussion of the tourist industry in Chapter 9 provides another perspective on the subject of differing images of Wales, and in doing so adds an interesting commentary on the changing economic landscape of Wales in the late twentieth century. Tourism, as Brewer explains, has been one of the major growth industries in Wales since the 1980s. Brewer argues that the development of a heritage industry associated with tourism has proved very attractive because of the low capital investment in relation to the jobs created and the facilities enhanced. She shows, from a broad range of Welsh examples, that the development of tourism and 'heritage' is actually about more than wealth creation and economic regeneration. Moreover, she argues that the question of regional identity and confidence is central and that new attitudes and opportunities arise from many of the Welsh projects discussed.

Whereas Brewer's discussion reflects on how the history of Wales is currently being commodified in the heritage industry, Susan Hutson's focus in Chapter 10 is the experience of young people coming to terms with life in modern Wales. Indeed, Hutson's discussion of the problems facing many young people is light years removed from the idyllic image of Wales found in tourist brochures. Hutson has spent many years researching this problem in Wales and in her chapter she describes some of the general issues affecting young people such as unemployment, access to benefits and changes in the housing market. This leads her to explore in detail the growing phenomenon of youth homelessness in Wales, showing that this is far from being a feature of the large metropolitan areas of the UK. Her research has shown that young people who are now finding themselves homeless are younger and more likely to find themselves sleeping rough than a decade ago. She examines the peculiarities of youth homelessness in both urban and rural Wales and, revealingly, gives first-hand accounts of young people themselves describing their situation.

In Chapter 11 Matthew Colton directs our attention to another dimension of the experience of younger generations in Wales – the issue of child welfare. The author of a number of key studies of child welfare, he focuses on the implications of the Children Act 1989 for the provision of child welfare in Wales. Informed by recent research, Colton assesses this matter in relation to three areas: family support services; protective services for children at risk of abuse and neglect; and care for children 'looked after' in residential child-care settings. As with Hutson's discussion of youth homelessness in Wales, Colton's discussion draws our attention to some serious problems with regard to the welfare of younger generations in Wales.

Chapter 12 continues this discussion of public-sector service provision, although here the focus is on a broader conceptualization of health and social welfare. Marcus Longley and Morton Warner reveal the extremely varied social determinants of ill health but also argue that the actual policies and services that respond to health problems are themselves varied in Wales. They outline the results of the 1996 Welsh health survey emphasizing medical and social epidemiology. Their discussion of the political responses to 'the health problem' is particularly illuminating and enables an understanding of a specific health strategy for Wales involving the NHS, local authorities and the voluntary and private sectors.

In their account of crime and criminal justice in Wales in Chapter 13, Adrian Barton, Fiona Brookman and David Smith examine another aspect of service provision and assess how this responds to social circumstances in Wales. Barton et al. point out that the criminal justice system in Wales is largely indistinguishable from that of England, but explain that the demands placed upon it within Wales do differ. To this end, they provide a general description of the elements of the criminal justice system such as the police, the Crown Prosecution Service, the courts, prisons and the probation service. They then identify recent patterns of criminal activity in Wales and examine sentencing and policing, comparing these patterns within Wales and with overall UK trends.

Education is another area in which it is conventionally understood that circumstances in Wales are indistinguishable from those in England. In Chapter 14 Gareth Rees and Sara Delamont take this as their starting-point for a discussion of education in Wales, arguing that, while the development of post-war education policies established similar systems in England and Wales, changes in policy since the 1980s have facilitated the creation of a distinctiveness to educational provision in Wales. Rees and Delamont make vivid comparisons of education and educational attainment in Wales with the rest of the UK. Their chapter also summarizes the debate over Welsh-medium schooling and the apparent differential achievements of such schools compared with English-medium schools. Of course, differences in social class, race and gender all contribute here and the chapter identifies the specific contribution (and outcomes) of each.

Questions of education and training also feature strongly in Chapter 15, in which Teresa Rees explores the implications of social change for women in Wales. Pursuing further the idea of change and difference, Rees highlights the significant increase in women's participation in education, training and employment in Wales in recent years. She is specifically concerned with the question of whether in Wales something approaching gender equality is being approached. Her discussion suggests that patterns of gender inequality are not, in fact, disappearing but, rather, are reformulating. This is seen most vividly in the lack of recognition of women's skills in the Welsh labour market (even though women are acquiring more qualifications), in the low wage rates of women workers in Wales and in the relative absence of women in senior decision-making positions.

Rees's chapter adds another contribution to an area which has been the subject of growing interest in Wales in recent years. The same can be said of Charlotte Williams in Chapter 16, although the issue she explores – the position of black and ethnic minorities – has so far been subject to rather less research in Wales. The principal question that Williams poses in her discussion is: 'what is it that is special about Wales in relation to an understanding of "race" and racism?'. In order to answer this question Williams begins by highlighting the spatial distribution of black and ethnic-minority populations in Wales and notes that, in contrast to many other areas of Britain, the majority of black and ethnic-minority populations in Wales have been resident over a number of generations. Cultural diversity, as she explains, has been 'part and parcel' of Welsh society since the nineteenth century. In spite of this situation, Williams argues that racism has nevertheless been a persistent problem in Wales throughout this period, yet there has been a noticeable silence in regard to this matter. In explaining why this is the case Williams suggests that representations of the Welsh as an oppressed people, and as a population with a strong sense of empathy for other oppressed peoples, has led to a complacency about issues of 'race' and racism. Williams concludes her assessment, however, by suggesting that the establishment of the National Assembly may herald a positive change with respect to how issues of 'race' and racism are addressed in Wales.

The reference to the future role of the National Assembly with which Williams ends her discussion is subject to a more systematic consideration by Alys Thomas in Chapter 17, in which she explores the evolving political arena in Wales. Throughout *Wales Today* many of the contributors point to the possible implications of the creation of the National Assembly in 1999. In her chapter Thomas contextualizes these recent developments within a longer, historical process of political change in Wales. Furthermore, she offers insights into the relationship between political change and questions of nation and national identity, arguing that the latter have often proved to be both a source of conflict in Wales and a catalyst for political change. Thomas argues that the National Assembly will change the political arena in Wales quite fundamentally, and will bring an end to discussions about whether or not there is a peculiarly 'Welsh politics'. As Thomas maintains, in future the question will not be '*Is* Wales different?', but rather '*Why* is Wales different?'. Thomas's examination of political institutions, administration and electoral behaviour provides us with some answers to the latter.

As with the chapter by Thomas, Andrew Thompson's discussion considers the implications of recent political developments in Wales, although here the emphasis is on exploring Wales's position within the European Union. 'Wales in Europe' has become the subject of growing discussion since the late 1980s, and it is an issue which will become an increasingly important matter once the National Assembly is operational. Thompson's chapter provides an overview of some of the main issues at stake in these discussions, most notably the mechanisms through which Welsh interests are represented in the EU. The main suggestion of the chapter is that, as the influence of the EU continues to grow, the ability of organizations in Wales to promote Welsh interests across the EU will be crucial for ensuring that the changes we are currently experiencing bring positive outcomes.

We want to take this opportunity of thanking all our contributors for the positive and good-humoured way in which they have responded to our cajoling in the preparation of the book. As Adrian Webb notes in the Foreword, each chapter is written by recognized experts in the particular field whose work is often highly technical and written for a different audience. It is a tribute to them that they have written their respective chapters in such a lively and accessible manner. As always, Penny Byrne has made a significant contribution and for that we are grateful. Teresa de Villiers and Cerys Davies critically read almost all early drafts and have had to live with the production of the book; their insights and patience have not gone unrecognized.

References

Day, G. and Rees, G. (1987). 'Editorial', *Contemporary Wales*, 1.

Hume, I. and Pryce, W. T. R. (1986). *The Welsh and their Country* (Llandysul: Gomer Press).

Rees, G. and Rees, T. (1980). *Poverty and Social Inequality in Wales* (London: Croom Helm).

Williams, G. (ed.) (1978). *Social and Cultural Change in Contemporary Wales* (London: Routledge & Kegan Paul).

Williams, G. (ed.) (1983). *Crises of Economy and Ideology: Essays on Welsh Society, 1830–1980* (Bangor: Sociology of Wales Study Group).

1   Social Change in Wales since 1945

R. MERFYN JONES

Wales experienced profound social change in the half-century which followed the Second World War. The structure, composition and location of the population shifted in a number of dramatic ways and class and gender relations were transformed. The rate of population growth was modest, rising from 2,598,675 in 1951 to 2,891,500 in 1991, but this rate of growth was nevertheless significant given the fact that the Welsh population had actually decreased during the terrible inter-war depression. In the early decades of the century the massive growth in the Welsh population had taken place on the coalfield but this was no longer the location of growth. The post-war period has witnessed a continuing decline in the old coalfield valleys and a growth along the south Wales coast, the north Wales coast and, interestingly, rural Wales also experienced population growth from the 1970s, reversing a century-long trend of depopulation.[1]

As it grew, the population also aged; at the beginning of the century the Welsh population was markedly younger than it was to be at the end of the century. In 1911 over half the population was twenty-four or under; by 1951 this proportion had declined to 35 per cent and it declined further to 31 per cent in 1991. If the number of young people in the population stabilized over the decades with only a slow rate of decline apparent after 1945, the proportion of older people in the population increased markedly over the same period. In 1951 only 11 per cent of the population was aged over sixty-five; by 1991 that proportion had increased to 17 per cent. The growth in those over seventy-five was even more marked: by 1991 there were twice as many people aged over seventy-five in Wales as there had been in 1961. Almost 10 per cent of women in Wales were over seventy-five. In the popular retirement area of Conwy in north Wales 27 per cent of the population was over sixty-five in 1991. The social repercussions of this ageing population in terms of family structures and welfare and health-care resources were, of course, profound (*DWS* 1954; Williams 1985; Wenger 1988; *DWS* 1996).

One of the reasons for the increasing longevity of the population was the improvement in medical care and health services which characterized the post-war situation in Wales. In the inter-war period Wales had an unenviable reputation for poor health which was exacerbated by the privations of the depression. Tuberculosis, for example, that classic disease of poverty and poor social conditions had come to be identified as a peculiarly Welsh scourge during the early twentieth century and in 1939 it was noted that seven of the Welsh counties had the highest incidence of TB mortality in the whole of England and Wales (Ministry of Health 1939). Aneurin Bevan, the founder of the National Health Service, knew these problems intimately through his acquaintance with the work of the Tredegar Medical Aid Society and, in this context, it is perhaps no accident that Aneurin Bevan and James Griffiths, the two crucial architects of the post-war welfare state, which was to change the social experiences of people in such a far-reaching way, were both Welsh. The establishment of the health service transformed the quality of health care in Wales, but even more profound was the impact of medical innovation and of new drugs. Tuberculosis was finally defeated in Wales through a combination of features – increased affluence, improved environment and health care and the influence of streptomycin which became increasingly available after the war. In the early 1950s there were still over a thousand deaths a year from tuberculosis. By 1961 there were fewer than 300 deaths, and in 1989 the death rate had fallen to under forty. The spread of antibiotics and the availability of x-ray revolutionized the health expectations of people throughout Wales in the post-war years. While Wales continued to suffer from a poor health profile at the close of the century, with a high incidence of heart disease, cancer and respiratory diseases, it is also true that the transformation of medical and health care has touched people's lives in a more profound way than almost any other development. The number of beds available in the health service in Wales declined in the 1980s from 26,000 in 1970 to 17,000 in 1995, but in the same period there was a significant increase in the number of patients treated (*DWS* 1954, 1962; Welsh Office 1995). For a country whose people's lives were so often blighted by disease and injury in the past the improvement in health care has vastly improved the way in which people can live.

The post-war planners of a reconstructed Wales identified housing as a major social problem responsible in part for the poor health of the people and the municipal housing schemes launched in the inter-war period now developed at a remarkable rate. The construction of council housing became a major priority and the aim was to provide housing of good quality with proper indoor toilets, an absence of damp, and provided also with gardens. The coincidence of this local authority housing explosion with the growing availability of new household appliances, such as washing machines and vacuum cleaners, and the growing affluence of the 1950s created a massive shift in the social environment of thousands of people. The giant Penlan estate in Swansea was constructed shortly after the end of the war and this was followed by other massive developments such as the Sandfields estate in Port Talbot. By the 1960s virtually every town and village in Wales had its council houses; 15,500 houses were built in 1953 and the annual rate of construction was to increase in the 1960s. Between 1955 and 1984 Welsh local authorities built 172,000 houses. Designed as the answer to poor housing conditions and the insanitary perils of the old housing stock, the council estates were, at first, remarkably successful and they were popular with potential and actual tenants; the new town of Cwmbran attracted many families from the surrounding valleys and the town quadrupled in size between 1955 and 1966 (DWS 1954, 1996; Riden 1988).

Many of the new estates, however, displayed grievous faults, the greatest of which was the all-too-common isolation of these estates from facilities such as shops and recreational opportunities. Examples of this isolation were to be found throughout Wales, from the mountain-top location of Penrhys in the Rhondda, well away from all the conveniences constructed in the surrounding Rhondda Valleys by a century of development, to small estates like Bro Silyn in the Nantlle Valley in Gwynedd which was located well away from the existing village. As the years progressed there was a further policy failure as the original solid housing proved to be too expensive and cheaper, far less durable houses were constructed instead. By the time of the economic downturn of the early 1980s these shortcomings, allied to the return of mass unemployment, conspired to produce profound social problems in many of the estates. They increasingly came to be perceived as the dwelling places of a new underclass, and the Conservative government not only attempted a futile effort at regeneration through the selling of council houses to their tenants, but effectively also brought the whole business of local authority council building to an end. In 1995 only 176 council houses were built in Wales, a far cry from the days of expansion and hope which characterized the social engineering of the 1950s.

If the reforms of health and housing helped to recast social life in Wales after the Second World War, the major influence was the reconstruction of the economy. The great and corrosive social ill of pre-war Wales had been unemployment. The Labour government elected in 1945 set out to prevent its recurrence through nationalization and state planning, including regional planning. The war had itself removed unemployment; the challenge after the war was to prevent its reappearance and the success of this policy marked the greatest single shift in Welsh social life. For thirty years from the end of the war until the late 1970s the Welsh people lived largely without any real fear of mass unemployment and without the poverty and misery that came in its wake.

The economy faltered in the 1970s and government policy shifted radically away from planning and towards free-market policies with the victory of the Conservative Party in 1979. Industries which had previously relied on state subsidy now found themselves mortally undermined. The closure of the giant Shotton steelworks in Flintshire in 1980 was a harbinger of the devastation that was to unfold. Between 1980 and 1985 the number of un-employed in Wales doubled from 60,000 to 120,000, and although these figures decreased during the late 1980s they remained stub-bornly high and rose again to over 100,000 in 1993 (DWS 1996). A generation was consigned to the dole and the social consequences in many parts of Wales were profoundly destructive as unemployment led inevitably to poverty and all its associated evils. In the late 1990s the situation in Wales appeared to have improved considerably and the unemployment rate fell to equal, or indeed to be lower than, the national average. These statistics, however, disguised a situation in which vast numbers of people had been removed from the unemployment registers to live instead on disability and other benefits. In large parts of Wales which were dependent on disappearing industries such as coal, the level of economic inactivity was deeply disturbing as whole areas appeared to be stuck in a cycle of poverty, deprivation and sickness. This patterning was, of course, regional and these areas of poverty coexisted with other parts of Wales which were booming: a great rift in living standards opened up by the 1990s between prospering north-east Wales and the much poorer areas to the west. But the greatest contrast was that between Cardiff and the M4 corridor on the one hand and the Valleys communities on the other. This was reflected in the huge disparity in GDP: the per capita GDP of South Glamorgan in 1993 was £17,157; a few miles to the north in the old Mid Glamorgan it was stuck at an astonishingly low £10,888 (Adamson 1996; DWS 1996). This divide between prosperous areas and their depressed neighbours became one of the most marked social characteristics of Welsh society in the late twentieth century. And this was a divide which undermined many of the old social categories. The distinction between working class and middle class, so fundamental to Welsh society for much of the century, now became less meaningful as the crucial social distinction came to lie between those in employment and those on benefit, between the workers and the poor (Rosser and Harris 1983).

Without doubt one of the most momentous changes which happened in Wales was the change in the composition of the traditional workforce. Before the Second World War the nature of the economy in Wales determined that there were very low levels of female participation in the labour market, much lower than in some parts of England, such as in Lancashire where there had long been opportunities for women not only in the textile industry but also in secretarial and clerical positions. Such opportunities were scarce in pre-war Wales, and although the war itself markedly increased the participation rate of women the Welsh economy remained very traditional in essence until the 1970s. But then, as the old, male-dominated, industries retreated and disappeared, women rapidly made progress in the labour market. In 1951 as many as 75.5 per cent of adult women in Wales were classified as being 'unoccupied or retired' as opposed to only 13.6 per cent of men. By 1993, however, there were almost as many working women in Wales as there were men. This amounted to a revolution of the most far-reaching significance (DWS 1954, 1996).[2]

It remained true that almost half the women in employment were in part-time jobs, that women's wages continued to be lower than men's and that women's careers were often frustrated by the 'glass ceiling' which prevented promotion, especially, and most shockingly, in the field of education. Nevertheless, the vast expansion in women's employment, allied to other profound social changes which affected women's role in society, led to a transformation in social life of the most fundamental kind (*Western Mail*, 25 September 1997, 29 October 1998). This shift has led to a redefinition of traditional gender roles, roles which lay at the heart of social organization and its most treasured unit – the family.

The changes in gender roles and expectations were rapid, and social attitudes did not always adapt to the new social realities. Many women still had to carry the double burden of paid employment and domestic work as husbands and male partners, basing their expectations on the gender roles of an earlier generation, failed to understand the full consequences of the changes. But even these traditional attitudes were changing rapidly by the end of the century and this gave rise in some quarters to an anxiety about masculinity and male roles. In the old industrial areas in particular men often found themselves out of work while their wives were in employment and this reversal of the traditional roles could lead to confusion and anger.

The changes in the role and status of women were not, of course, restricted to changes in the labour market. They also reflected profound changes in women's ability to control their fertility and the reproductive process. Contraception had existed throughout the century, but birth-control advice was rarely heeded in pre-war Wales and indeed was often actively dismissed and resisted. The Second World War brought some changes in attitude as the war saw heightened sexual activity and a growing readiness to use condoms for health as well as contraceptive reasons. But the condom was essentially the responsibility of the male and women remained vulnerable. The growing availability of the contraceptive pill during the 1960s changed this situation fundamentally. The Abortion Act of 1967 gave women further control over reproduction. These changes had a profound and widespread impact on many aspects of social life. With the threat of pregnancy removed women could not only plan their families around careers and employment but sexual activity and reproduction could be effectively separated. The revolution in attitudes towards sexuality and sex which was established in the 1960s was the consequence of many forces but chief amongst them was the power which effective contraception now gave to women (see Aaron *et al.* 1994).

The debate concerning the value of the family and the dangers to its existence caused growing concern to many social-policy makers and politicians during the 1980s and 1990s.[3] This was a debate which would have been unthinkable in the 1940s and 1950s, when the inviolability of the family appeared unchallenged. Wales has witnessed a profound shift in attitudes towards the family and marriage. This change has affected Britain and the United States much more than other European countries and its impact in Wales has been dramatic. In the 1940s 26 per 1,000 people over the age of fifteen got married every year. By 1993 this rate had been halved and, despite the overall increase in the population, the number of marriages decreased from some 23,000 annually in the 1960s and 1970s to 15,000 in 1994. The changes can be measured even more clearly in the number of what used to be called 'illegitimate' births, children born outside marriage. In 1951 3.8 per cent of total births were in this category, while in 1995 almost 40 per cent of births in Wales were to unmarried partners, one of the highest rates to be found anywhere. These statistics need to be treated with some caution as the great majority registered a father as well as a mother on the birth certificate; a high proportion were therefore likely to be born into settled partnerships even if the parents were not married. There is, however, no avoiding the seriousness of the challenge which this trend posed to traditional marriage and therefore to a fundamental feature of the structure of traditional social life. The growth in divorce further weakened the previously unchallenged position of the nuclear family in society. From the 1980s there were some 10,000 divorces annually in Wales (*DWS* 1954, 1996).

Attitudes towards homosexuality also underwent a significant change in the post-war period. Homosexual activity remained illegal until 1967, but social prejudices were only slowly overcome. It was often assumed that Wales was particularly prejudiced, and there were certainly problems in some rural areas. Nevertheless, the response of the Welsh public and media to the alleged behaviour of Ron Davies in 1998, when polls demonstrated only a minority had reacted negatively to his behaviour, suggested that attitudes in Wales were in fact as open and tolerant as elsewhere, if not more so (BBC Wales poll, October 1998).

These changes in social attitudes and behaviour coincided with a profound change in the influence of religion in Wales. For decades the chapels of Wales were amongst the country's most distinctive and socially significant buildings. Not only did they draw large congregations but they also shaped and influenced social mores and cultural expression. The social influence of the chapels, as regards sabbatarianism, in fact came to outweigh their significance in narrowly religious terms. The chapels had been in retreat since the beginning of the century, but membership figures and congregations stood up remarkably well until the Second World War, particularly in rural areas but also in many industrial centres. The moral authority of the chapels remained powerful even in the 1950s, but the days of their hegemony were gone and the virtual emasculation of Nonconformity as a real social force during the last four decades of the century was one of the most remarkable changes to affect the way in which the Welsh people have lived.

This decline in religion was accompanied by the decline of many other organizations and movements which had shaped society in large areas of Wales. For much of the twentieth century Wales's rural and industrial communities were characterized by a high level of social interaction through voluntary bodies and organizations. Life in the mining communities continued to revolve around the Miners' Institute and Welfare Hall and the Miners' Union, even as the industry declined. Many of the Welfare Halls, previously famous for their high level of cultural and political activity, their debates and libraries and dramas, became little more than drinking clubs and many of the amateur societies and voluntary associations which had previously blossomed within the cultural space they provided withered with them. Wales in the 1940s and 1950s still possessed a highly organized democratic working-class culture blessed with articulate expression (Brennan *et al.* 1954; Francis and Smith 1980). The economic changes which gathered such monumental speed from the 1980s undermined much of this cultural apparatus which had sustained these communities and shaped the way in which their people lived.

In rural Wales other forces also led to the loss of traditional structures. During and after the Second World War rural Wales underwent a transformation as the patterns of agriculture were threatened by new economic forces and by the advent of machinery. The old system of mutual co-operation and the existence of a rural economy which relied as much on barter and 'labour debts' as on any money economy, was swept away in the post-war period as many of the cottages with a small plot of land, so characteristic of much of rural Wales, disappeared. The revolutionary impact of machinery was as profound in Wales as elsewhere. In 1942 there were only 6,710 tractors in the whole of Wales, by 1952 there were 30,240 and in 1957 there were 42,515. As smallholdings became uneconomical they were swallowed up by their neighbours and it became common for a single farmer to manage the land which had previously sustained a dozen or more families. The number of holdings under twenty hectares in Wales was reduced by 35 per cent between 1971 and 1995 (DWS 1954, 1996; Welsh Office 1996).[4]

At the same time as these changes affected agriculture, so another significant process was changing further the structure of rural life: inward migration. For the first time for a century the population of rural Wales started to increase but this increase was not internally generated; it came from outside as urban dwellers, largely from England, moved in, often to inhabit the cottages which became available as the number of holdings declined.[5] By the 1980s there was at least one village in Wales, Rhyd near Penrhyndeu-draeth in Gwynedd, which had witnessed a complete population transfusion. All the original population moved out during the 1960s and 1970s and the village came to consist entirely of holiday cottages and migrants from England. Whole sections of rural Wales witnessed a massive population change, as did the commuter areas of the north-east, close to Merseyside and Manchester, and the north Wales coast, popular with the Lancashire retired. As these migrants moved in they inevitably changed the fabric of rural life and the folk memories and kinship ties which had sustained them.

These processes also deeply affected the distribution of Welsh-speakers in Wales. Until the 1960s a large swathe of western Wales was still an area in which Welsh was spoken by over 80 per cent of the population. By 1991 there were fewer than thirty scattered areas in which over 80 per cent of the population spoke Welsh and Welsh ceased to be the natural living language of any large geo-graphical area in Wales (Aitchison and Carter 1994). Instead, it became increasingly identified with certain networks which were to be found throughout Wales and in increasing numbers in Cardiff and other areas not previously associated with a high level of

Welsh-speaking. Thus the changes which affected Wales over the last three decades of the century profoundly affected some of the most fundamental features of social life, including the language spoken by individuals and the contexts in which that language was employed.

During the last decades of the twentieth century, therefore, there was a remarkable series of social developments which changed industrial and rural communities alike. Many were unsettled and disturbed by these developments while others saw elements of hope and confidence about them. A prime concern was the perceived social dislocation and dysfunctionality which became visible in a number of communities especially in the poorer areas. Far too many parts of Wales were blighted by poverty and its consequences, including poor diets and crime. The number of registered drug addicts rose dramatically during the early 1990s, for example, and acute concern was expressed at the effect of hard-drug use in many communities. This was often associated with a rise in crime of all sorts. Wales had once been portrayed as 'gwlad y menig gwynion', a virtually crime-free area. The situation had never, in fact, been so rosy, but it still remained true that the number of offences committed in Wales in the early twentieth century was remarkably low. There was a rise in the inter-war period and again during the Second World War but the crime rate only began to rise steeply from the 1950s onwards. From then on the crime figures doubled in each decade, and by 1989 there were 6,818 indictable offences per 100,000 of population committed in Wales as compared with a mere 222 in 1911 (Jones 1996). These statistics need to be treated with great caution, and much of the rise is due to the creation of new offences and improved reporting and registering of crimes. Nevertheless, even if these elements are stripped out it is clear that by the 1980s crime was a serious problem in large parts of Wales, and south Wales, in particular, gained an unenviable reputation as a centre of car theft. Other problems were often alcohol-related and it was estimated in 1990 that as many as a third of Welsh men regularly consumed more alcohol than the recommended limit.

If social dislocation was most apparent in areas of poverty and economic decline, there were also elements of social malaise to be discovered in more middle-class areas. The densely structured and organized nature of earlier communities was now replaced by a collapse of neighbourliness and the rise of private living. In many estates of executive housing across Wales the common complaint was that people did not know their own neighbours and that children did not seem to play any more, preferring instead to interact with television and computer screens. An apposite metaphor for this new, atomized, society, the existence of which was in such sharp contrast to the older social solidarities which prevailed in Wales, is digital television which was itself launched in 1998. Whereas previously most people chose from a small number of TV channels, all of which attempted to serve a full menu, they were now confronted by hundreds of different niche channels all catering for different tastes. As television, the most powerful medium and a profound influence in virtually every household, fragmented so did life in many increasingly suburban environments follow the same pattern as networks appropriated the space previously occupied by community. This trend was further confirmed by the immense retailing strength of the supermarket chains which had led, by the 1990s, to the decimation of town shopping centres and to radical change in people's shopping habits.

But if change possessed its negative elements it also contained many positive features. The fragmentation noted above can also be interpreted as a move towards greater choice and cultural diversity. Despite the persistence of racial attacks on individuals, it was clear by the 1990s that Wales was enriched by its ethnic and cultural diversity. The concept of a multicultural Wales had long been resisted in the past, but by the end of the century it was widely acknowledged and valued.

As we have seen, the improvement in social conditions and in health care had led to increasing longevity. The vast growth in the number of restaurants, and the quality of food provided, suggested that prosperity had brought a distinctly enriched lifestyle to many in Wales. Education was a treasured avenue of social mobility in Wales before the Second World War but only a small minority were ever able to get into university: the whole of the University of Wales had only 4,105 students in 1946–7 (DWS 1954). By 1997 there were 54,000 university students in Wales (HEFCW 1998).

As educational and career opportunities widened so did the pattern of leisure activity. Sport, of course, remained a Welsh passion, but there were endless choices available which had never existed previously. Whereas the miners had traditionally enjoyed a fortnight in Porthcawl or Barry Island as their annual holiday, their successors were more likely to fly abroad. There was a massive increase in the number of charter flights leaving Cardiff Airport, from 117,000 in 1971 to 855,000 in 1995, and leisure parks and the attractions of the Welsh National Parks became increasingly popular.

Social change in Wales has, of course, mirrored wider changes in the United Kingdom and further afield – the technological revolution which allowed for tele-cottaging in remote mid-Wales villages and cyber cafés in many a high street brought similar developments on a global scale. There were, however, some Welsh developments which were more emphatically Welsh if only because of the contrast they invoked with the past. The decline of religion was a general British and European phenomenon, for example, but in Wales it carried a particular charge and poignancy as the chapels were demolished. Economic modernization affected all countries, but few experienced the total transformation of their economic base as was witnessed in Wales. Moreover, in few other regions did the number of women in employment rise so dramatically from what had historically been a low base. What is clear at the end of the century is that Welsh society has changed fundamentally and in diverse ways and the pace of that change has been bewilderingly rapid and far-reaching.

Notes

1. This chapter draws heavily on the annual *Digest of Welsh Statistics (DWS)* available since 1954, but it is also informed by more than 300 interviews conducted with people in Wales, 1995–8. For a general discussion of social change in Wales, see Herbert and Jones (1995); Jones (1992); for an earlier analysis, see Williams (1978).
2. In 1993 there were 484,400 males in employment in Wales, of whom 44,900 were part-time workers, while there were 475,100 women in employment, of whom 221,500 were part-time.
3. One of the most high-profile contributions to this debate was made by John Redwood, then Secretary of State for Wales, on the St Mellons estate, Cardiff, in 1993.
4. Traditional Welsh rural societies are also discussed in a number of important community studies. See Owen (1986).
5. The changes in rural Wales are discussed in detail in Cloke *et al.* (1997).

References

Aaron, J., Rees, T., Betts, S. and Vincentelli, M. (eds.) (1994). *Our Sisters' Land: The Changing Identities of Women in Wales* (Cardiff: University of Wales Press).

Adamson, D. L. (1996). *Living on the Edge: Poverty and Deprivation in Wales* (Llandysul: Gomer).

Aitchison, J. and Carter, H. (1994). *A Geography of the Welsh Language, 1961–1991* (Cardiff: University of Wales Press).

Brennan, T., Cooney, E. W. and Pollins, H. (1954). *Social Change in South West Wales* (London: Watts).

Cloke, P., Goodwin, M. and Milbourne, P. (1997). *Rural Wales: Community and Marginalization* (Cardiff: University of Wales Press).

Digest of Welsh Statistics (DWS) (1954–96). Annual publication (London: HMSO; Cardiff: Government Statistical Service from 1964).

Francis, H. and Smith, D. (1980). *The Fed: A History of the South Wales Miners in the Twentieth Century* (London: Lawrence & Wishart).

HEFCW (1998). Annual Report (Cardiff: Higher Education Funding Council for Wales).

Herbert, T. E. and Jones, G. E. (eds.) (1995). *Post-War Wales* (Cardiff: University of Wales Press).

Jones, D. V. (1996). *Crime and Policing in the Twentieth Century: The South Wales Experience* (Cardiff: University of Wales Press).

Jones, R. M. (1992). 'Beyond identity? The reconstruction of the Welsh', *Journal of British Studies* (October), 330–57.

Ministry of Health (1939). *Report of the Committee of Inquiry into the Anti-Tubercular Services in Wales and Monmouthshire* (London: HMSO).

Owen, T. (1986). 'Community studies: an overview', in I. Hume and W. T. R. Pryce (eds.), *The Welsh and their Country* (Llandysul: Gomer).

Riden, P. (1988). *Rebuilding a Valley: A History of Cwmbran Development Corporation* (Cwmbran: Cwmbran Development Corporation).

Rosser, C. and Harris, C. (1983). *The Family and Social Change: A Study of Family and Kinship in a South Wales Town* (London: Routledge & Kegan Paul).

Welsh Office (1995). *Welsh Health Survey* (Cardiff: Welsh Office).

Welsh Office (1996). *A Working Countryside* (London: HMSO).

Wenger, C. (1988). *Help in Old Age* (Bangor: CSPRD).

Williams, G. (ed.) (1978). *Social and Cultural Change in Contemporary Wales* (London: Routledge & Kegan Paul).

2 Social Wales

DAVID DUNKERLEY

Introduction

The traditional view of Wales is that it is divided between north and south and that this division can be perceived in terms of history, industry, 'Welshness' and rural/urban areas. This view recognizes that different areas of Wales differ along a number of dimensions, be they social, economic, cultural or historical. This chapter concentrates on the social dimensions of Wales, particularly aspects of its population and population change and its social composition. The picture that emerges is of a heterogeneous country and one that differs from the rest of the UK in some important respects. It is a picture also of a country of profound social contrast where the north/south divide is not particularly helpful as a description. The picture is one of great social differences between and within counties and even wards. The chapter is largely descriptive and does not seek to suggest solutions to the social problems identified. But this description moves away from the warm popular myths about social Wales through the use of cold statistics and trends. This demystification is obviously important given the aim of providing an objective statement about the demography and social structure of Wales.

Population

Along with the regions of England and the rest of Europe, the population of Wales continues to grow, but the rate of growth (both in Wales and Europe more generally) has diminished progressively during the second half of this century. Furthermore, there are differences in population change within different parts of Wales with some experiencing rather large growth while others have seen a negative growth in their population.

Table 2.1. *Population of Wales* (000s)

	1981	1986	1991	1996
Isle of Anglesey	68.0	69.5	69.3	67.1
Gwynedd	111.9	112.2	116.0	117.8
Conwy	99.0	101.6	108.5	110.6
Denbighshire	86.7	89.3	91.7	92.2
Flintshire	138.6	138.3	142.7	144.9
Wrexham	119.2	120.3	122.9	123.3
Powys	112.2	113.6	120.1	124.4
Ceredigion	61.2	62.6	66.6	69.5
Pembrokeshire	107.4	109.8	113.0	113.6
Carmarthenshire	165.1	164.0	170.5	169.1
Swansea	229.3	228.1	231.6	230.2
Neath Port Talbot	142.7	139.0	139.4	139.5
Bridgend	126.2	128.3	129.4	130.1
Vale of Glamorgan	113.2	117.6	119.2	119.4
Cardiff	286.8	287.8	300.0	315.0
Rhondda Cynon Taff	238.4	233.2	237.4	240.1
Merthyr Tydfil	60.5	58.6	59.9	58.1
Caerphilly	171.8	169.0	171.5	169.1
Blaenau Gwent	75.7	73.5	73.0	73.0
Torfaen	90.7	90.1	91.4	90.5
Monmouthshire	76.5	79.0	80.4	86.8
Newport	132.4	134.0	136.9	136.8
Wales	2813.5	2819.6	2891.5	2921.1

Source: Welsh Office 1998.

In the fifteen-year period covered in Table 2.1 the variations in population growth can be seen – with a very sizeable increase in

Cardiff of 28,000 through to the population decreases in Anglesey, Neath Port Talbot, Merthyr Tydfil, Blaenau Gwent, Torfaen and Caerphilly. The overall figures (the latest available at the time of writing) relate to 1996; modest growth in population is projected to 2006. The gender balance in the principality as a whole was roughly equal – 1,428,100 males and 1,493,000 females. This pattern of slightly more females than males prevails throughout Wales although there are, again, some proportional variations – Cardiff, for example, was populated by 6,000 more women than men.

Population change is dependent upon two principal factors, the greater or fewer number of births over deaths and inward or outward migration. Taking the former and ignoring the latter for the present, there will be an obvious growth in population if births are greater than deaths over a given period. In Wales, as elsewhere in advanced industrial nations, there has been a very substantial drop in mortality over the course of the twentieth century with the effect that the possibility of population replacement has also declined from the position witnessed in the nineteenth century. Nevertheless, even if the short period 1991–1996 is taken, Wales experienced a natural increased change in population of 7,800 made up of 180,300 births and 172,500 deaths. This upward natural change was not a universal characteristic – for example, Carmarthenshire's natural change was minus 2,300 and Conwy's was minus 2,400. On the other hand Cardiff experienced a natural change of plus 5,900 in the same period.

As far as migration is concerned there was a net migration into Wales between 1991 and 1996 of 18,200 people but, again, the pattern is not one of growth everywhere. Thus, Anglesey had a net outward migration of 2,200. Other areas experiencing negative migration were Swansea (1,800), the Vale of Glamorgan (900), Merthyr Tydfil (2,300), Caerphilly (5,000), Blaenau Gwent (600) and Torfaen (2,200). Areas experiencing quite large inward migration included Cardiff (8,800), Monmouthshire (6,300), Conwy (4,600) and Powys (4,900).

Table 2.2 compares Wales with the rest of the UK and with England, Scotland and Northern Ireland in terms of the distribution of the population by age. Two notable features from this table are that Wales has the lowest proportion of sixteen- to forty-four-year-olds in the UK and by far the highest proportion of

Table 2.2. *Resident population by age, 1996 (%)*

	0–4	5–15	16–44	45–59	60–64	65–79	80+	All
UK	6.4	14.2	41.0	18.0	4.7	11.7	4.0	100.0
Wales	6.1	14.5	38.5	18.5	5.1	13.1	4.3	100.0
England	6.4	14.1	41.0	18.0	4.7	11.7	4.1	100.0
Scotland	6.1	13.9	41.8	17.9	5.0	11.6	3.6	100.0
N. Ireland	7.5	17.5	42.1	16.0	4.2	9.9	2.8	100.0

Source: Regional Trends, 33 (1998).

people of pensionable age. The fact that over 17 per cent of the population of Wales is aged sixty-five years and over raises some general issues about an ageing population.

An ageing population is by no means unique to Wales; indeed, it is a feature of all the advanced industrial nations. It has come about for a variety of reasons but the combination of lowered fertility and mortality decline has led to a greater proportion of older people in these societies. As with natural population change this is not something that has happened only in recent years but can be traced back for the best part of this century. Historic events have affected the trend. For example, during the depression of the 1930s fertility rates plummeted; after the Second World War they rose sharply (the so-called 'baby boom') and dropped back again from the 1960s onwards.

One quite dramatic way of demonstrating the way in which the Welsh population is ageing is by looking at the median age. Currently it stands at around thirty-nine, ten years more than fifty years ago. It is interesting to compare this with sub-Saharan Africa where the median age has remained roughly the same (at a mere eighteen years) over the past fifty years (United Nations, 1995, 468).

A further indication of the ageing population is the so-called 'dependency ratio' – that is, the proportion of people of pensionable age as a percentage of the population aged sixteen to sixty-four. Wales, as indicated above, has a low proportion of the economically active age group and a high dependent aged population generating, in turn, a high dependency ratio and one that has almost doubled since 1950. Declining mortality will increase this ratio further in the next century.

The policy implications of such a demographic profile are obvious if more and more people are economically inactive through age. The major problem is that, as the dependency ratio gets greater, so the actual cost of supporting older people increases. The impact on the health service and social services is correspondingly increased. The Green Paper on pensions published in December 1998 is, in part, a response to this problem since the projected increase in retirees over the next twenty years will place an impossible burden on the social security system.

Within Wales there are significant differences relating to longevity. One useful way of looking at this is by taking the 'standardized mortality ratios' (SMRs), the number of actual deaths in each authority in a given period as a percentage of deaths that would have been expected if the local populations had experienced the specific mortality rates in Wales as a whole during the same period. From Table 2.3 it is clear that the SMR differs widely in different Welsh authorities. With a few exceptions, the general pattern is that the SMR is much higher in industrial south Wales and lowest in rural Wales. Thus Merthyr Tydfil (126), Blaenau Gwent (109) and Rhondda Cynon Taff (115) compare very badly with Ceredigion (86), Powys (86) and the Vale of Glamorgan (87). This kind of divide across Wales is explored further below.

Turning now to fertility rates, it has already been indicated that Wales, alongside all European countries, has experienced an overall decline in fertility. This has been at such a rate that fertility is now at a level that makes it impossible to replace the extant population. In other words, if population change were dependent solely on the difference between birth rates and death rates then Wales would experience a decline in its population. A useful measure used by demographers is the total period fertility rate (TPFR) – the average number of children who would be born to a woman if the current pattern of fertility persisted throughout her childbearing years. At the beginning of the twentieth century the TPFR in Wales was just under four children per woman. At this level the population was easily capable of being replaced. Over the last thirty years, however, the TPFR dropped considerably in Wales to 1.82 children per woman in 1996 (well below the figure of around 2.1 needed for population replacement). Although slightly higher than the UK rate of 1.72, within Wales there are again quite considerable differences. At the extremes, Merthyr Tydfil has a TPFR of 2.09

Table 2.3. *Standardized mortality ratios, 1992–1996*

	Males	Females	All
Isle of Anglesey	99	94	97
Gwynedd	95	91	93
Conwy	91	85	88
Denbighshire	93	94	93
Flintshire	98	101	99
Wrexham	102	106	104
Powys	86	86	86
Ceredigion	87	85	86
Pembrokeshire	93	89	92
Carmarthenshire	101	98	100
Swansea	96	99	97
Neath Port Talbot	108	107	108
Bridgend	104	103	103
Vale of Glamorgan	89	85	87
Cardiff	100	96	98
Rhondda Cynon Taff	115	116	115
Merthyr Tydfil	126	129	128
Caerphilly	106	114	109
Blaenau Gwent	117	119	118
Torfaen	107	108	107
Monmouthshire	89	87	88
Newport	100	105	102
Wales	**100**	**100**	**100**

Source: Welsh Office 1998.

whereas Ceredigion's TPFR is 1.50. The divide in Wales suggested in relation to SMRs appears also to exist, with TPFRs in industrial south Wales (other than Cardiff) having rates well above the Welsh average and rural Wales (with the notable exception of the Isle of Anglesey at 2.03) having lower rates than the average for the principality.

The overall decline in fertility rates has been largely caused by two factors – the reduction in the number of women having three or more children and the increase in the number of childless women. Coupled with this has been the trend over the last two decades for women to have their children rather later in life. In Wales, the modal age of childbirth is now twenty-five to twenty-nine (11,530 births in 1996). Indeed, in 1996 there were more births to women in the thirty to thirty-four age group (8,727) than in the twenty to twenty-four age group (7,906).

One phenomenon that has generated much public debate in Wales has been the growth in the number of births occurring outside marriage. The comments of the former Secretary of State, John Redwood, on this during a visit to the St Mellons area of Cardiff are possibly remembered more than most of his activities during his period of office. It is the case that there has been a considerable growth in births outside marriage in Wales, in the UK and throughout Europe. Whether this constitutes the grounds for a moral panic is outside the remit of this chapter. Overall there are proportionately more births outside marriage in Wales (41 per cent) than the rest of the UK (36 per cent). As Table 2.4 shows, there are again considerable variations throughout Wales in the percentages of births outside marriage. In both Merthyr Tydfil and Blaenau Gwent over a half of all births occur outside marriage whereas in Monmouthshire just over a quarter do so.

Using the overall percentage is, however, rather deceptive since it ignores the fact that there has been an increasing trend of couples cohabiting – a feature of a changing family pattern throughout Europe. Cohabiting does not, of course, imply an unstable relationship *per se* but merely a different family pattern from that dominant throughout the twentieth century. This is a relatively new trend, given that in the 1960s marriage had never been so popular. Since the 1970s marriage has, however, lost its popularity regardless of whether children are present or not.

Table 2.4 shows, in fact, that the actual numbers of sole registrations of live births are relatively low. In Wales only 9 per cent of registered births were sole registrations in 1996. The validity of the suggestion of large numbers of feckless single mothers is somewhat diminished by this figure.

Table 2.4. *Live births by mother's marital status* (1996)

	Within marriage	Outside marriage		All	% outside marriage
		Sole registration	Joint registration		
Isle of Anglesey	507	68	224	799	37
Gwynedd	806	101	440	1347	40
Conwy	726	107	388	1221	41
Denbighshire	594	99	339	1032	42
Flintshire	1134	134	485	1753	35
Wrexham	854	132	473	1459	42
Powys	876	76	397	1349	35
Ceredigion	410	35	164	609	33
Pembrokeshire	793	107	387	1287	38
Carmarthenshire	1255	110	549	1914	37
Swansea	1496	247	852	2595	42
Neath Port Talbot	917	154	570	1641	44
Bridgend	967	141	524	1632	41
Vale of Glamorgan	914	133	428	1475	43
Cardiff	2398	477	1159	4034	41
Rhondda Cynon Taff	1508	276	1157	2941	49
Merthyr Tydfil	386	97	315	798	52
Caerphilly	1208	245	760	2213	45
Blaenau Gwent	415	90	367	872	52
Torfaen	680	119	386	1185	38
Monmouthshire	675	51	208	934	28
Newport	1005	216	583	1804	44
Wales	**20524**	**3215**	**11155**	**34894**	**41**

Source: Welsh Office 1998.

Poverty and Prosperity

Social structure can be viewed in a range of ways. Social class remains a key descriptor alongside (and, indeed comprising in part) measures to show the distribution of income, wealth and poverty. In this section the social structure of Wales will be described and analysed using these kinds of indicators and measures.

Until December 1998 when new criteria for the allocation of individuals to particular (and now different) social classes were introduced, the Registrar General's classification of the working-age population into five broad classes was accepted as the benchmark against which individuals and groups could be compared across the country. Essentially, the classification was based upon occupation. Taking the latest figures available at the time of writing, Table 2.5 summarizes the social-class distribution of Wales and enables a comparison to be made with the rest of the UK and with England, Scotland and Northern Ireland.

Table 2.5. *Social class*[a] *of working-age*[b] *population, Spring 1997 (%)*

Social class	Wales	England	Scotland	N. Ireland	UK
(I)	4.4	4.8	4.5	3.0	4.7
(II)	21.9	25.8	23.4	20.7	25.2
(IIIN)	18.1	20.5	19.9	17.7	20.3
(IIIM)	17.5	17.8	18.5	17.3	17.8
(IV)	17.7	14.4	15.1	13.9	14.6
(V)	5.9	4.6	5.3	5.7	4.7
Other[c]	14.6	12.1	13.2	21.6	12.6
Working-age population (000s)	1729	29818	3147	985	35678

Source: Adapted from *Regional Trends*, 33 (1998).

[a] Based on occupation.

[b] Males aged 16–64 and females aged 16–59.

[c] Includes members of the armed forces, those not stating social class, those whose previous occupation was more than eight years ago or those who had never had a job.

Key: (I) professional occupations, (II) managerial and technical occupations, (IIIN) skilled occupations non-manual, (IIIM) skilled occupations manual, (IV) partly skilled occupations, (V) unskilled occupations.

Comparing Wales with the UK as a whole, it is very clear from Table 2.5 that the working-age population is under-represented in the higher social classes and over-represented in the lower social classes.

The greater percentages in partly skilled and unskilled occupations is particularly marked. Although Table 2.5 provides a quick snapshot of the social-class position of working-age population, it is extremely limited in providing any detailed analysis of wealth or deprivation, based, as it is, on occupation. It excludes key material and social variables that might give a better and more comprehensive picture.

A variety of such indicators have been used in various influential studies (see, for example, Carstairs and Morris 1989; Jarman, 1984 and Townsend *et al.* 1988). Following publication of the 1991 Census data more sophisticated analysis of social structure was made possible. Unfortunately, Wales was not included in the major study commissioned by the Department of the Environment to develop a multivariate combined index of deprivation. However, the former South Glamorgan County Council took the bold step of developing an 'Economic and Social Deprivation Indicator' based on the 1991 Census results. The following discussion is based heavily upon this original and innovative study. Although the data were derived in 1991 the patterns of inequality remain valid in the late 1990s. It should also be noted that the analysis was undertaken before local government reorganization in Wales so the former local authority areas are referred to in the analysis.

The South Glamorgan study used both material variables and social variables in its analysis. Obviously, this gives a far more thorough picture than simply taking occupation as above. Five *material* variables were included:

- total unemployment;
- no car;
- public rented housing;
- overcrowding;
- sharing or lacking amenities such as a bathroom or indoor lavatory.

The five *social* variables were:

- limiting long-term illness;
- sixteen/seventeen-year-olds not in full-time education;
- minority ethnic population;
- lone-parent households;
- dependent children in households with no adult in employment.

The two groups of five variables generate two overall indices that show material and social deprivation (or not) respectively; these are also combined to produce a composite index. Using the census data enables these indices to be produced at county, district and district ward levels. For the sake of brevity, only the composite index is discussed in this chapter.

Table 2.6. *Material and social deprivation by county, 1991*

Rank	County	Deprivation score	Population (000s)	Households (000s)
1	Mid Glam.	16.63	534.1	205.6
2	West Glam.	9.26	361.4	143.7
3	Gwent	7.73	442.2	172.9
4	South Glam.	4.39	392.8	156.1
5	Gwynedd	−13.42	235.5	96.1
6	Dyfed	−17.43	343.5	137.4
7	Powys	−20.29	117.5	46.9
8	Clwyd	−20.66	408.1	161.2

Note: In Wales as a whole there were 2,835,100 inhabitants and 1,119,900 households.

It is clear from Table 2.6 that the former Mid Glamorgan had the highest level of deprivation in 1991, indeed much higher than any of the other Welsh former counties. The range of most to least deprived is quite considerable, given the relatively high scores of least deprivation for Clwyd, Powys and Dyfed.

It needs to be recalled, however, that these former counties, by comparison with current local authority arrangements, covered very large geographical areas in the main. It would follow, therefore, that in any one county there was likely to be an enormous range of material and social conditions. This can be seen if the same methodology is applied at district level and ward level.

The districts in Table 2.7 correspond much more closely to the present county structure of Wales. In 1991 the most deprived district in Wales was Merthyr Tydfil, followed by other districts in south Wales (Swansea, Rhondda, Newport and Cynon Valley). Generally, it is the more rural districts that record the least

Table 2.7. *Material and social deprivation: the ten most and least deprived districts, 1991*

	District	Deprivation score	Population	Households
	Most deprived districts			
1	Merthyr Tydfil	18.49	59317	23065
2	Swansea	15.80	181906	72655
3	Rhondda	13.86	78344	30797
4	Newport	13.65	133318	52553
5	Cynon Valley	13.54	65171	25499
6	Rhymney Valley	13.41	103400	38761
7	Blaenau Gwent	11.61	76122	29713
8	Cardiff	10.22	279055	111113
9	Port Talbot	7.33	51023	19920
10	Torfaen	5.28	90527	35529
	Least deprived districts			
1	Monmouth	−23.21	76068	29379
2	Alyn and Deeside	−20.23	73494	27878
3	Glyndwr	−18.84	41870	16424
4	Vale of Glamorgan	−18.80	113725	43565
5	Brecknock	−17.91	41145	16175
6	Delyn	−17.63	67850	25592
7	Colwyn	−16.62	55070	22727
8	Radnor	−16.10	23630	9555
9	Carmarthen	−15.11	55119	21435
10	Montgomeryshire	−14.84	52692	20722

deprivation. As with the county distribution observed in Table 2.6, the extremes between the most and least deprived districts is very considerable with the deprivation scores varying from 18.49 to minus 23.21. The districts closest to the Welsh average of zero were Rhuddlan in Clwyd and Islwyn in Gwent.

When the deprivation scores are used at ward level a different pattern again appears. In 1991 the most deprived ward in Wales was Pillgwenlly in Newport with a score of 22.25. Three Cardiff wards were the next deprived – Ely (21.90), Adamsdown (20.96) and Butetown (19.82). Others in the ten most deprived wards in Wales were Townhill in Swansea, Tylorstown in Rhondda (which, incidentally had the highest material deprivation score in Wales in

1991), Gurnos in Merthyr Tydfil, Splott and Riverside in Cardiff and Penderry in Swansea.

Rhiwbina in Cardiff was clearly the least deprived ward in Wales with a deprivation score of minus 20.40. Interestingly, the ten least deprived wards were to be found in south-east Wales. In rank order they were Cowbridge (Vale of Glamorgan), Cyncoed (Cardiff), Dinas Powys (Vale of Glamorgan), Caerleon (Newport), Radyr and St Fagans (Cardiff), Magor with Undy (Monmouth), Llantwit Fardre (Taff Ely), Creigiau (Taff Ely) and Ton-teg (Taff Ely).

One further interesting comparison that can be made across Wales is by looking at the distribution of deprived wards. As the SGCC Report states,

> Cardiff (10) has the largest representation by district in the fifty most deprived wards followed by Newport with six. Four are Swansea wards, whilst Cynon Valley, Ogwr, Rhondda, Rhymney Valley, Taff Ely and Wrexham Maelor each have three wards in the top group. (SGCC 1991, 45)

Cardiff presents an interesting case of deprivation extremes in that 40 per cent of its resident population in 1991 were living in the ten of the fifty most deprived wards in Wales and, at the same time, almost 30 per cent of its population were in eight of the fifty least deprived wards in Wales. This can be compared with the neighbouring Vale of Glamorgan where the figures were 5 per cent and 34 per cent respectively. These extremes can be seen in Table 2.8.

Table 2.8. Incidence of extremities of economic and social deprivation

District	Total population (000s)	Population in wards (%)		
		Most deprived	Least deprived	Total (%)
Cardiff	279.1	40.0	29.2	69.2
Newport	133.3	29.9	11.6	41.5
Vale of Glam.	113.7	5.0	34.4	39.4
Swansea	181.9	22.8	12.4	35.2
Taff Ely	95.4	9.1	17.4	26.5
Wrexham Maelor	115.3	6.9	11.3	18.2
Ogwr	132.4	7.9	9.4	17.3
Torfaen	90.5	4.5	6.0	10.5

Taking Wales as a whole, 11.4 per cent of the total population lived in the fifty most deprived wards and 9 per cent lived in the fifty least deprived wards.

An interesting comparison of the different parts of Wales has been undertaken by Morgan and Price (1998) for the Institute of Welsh Affairs as part of the argument for EU Objective 1 funding after 1999. Their paper, entitled *The Other Wales*, sets out to redefine the mental map of Wales. They argue essentially that the traditional perception of a divide between north and south Wales is no longer valid and that in the late 1990s a new east/west divide has become apparent. In fact, the statistical office of the European Commission (EUROSTAT) has accepted this new configuration. On the basis of analysis of a range of socio-economic indicators Morgan and Price suggest that the case of Objective 1 status is strong in north-west Wales, west Wales and in the Valleys. Objective 1 status is awarded to those areas in Europe lagging behind in development, especially with regard to income, employment, the productive system and infrastructure. The key criterion is that a region can be designated Objective 1 where the per capita GDP is less than 75 per cent of the EU average. In recent years Portugal and Ireland, for example, have had Objective 1 status, as has Merseyside in the UK. Considerable financial support follows the awarding of the status, especially in the form of infrastructure projects. The fact that Morgan and Price are able to make out a strong case for the above areas of Wales gives an idea of the extent of deprivation in those areas, many of which have been discussed above. They conclude:

> On the evidence presented for the key indicators of unemployment, economic inactivity, long-term illness, manufacturing employment, earnings and GDP the disparity in economic performance and social conditions between the east and west could not be more unambiguous. (Morgan and Price, 1998, 14)

Conclusion

In the brief space available, this chapter has described the demographic profile of Wales together with a more detailed analysis of the distribution of socio-economic deprivation across the country. What we see is a poor country that is deeply divided, with sharp contrasts between one area and another. And yet Wales is often portrayed in a kind of romantic timeless way as a land of mountains and lakes and beaches, of high culture and innovation. This is certainly the portrayal of Wales by the Welsh Development Agency in its advertisements on long-haul British Airways flights. It is also a view to be seen in Jan Morris's *Wales: Epic Views of a Small Country* (1998). One reviewer (Stephen Moss) writing in the *Guardian* (2 January 1999) asks the question, 'But where is the other Wales, of rundown estates, rising drug use and social dislocation; the Wales that has lost its industrial heart and is unconvinced by talk of its timeless, mystical soul?' This chapter goes some way towards exposing this other Wales.

References

Carstairs, V. and Morris, R. (1989). 'Deprivation, mortality and resource allocation', *Community Medicine*, 11/4, 364–72.

Jarman, B. (1984). 'Under-privileged areas: validation and distribution of scores', *British Medical Journal*, 289, 1587–92.

Morgan, K. and Price, A. (1998). *The Other Wales: The Case for Objective 1 Funding Post 1999* (Cardiff: Institute of Welsh Affairs).

Morris, J. (1998). *Wales: Epic Views of a Small Country* (London: Viking).

Moss, S. (1999). 'Mislaid in Wales', *Guardian* (2 January).

Office for National Statistics (1998). *Regional Trends*, 33 (Newport: ONS).

South Glamorgan County Council (1991). *Economic and Social Deprivation in Wales* (Cardiff: SGCC).

Townsend, P., Philimore, P. and Beattie, A. (1988). *Health and Deprivation: Inequality and the North* (London: Croom Helm).

United Nations (1995). *World Population Prospects: The 1994 Revision* (New York: United Nations).

Welsh Office (1998). *Digest of Welsh Local Area Statistics 1998* (Cardiff: Welsh Office).

3 Poverty and Social Exclusion in Wales Today

DAVID ADAMSON

Introduction

Poverty is no stranger to Welsh society. Images of hunger-marching miners during the Great Depression of the early 1930s have become a symbol of the poverty that has punctuated the modernization process in Wales. However, as elsewhere in Britain and Europe, the emergence of a welfare state in post-war society was believed to have eradicated poverty. Provision of health services, high-quality housing and a greater equality of educational opportunity were believed to have eliminated the primary causes of poverty. Wales, along with the rest of Britain, experienced increases in the standard of living throughout the 1950s and 1960s as the belief that Keynesian economic policy had eradicated the boom and slump of the economic cycle sustained itself until late into the 1960s.

The challenge to this belief emerged as a deepening economic crisis characterized the British economy from the early 1970s onwards. The primary effect of inflation and a collapsing economy was the creation of a high level of unemployment. The ditching of Keynesian strategy by the Conservative government elected in 1979 heralded the political acceptance of a high rate of unemployment as the price to pay for reducing the rate of inflation. This policy shift was acutely felt in Wales where traditional industries, such as steel making and mining, were amongst the first to succumb to the mass redundancies of the early 1980s. The rate of unemployment in Wales increased by 1983 to twice the British average and remained there throughout the 1980s. The 1991 Census revealed pockets of unemployment in the south Wales Valleys as high as 51 per cent of the male population of working age. Against the background of an increasingly poor economic performance poverty once again was evident in Wales.

A major attempt to understand this re-emergence of poverty was in *Poverty and Social Inequality in Wales* (Rees and Rees 1980). This book highlighted emerging levels of deprivation in both urban and rural Wales and began to draw together for the first time the links between different spheres of public provision and poverty. The book dealt with issues such as housing, health and education, and the complex connections between them and the nature of poverty. However, despite academic interest in the emergence of poverty the political climate prevented the creation of a political agenda that accepted the existence of poverty, and sought its eradication. Rather, the politics of the Thatcher government denied the existence of poverty, other than to recognize it as a consequence of the failing of the individual. It did not recognize structural causes of poverty or any link between the collapse of the economic environment in Wales and increases in the measured levels of deprivation. Those levels continued to increase throughout the late 1980s and early 1990s. Concerns expressed by practising professionals in the fields of health, housing and education were largely ignored by all the major political parties. It was possible to write in 1995 that Wales suffered an invisible crisis, a crisis of poverty which was being ignored by all the major institutions, political parties and mainstream society in Wales (Adamson 1996). It was a crisis that had thrown up to a quarter of the population into poverty.

Throughout Europe the period from the 1980s onwards saw the rise of what has been termed 'the new poverty'. In the context of massive economic change characterized by the demise of traditional, heavy manufacturing industry and its replacement by an increased tertiary and service sector, poverty has emerged as a major social problem in all European states. As European economies have responded to changes in the global structure of manufacturing, higher levels of unemployment have become the norm. Additionally, changing working conditions have eroded wage levels and the legal rights of those in work, ensuring that employment is no guarantee against poverty. The 'new poverty' has a number of important characteristics. The first part of this chapter will concern itself with these features and how they suggest that a process of 'social exclusion' has emerged.

Characteristics of Contemporary Poverty

Poverty is conventionally seen as an absence of economic or financial resources experienced by an individual, a family or a community. Early studies were concerned with the analysis of absolute poverty whereby the most basic needs of life such as food, clothing and shelter were unavailable to some populations. Whilst such conditions still prevail in parts of the developing world, poverty studies in modern industrialized nations have concerned themselves with the existence of relative poverty. Relative poverty is defined in comparison to the accepted standards of living prevailing in the society studied. To be relatively poor is to lack the resources to maintain the lifestyle accepted as normal by the wider society. Early poverty studies were concerned with establishing minimal standards of diet and housing. Contemporary studies measure poverty against current lifestyle standards that might include ownership of a warm coat or the ability to take an annual holiday.

The nature of relative poverty or deprivation raises difficulties with its measurement. The numbers experiencing poverty in a society will vary according to the criteria used in defining it. Sociologists use established poverty indices that amalgamate a range of poverty indicators to produce a poverty score (more information on poverty scores is to be found in Chapter 2 by David Dunkerley). This allows comparison between communities and regions. Numerous indices exist, such as the Department of Environment Index used in many government studies or the Breadline Britain Index which has been employed in television programmes on poverty. The most influential in Wales is the Welsh Office Index of Deprivation that is employed to determine important allocations of government and European funds to communities in Wales. This index combines data on unemployment, housing tenure, educational qualifications and benefit dependency. Because each index produces different results it is difficult to arrive at a clear understanding of how many people experience poverty in Wales. The European Union European Threshold of Decency suggests that those whose income is less than half of the national average are in poverty. By this measure approximately 20 per cent of the Welsh population currently are poor.

The multi-dimensional character of contemporary poverty

Studies of this relative deprivation developed throughout the 1970s and 1980s and established considerable evidence for the existence of sections of the population who experience major inequalities in almost every aspect of their lives. Poor people have a higher rate of failure in the education system. This disadvantages them in the labour market and they experience poor wages and precarious employment. Poor people compete unfavourably in housing markets and tend to be housed in social or privately rented accommodation. Poor people also are more prone to illness and poor health. Mortality rates and morbidity rates are significantly higher for people in lower income categories or who are unemployed. Direct causal links exist between poor health and poverty (Townsend and Davidson 1988). In this way modern poverty is seen to have many dimensions which stem initially from the absence of income or financial resources but combine to form a complex web of related conditions.

In this context of multi-dimensional deprivation and the existence of interlocked and interrelated features of a poor lifestyle we can identify the existence of a poverty trap. Two meanings exist for this term. The first refers to a technical situation where those with low incomes or benefit dependency lose benefit entitlement if their income from other sources increases. The loss of benefit is more than the increase in income and a net loss of income results. For example, an individual in low-paid work who receives a small pay rise may lose eligibility to Family Income Support, Housing Benefit and free school meals. The net loss of income will far outweigh the small pay increase.

The second sense of the term 'poverty trap' refers to the way in which the poor become locked in poverty by the considerable disadvantages they suffer in all aspects of their consumption of goods and services. There are many examples, but in Wales the most recent is the introduction of electronic 'tokens' for purchasing basic utilities such as gas, electricity and water. The price paid for the service is considerably more expensive than customers able to complete a banker's standing order for payment. In Wales this practice has lead to considerable concern about poor families 'self-disconnecting' (Drakeford 1995) from the water supply, following compulsory use of such tokens. The problem is exacerbated where no local purchase point is available and customers have to finance a bus or taxi ride to the nearest place of purchase.

The poor are frequently excluded from opening bank accounts and have to pay excessive interest rates for any money they borrow, whether from illegal loan sharks or legal, high-interest traders in clothing tokens or television-meter purchase schemes. Finally, lack of transport often forces poor people to purchase basic foodstuffs at high prices in local stores where fresh produce is not available, thus contributing to the link between poverty, poor diet and disease. These examples demonstrate that the poor experience conditions that exaggerate their basic lack of financial resources and compound the basic effects of poverty.

The spatial organization of poverty

In the early 1980s, as the impact of economic change began to have adverse effects in Britain, there was an emerging concern about growing regional inequalities. Identified initially as a north/south divide the negative effects of economic change and government policy were more evident in regions such as the North East of England where unemployment and poverty were increasing dramatically. In contrast, the South East benefited as the economy moved from heavy manufacturing to industries such as electronics, textiles and a large service sector. Concern was also growing about the effects in the Celtic Fringe countries of the United Kingdom as Scotland, Northern Ireland and Wales became characterized as low-wage economies with high levels of unemployment. Wales did particularly badly as the key industries of steel production and coal mining were badly hit, along with the wider manufacturing sector.

These regional inequalities also masked increasing differences of wealth and income within the region. A process of 'polarization' was emerging across Europe whereby those in secure employment were increasingly financially better off, while those in precarious, low-paid jobs and the unemployed experienced declining standards of living (Gaffikin and Morrisey 1991). Within Wales this polarization was especially marked (Morris and Wilkinson 1995) as rural Wales, the south Wales Valleys and the industrialized region of north Wales faced extreme levels of unemployment. In contrast, the M4 corridor was enjoying an economic renewal as an aggressive inward investment strategy brought overseas investment to the area. Similar gains were evident along the A55 expressway along the north Wales coastal route. However, these new sources of employment were physically remote from the Valleys region or the rural hinterland of the A55 and required skills not possessed by the vast army of labour shed from the traditional industries (Rutherford 1991). The result was a growing internal divide within Wales as the Valleys and rural regions fell increasingly into a spiral of economic decline.

There were further highly localized effects within this emerging pattern of poverty. The 1991 Census revealed considerable disparities between neighbouring communities as local authority housing estates emerged as locations with a specific concentration of poverty indicators (Adamson 1998). The growth in private house ownership in the 1980s and the related policy of selling council houses had ensured that those left in local authority accommodation either occupied the least desirable houses or were those who could not afford to buy their properties. Additionally, housing associations had emerged as primary competitors in the social housing market and their properties were seen as more socially desirable and in better condition than the ageing council house stock. Many of the housing estates built since the war were in hilltop locations, remote from the wider Valleys communities, and lacked basic amenities and transport connections. They had become difficult to let and unpopular with prospective tenants. Consequently, they were increasingly allocated to those with the most urgent housing need, which often correlated with states of extreme poverty. Such locations became associated with benefit-dependent families and a growing population of poorly qualified, long-term unemployed people.

Poverty and Social Exclusion

The existence of local authority housing estates throughout Wales where high levels of unemployment are matched by high levels of lone parenthood has created in the eyes of the wider community locations which are seen as 'dangerous places' (Campbell 1995). They have become associated with high levels of car and property crime, a high incidence of drug abuse and are seen as sites of extreme youth disaffection. Media portrayal of communities such as Penrhys and Ely in south Wales have drawn comparisons with the highly marginalized communities of England's peripheral city estates (Power 1994). In the 1995 Regional Research Programme survey (Adamson and Jones 1996) such locations in the Rhondda and Cynon Valleys were seen by the wider population as sources of a more generalized decline of community values which were promoting practices of criminality and drug abuse. This perception caused a clear stigmatization of such communities, creating practical social divisions between them and the traditional Valleys communities (Adamson 1998).

This suggests that the poor populations in Wales suffer practices of prejudice and stigmatization that shape and structure their dealings with the wider society. The existence of a 'postcode prejudice' prevents such communities from participating in the wider society. This situation is inadequately described by conventional studies of poverty and deprivation and increasingly the term 'social exclusion' is being adopted to explain fully the multi-dimensional experience of contemporary poverty.

Defining social exclusion
Drawing from debates in France which emerged in the 1950s (Silver 1994) the term social exclusion has become the main basis for describing and analysing the key features of the 'new poverty' in Europe. This term is now firmly on the British political agenda with its adoption by the British Labour Party (Levitas 1996). The election of that party in 1997 saw an acceptance by government of the severity of the problem of poverty in British society. In keeping with its European counterparts this government has recognized that resource-based poverty leads to practices and processes of social exclusion whereby those in poverty are prevented from enjoying the benefits of full citizenship. To understand this better it is necessary to look more closely at the concept of social exclusion to provide some definition and to develop a more sociologically useful meaning for the term than is found in contemporary British political debate.

Room highlights the difference between analysing poverty from the perspective of social exclusion and more traditional approaches. His definition is one that draws attention to the relationships the poor have with the wider society rather than their material circumstance.

The notion of poverty is primarily focused on distribution issues: the lack of resources at the disposal of an individual or household. In contrast notions such as social exclusion focus primarily on relational issues; in other words inadequate social participation, lack of social integration and lack of power. (Room 1995, 105)

Room's analysis draws attention to the way individuals are able to behave and participate as citizens in society. Those in disadvantaged positions are excluded from full citizenship. Their poor interaction with and prejudicial treatment in all spheres of social and public life denies them the rights of citizenship. A process of social exclusion can be said to exist where society operates practices of prejudicial treatment on the basis of an individual's poverty. This perspective draws on French political theory (Silver 1994) which sees it as the responsibility of the state to secure social cohesion. Where an individual is not integrated with the wider society this perspective regards it as a failure by the state and not the fault of the individual. This is in considerable contrast to what has become known as the Anglo-Saxon understanding of poverty which consistently blames the poor for creating their own poverty. This was most apparent in the nineteenth-century British Poor Law system and the distinction it made between the eligible and ineligible poor. Whilst the Poor Law has long disappeared, the beliefs which saw poverty as the consequence of individual laziness and personal incapacity remain a strong element of British culture. This was perhaps never more apparent than in the reforms to the welfare and benefits system which Conservative governments initiated in the 1980s and early 1990s.

This long-standing view has also been expressed in a relatively recent explanation of poverty that has seen the term 'underclass' applied to the poor in Britain. Drawing from American experience, writers such as Charles Murray (1989) have suggested that the poor adopt a poor lifestyle from choice. For Murray, members of the underclass prefer to secure a livelihood through crime rather than legitimate work. He claims that they prefer to live outside of marriage with illegitimate children and develop deviant social values in contrast to the dominant values of the wider society. Studies in Britain, including the large-scale ESRC Social Change and Economic Life Initiative, have rejected Murray's portrayal of the poor. Analysis of the social values of the long-term unemployed suggests that there is no lessening in commitment to the work ethic (Gallie 1994). The 1995 Regional Research Programme survey found no change in commitment to finding work even in those who had experienced long-term unemployment and who lived in the most marginalized and socially excluded communities (Adamson and Jones 1996). Recent research (Jones 1999) has demonstrated a continued 'labour force attachment' in young unemployed people from the most marginalized communities in the Rhondda Valley. Consequently, the evidence for the existence of a group of poor people who actively choose to be poor is weak and more structural explanations of poverty are required which link the increase in poverty to changes in the social and economic organization of Welsh society.

The term social exclusion provides us with such an approach and permits the development of a model of poverty which seeks explanation in structural economic shifts and the response of the wider society to those who experience the poverty it creates. Social exclusion allows us to understand fully the real-life consequences of poverty and the way it structures and limits the lives of those who experience it. Unlike poverty, social exclusion is a process rather than a condition and it is one in which the whole society participates to create practices that prevent poor people participating as full members of society. The following section will examine this process in detail and draw on research which records the first-hand experience of social exclusion.

Understanding social exclusion

In 1993 the Regional Research Programme based at the University of Glamorgan began a study of the 'new poverty' in Wales with a specific focus on the experience of the Rhondda Valleys. Employing newly available 1991 Census data the project attempted to assess the extent of polarization between the poor and better-off communities which had been identified in earlier studies of the Census material for Wales (Morris and Wilkinson 1995). Disparities were found to exist within ward areas of south Wales where analysis of the smallest statistical area in the Census, the enumeration district, revealed that polarization was occurring even within generally deprived areas. It was also found that high levels of male unemployment coincided with high levels of lone parenthood. Of the ten wards with the highest level of male unemployment, nine also had the highest level of lone parenthood. Whilst no causal link was established between the two factors it was not difficult to hypothesize that the absence of work was preventing both male and female entry into adulthood through traditional routes of courtship, early marriage and early parenthood.

These data, set against a growing European debate about social exclusion, suggested a useful application of the term to the pattern of poverty in Wales. Site visits to the locations with the highest rates of lone parenthood and unemployment confirmed the physical locations as hilltop local authority estates, suffering from physical and social isolation and a decaying housing stock. Such sites lacked social and public facilities and basic amenities such as shops, surgeries and play areas were absent. Many locations were physically degraded with contamination by rubbish and scrapped cars. Housing voids were boarded and derelict, and subjected to stripping of roofing materials and arson. Unsurprisingly, such estates were perceived as difficult to let and were populated by transient tenants awaiting transfer to better estates or by young people with no housing alternatives. The wider community held deep-seated prejudice against these locations and they were perceived in the wider public eye as the source of crime and social decay that was contaminating the whole of Rhondda culture. The Census data, the physical observation of communities and the survey evidence suggested that four fields of social exclusion exist.

Four fields of social exclusion
1. Material
This field relates to an individual's or a family's economic status and includes factors such as housing tenure, work status, benefit dependency, educational qualification, car ownership and owner-ship of consumer-durable goods. Factors in this field can determine the level of opportunity that exists and the extent to which the individual is able to participate in the labour and housing markets. Unemployment and benefit dependency are the primary triggers of social exclusion. This field closely coincides with conventional analyses of poverty and the use of standardized poverty indicators provides well-tried methods for identifying communities at risk of social exclusion. Communities with high levels of unemployment and benefit dependency, low educational qualification, lack of work training and low car ownership are precarious communities and highly susceptible to developing the compound features of social exclusion.

2. Environmental

This field refers to the physical environment and includes housing quality, housing density, housing cost as proportion of income, transport links, location and its proximity to key services, especially education and health. Many estates in the Valleys demonstrate acute environmental decline as poorly conceived housing and estate design became exacerbated by the collapse of repair and maintenance programmes in the 1980s. Environments became degraded by the failure of statutory bodies to collect waste and control rodent infestation. Lack of play facilities and public green space add to the environmental deprivation and absence of public facilities prevents personal and social investment in the community. The appearance of a community also does much to influence its standing in the eyes of the wider community.

3. Social

This field refers to an individual's overall status set, including marital and parental status, age, disability and incapacity. It will also include analysis of family and neighbourhood relationships such as the extent of contact with siblings and parents, neighbours and the extent of communal support networks. Such factors determine the individual and, ultimately, the communal ability to resist and adapt to negative socio-economic change. Where high levels of community support exist, social exclusion does not necessarily follow from poverty. The estates visited were significantly populated by young people housed away from their home community with its associated social and family networks. These important sources of potential support were often absent for young people allocated housing on isolated estates. Some consequences include the breakdown of transmission of parenting skills between generations and the creation of barriers for the emergence of strong community linkages between households.

4. Relational

This refers to the standing of the individual, family and community in relations with external agents. Residents of estates defined as 'problem' will experience relations characterized by 'labelling' and self-fulfilling prophecy. Merely to give one's address is sufficient to be regarded by key professional and institutional gatekeepers as deviant or difficult. Contacts with doctors, teachers, the police and other public agents are characterized by the operation of stereotypes. Key indicators of a negative perception of a community will include levels of referral to police, education and health authorities and numbers registered on 'at risk' or special-needs registers. At the communal level localities with high prosecution/victimization rates, social-work caseloads and health problems will be defined by professionals as risk areas for all residents. It is this field which most clearly represents the 'relational' aspects identified by Room (1995).

Opportunity to test more closely this model of social exclusion arose in 1998 when the Regional Research Programme was commissioned by a local authority in south Wales to conduct a detailed social-exclusion audit of a highly disadvantaged community. The research strategy centred on deriving the views of the residents of the estate and surrounding area. Discussion groups were created in various age ranges to assess the reality of social exclusion to those who experience it. Three major themes emerged from the group discussions that emphasized the issues of stigmatization by and isolation from the wider community.

The experience of social exclusion
1. Invisibility
Residents of all ages reported a sense of 'invisibility' in their dealings with the wider society. Like many such locations their estate was hidden from the main roads and no signposts pointed to its existence. Residents felt that they were being left to cope unaided with the problems encountered on the estate and they felt abandoned by all agencies with a statutory responsibility for providing services. Residents felt that no one listened when they complained and that any attempt to claim the rights enjoyed by the wider community were interpreted as 'them being difficult'. Residents felt that they were being ignored and forgotten by the agencies which should have carried responsibility for the estate and its environment.

2. Stigma
The sense of stigma attached to the community was overwhelming. Residents were acutely conscious of the reputation suffered by the community and were highly articulate about its effects on their relations with a range of public and commercial agencies. All age

groups reported their own practice of not declaring exactly where they lived. For older people this stemmed from a sense of shame. For younger people it was because of the trouble it often invited both from agencies like the police and from their peers from other villages who often reacted violently. Local media were felt to exacerbate the problem of stigma with their coverage of offenders from the community. This was felt to give an unfair impression of the majority of honest individuals and families who lived on the estate. In interviews with local professionals references to drug use were common and an imagery of a highly deviant community appeared well established within the surrounding area. Young people were convinced that they had been rejected for job opportunities because of their place of residence.

3. Exclusion from services

Even a rapid survey of the physical environment of the estate revealed an acutely neglected community. Housing voids were boarded and derelict with gaping roofs and rubbish-strewn gardens. No telephone or post box was provided and the bus service was virtually non-existent. Residents reported acute difficulties in accessing a wide range of services taken for granted in less deprived and isolated communities. There were no leisure facilities and, outside of the local community development initiative, there were no facilities of any kind for either adults or children. Two crucial areas of service provision presented extreme difficulties for residents. First, health facilities were very difficult to access. GP practices were difficult to reach by public transport and necessitated physically demanding walks. Local hospitals provided only limited services and the nearest general hospital was nearly twenty miles away with few public transport links. Residents with young children were particularly concerned about accessing casualty and emergency services. Secondly, the local authority was seen as very remote from the needs of the residents. The housing department had a local office but relations between staff and residents had almost completely broken down. The repair service on the estate was seen as ineffective and residents blamed allocation policy for introducing drug users and criminals to the estate. Basic public health provision on the estate was absent with accumulations of rubbish and numerous reports of rodent infestation.

Conclusion

The conditions identified by the study described above are typical of those experienced by many socially excluded communities throughout Wales. Whilst the problems are associated with the urban areas of the south Wales Valleys, problems are equally evident in rural Wales. The multi-dimensional and spatial characteristics of poverty described earlier require us to move beyond an understanding simply of the financial characteristics of poverty to a fuller understanding of the pattern of relations which poor people and communities experience with the wider society. The existence of stigma and social exclusion suggests that society is actively prejudiced against the poor. Many of the problems which poor people experience are either caused by or exacerbated by their relationship with the wider community. This process of social exclusion is central to understanding contemporary poverty. It creates a demand that social policies are developed which break the cycle of poverty, stigma and social exclusion that currently exists. Policies that provide training, social and community facilities, improve the environment of deprived locations and reduce crime and disaffection are particularly valuable.

The government is now recognizing this need in England with its Social Exclusion Unit and in Wales with the 'People in Communities' Programme initiated by the Welsh Office. The poor communities in Wales were not always poor. As recently as twenty years ago they enjoyed higher levels of employment, greater stability and higher levels of community cohesion. The residents of such communities have not chosen to lose that, rather it has been imposed by complex economic and social processes that are beyond their control. It is necessary for the wider society to recognize this and fund programmes that combat the social exclusion that now exists. This process has begun as communities themselves develop grass-roots action programmes (Adamson 1997) which are tackling the deep-seated problems they face. This in itself challenges the negative stereotypes held by the wider society as highly marginalized communities develop innovative and progressive social activities to turn their communities into desirable places to live.

References

Adamson, D. (1998). 'The spatial organization of difference and exclusion in a working class community', in K. C. Mep (ed.), *Full Employment: A European Appeal* (London: Spokesman, for the Bertrand Russell Peace Foundation), 64, 141–52.

Adamson, D. L. (1996). *Living on the Edge: Poverty and Deprivation in Wales* (Llandysul: Gomer).

Adamson, D. L. (1997). *Social and Economic Development in Wales: The Role of Community Development* (Merthyr Tydfil: Community Enterprise Wales).

Adamson, D. L. and Jones, S. (1996). *The South Wales Valleys: Continuity and Change* (Pontypridd: Regional Research Programme, University of Glamorgan).

Campbell, B. (1995). *Goliath: Inside Britain's Dangerous Places* (London: Methuen).

Drakeford, M. (1995). *Token Gesture: A Report on the Use of Token Meters by the Gas, Electricity and Water Companies* (Cardiff: University of Wales, Cardiff).

Gaffikin, G. and Morrisey, D. (1991). *The New Unemployed* (London: Zed Books).

Gallie, D. (1994). 'Are the unemployed an underclass? Some evidence from the Social Change and Economic Life Initiative', *Sociology*, 28/3, 737–57.

Jones, S. R. (1999). 'Breakdown of the work ethic? An analysis of labour force attachment in a marginalised community', unpublished M.Phil. thesis (Pontypridd: University of Glamorgan).

Levitas, R. (1996). 'The concept of social exclusion and the new Durkheimian hegemony', *Critical Social Policy*, 16, 5–20.

Morris, J. and Wilkinson, B. (1995). 'Poverty and prosperity in Wales: polarization and Los Angelesization', *Contemporary Wales*, 8, 29–45.

Murray, C. (1989). 'Underclass', *Sunday Times* (London).

Power, A. (1994). *Area-Based Poverty, Social Problems and Resident Empowerment* (London: Welfare State Programme Suntory-Toyota International Centre for Economics and Related Disciplines, London School of Economics).

Rees, G. and Rees, T. L. (eds.). (1980). *Poverty and Social Inequality in Wales* (London: Croom Helm).

Room, G. (1995). 'Poverty in Europe: competing paradigms of analysis', *Policy and Politics*, 23/2, 103–13.

Rutherford, T. (1991). 'Industrial restructuring, local labour markets and social change: the transformation of south Wales', *Contemporary Wales* 4, 9–44.

Silver, H. (1994). 'Social exclusion and social solidarity: three paradigms', *International Labour Review*, 133/5–6, 531–78.

Townsend, P. and Davidson, N. (eds.) (1988). *Inequalities in Health: The Black Report and the Health Divide* (London: Penguin).

4   The Welsh Economy

RALPH FEVRE

Introduction

Throughout the twentieth century the Welsh economy has struggled to create enough jobs and to match the rate of economic growth elsewhere in the United Kingdom (Morgan 1981; Fevre 1989). In order to make up the shortfall in jobs, and growth Wales depends on companies from outside Wales and on government intervention. This dependence on outside companies means that Wales does not always get the best *type* of jobs, and dependence on government intervention means that the Welsh economy is subsidized. Wales receives a proportionately greater share of taxpayers' money than England, or the UK as a whole, but less than Scotland or Northern Ireland (Blackaby *et al.* 1996, 223; Drinkwater 1998, 225; Lovering 1999a, 33). Much of this money goes in social security benefits to the people for whom the Welsh economy has been unable to create jobs. These benefits account for twice the proportion of personal incomes in Wales that they do in the South East of England and over 40 per cent of public spending in Wales goes in social security[1] (Lovering 1999a, 32–5). The first half of this chapter will describe the sorts of jobs created in Wales's dependent economy and in the second half we will look at the effects of all this on Welsh prosperity.

The Private Sector

Wales is not very good at growing successful companies from small beginnings and in the 1990s the rate of company *failure* in Wales exceeded the rate elsewhere in the UK. If smaller firms accounted for a greater share of employment than they used to, this was because larger firms were shrinking and not because there was a dynamic small-firm sector (Lovering 1999a, 19). There are a handful of home-grown success stories, of which the best-known are all retail enterprises which sell at the cheaper end of the markets for groceries or apparel (Guy 1995, 174). For the most part successful Welsh companies do not create jobs which demand highly skilled workers and pay high wages but, as we will see, nor do most of the companies that move into Wales from elsewhere. Some of the better new jobs have been brought in by *foreign* companies but most of the new jobs created between 1985/6 and 1995/6 came when companies based elsewhere in the UK opened new branches in Wales[2] (Atkinson 1997, 6).

Agriculture

At the time of writing Welsh agriculture is in considerable difficulty. Of farm revenue 90 per cent is earned from rearing cattle and sheep and from milk production (there is long-term potential for the development of forestry but this sector employs few people – Blackaby *et al.* 1996, 281). Even before crises such as the ban on British beef sales on the continent, these activities, like other Welsh industries discussed below, were dependent on subsidies (Midmore *et al.* 1994; Blackaby *et al.* 1996, 275). They generally take the form of small-scale, low-productivity production and farm incomes have been suffering for some time (Blackaby *et al.* 1996, 277–8). Yet agriculture is much more important in terms of employment to Wales than any other region except Northern Ireland (Blackaby *et al.* 1996, 277–8). Employment in farming may have been declining for decades but total employment in agriculture, forestry and fishing still stands at 7.3 per cent of all employment in Wales – there are 36,000 farmer-proprietors and 12,000 non-whole-time farm workers – and a quarter of all Welsh firms are in agriculture (Lovering 1996, 8–9; Blackaby *et al.* 1996, 231–2).

Manufacturing

Wales lost proportionately more manufacturing jobs than any other part of the UK in the 1979–83 recession but after that time manufacturing employment (and output) grew more quickly in Wales than elsewhere (Blackaby *et al.* 1996, 221). In fact, between

1986 and 1996 Welsh manufacturing employment grew by 6 per cent whereas in the UK it fell by 16 per cent (Atkinson 1997, 9). Because of the job losses in the early 1980s this expansion of manufacturing was needed in order to get manufacturing employment in Wales back to the same sort of level that it was elsewhere in the UK (Blackaby *et al.* 1996, 237). So, by 1995, Wales had 5.0 per cent of the UK population but 5.7 per cent of UK manufacturing employment (*Welsh Economic Review* 1997).

Manufacturing provides jobs for 30 per cent of men and 12 per cent of women in Wales (Lovering 1999a, 51n). Some of these jobs require skilled workers and pay high wages, but many of the better jobs are actually in the automotive and electronics sectors which expanded rapidly in Wales *before* the recession which began in 1979 and grew much more slowly thereafter, or even declined (Drinkwater 1998, 226; Lovering 1999a, 18). Jobs were also gained in the office machinery and data processing sector in the 1980s, but half the job increase here was wiped out in the early 1990s (Lovering 1999a, 18).

Wales has a problem attracting, and keeping, the *right sort* of jobs. It has had most success (in the 1980s, for example) in attracting the wrong sort of jobs, namely jobs with employers who are attracted to Wales by low labour costs (Blackaby *et al.* 1996, 266). Firms which come to Wales to take advantage of low labour costs are unlikely to be at the leading edge of their industry or even in the sort of sector that prizes skills and innovation. This is why firms in Wales spend so little on research and development (R&D). Spending on R&D per head as a proportion of output in Wales averaged a third of the UK ratio in the first half of the 1990s (Blackaby *et al.* 1996, 229; Lovering 1996, 12). Wales also has too few professional managers and scientists and too many manual workers (and too many of these are in repetitive assembly and construction – Blackaby *et al.* 1996, 243). Although the numbers of professional engineers, scientists and technologists have grown (Morgan and Price 1996, 95), these sorts of jobs are still less common in Wales than they are elsewhere in the UK (Blackaby *et al.* 1996, 243), even within the same industry (see Lovering 1996, 12, on electronics).

For the most part manufacturing firms do not relocate their headquarters or research and innovation departments to Wales. Instead they move routine assembly operations here. Often the

Welsh operation is only a part of the process the firm controls and important decisions are made elsewhere (Brand *et al.* 1998, 52). This does not mean, however, that investment in manufacturing in Wales is low:

> In 1994 manufacturing productivity in Wales (gross value added per employee) was 3.9 per cent above the UK figure and was the fourth highest region in the whole of the UK. This higher level of productivity can be attributed to the higher levels of investment recorded in Wales throughout the 1980s and 1990s. Manufacturing investment per employee in Wales in 1992, for example, was over 25 per cent higher than the UK average. One of the consequences of this is that the growth rate of the Welsh economy has been consistently above that of the rest of the UK for most of the last decade. (Morgan and Price 1996, 95)

In fact, much of this high level of investment occurred either in the two large steel works in south Wales or in the plants of foreign-owned companies which have invested in Wales and it is these employers who are responsible for improvements in the productivity and profitability of Welsh manufacturing (Blackaby *et al.* 1996, 222).

Foreign direct investment

Foreign-owned companies have been responsible for many of the better jobs created in Wales and foreign direct investment (or FDI) has generally been the success story of Welsh manufacturing. This success, however, simply underlines the failure of the Welsh economy to create enough jobs without outside intervention. FDI does not alter the fact that Wales has a dependent economy, because the economic growth which allowed jobs to be created originally occurred in foreign companies outside Wales. Moreover, most FDI has depended on foreign companies being induced with government subsidies to bring jobs to Wales. For many commentators FDI is itself a sign of weakness and dependence. The fact that Wales gets more than its fair share of FDI within the UK (see below) may not be a good sign. Whereas the UK as whole has been getting more than its fair share of FDI within Europe, UK companies actually invest more overseas than foreign companies do in the UK and this is very far from being the case in Wales, which is a net importer of investment (Atkinson 1997, 6).

European countries have been particularly successful in attracting FDI (Atkinson 1997, 6) because companies need to

> get round trade barriers, mainly of a non-tariff variety, that are erected round the European Union. These barriers are aimed at restricting direct imports in order to protect domestic industries and domestic jobs. Thus multinational firms are forced to produce their goods within the Union rather than produce them elsewhere and export them to Europe. But there are many regions within Europe that would like this kind of investment, not least relatively low-income countries like Greece, Portugal and Spain. Governments are thus engaged in a competitive game of throwing money at would-be investors while simultaneously trying to convince them that their costs of production are lower than everyone else's. (Mainwaring 1996, 20)

From 1993 various restrictions were put on the size of financial packages that could be used to attract companies to Wales but investors could still get the taxpayer to pay for 40 per cent of their initial capital outlay. Between 1993 and 1996 the level of financial help given in Wales was second only to Scotland and far in excess of anything given to any English region (Gripaios 1998, 45).

The Welsh proportion of all UK FDI *projects* peaked in 1991/2 at over 20 per cent, but the Welsh proportion of all jobs created by FDI continued to increase (Atkinson 1997, 6; Blackaby *et al.* 1996, 229). In 1995–6 there was an increase of 8.4 per cent in the number of manufacturing workers employed in foreign-owned factories and 1996 was a record year with 15,000 jobs created by FDI (Blackaby *et al.* 1996; Drinkwater 1998, 228). Almost all of these jobs were created in a location which qualified for government subsidy and which was near a motorway (Blackaby *et al.* 1996, 227). In the mid-1990s the greatest concentration of workers in overseas-owned plants was in Rhondda Cynon Taff and Bridgend, each with over 7,000 jobs (Drinkwater 1998, 242).

In 1983 FDI was responsible for 17 per cent of manufacturing jobs in Wales. By the mid-1990s over a third of the people who worked in manufacturing plants which opened in Wales 1966–92, and were still in operation, were employed by foreign-owned firms (Blackaby *et al.* 1996, 222). Many of these jobs had been created when an existing project was expanded[3] (Atkinson 1997, 6) but some commentators are sceptical about recent claims for high growth rates in FDI jobs. According to Lovering, most 'new' FDI jobs created between 1985 and 1994 were actually existing jobs which were moved under the heading of FDI when a foreign-owned company took over a British one. At the same time FDI projects got rid of 18,000 jobs through divestment, closure or contraction, leaving a net gain between 1985 and 1994 of about 4,000 jobs (Lovering 1997, 14–15; 1999a, 5). All the same, it may well be that employment in Welsh manufacturing would have actually declined without FDI (Morgan 1997).

According to the *Welsh Economic Review* (1997) over 40 per cent of foreign manufacturing employment in Wales is in US-owned companies, 27 per cent in European-owned companies and just over 20 per cent in Japanese-owned companies (also see Munday and Peel 1998, 54–5). Blackaby *et al.* (1996, 229) also note that

> The vast bulk of recent inward investment has come from the USA, followed some way behind by Japan and Germany. In the financial year 1994–5, 55 per cent of inward investment into Wales came from North America, 25 per cent from the Far East and 5 per cent from Europe.

Over 50 per cent of the employment generated in foreign-owned manufacturing plants is in the following sectors: electrical, electronic engineering, motor component manufacturing and chemicals. While these sectors usually contain high-paying jobs,

> More recent evidence indicates that the new jobs created by overseas firms have far lower wages attached to them compared with the more traditional employment which they replaced. For example, a worker in a new overseas electronics plant could now expect to earn £173 a week, whereas a coalminer would typically have earned around £330 and a steelworker £314 a week. However, without overseas assistance these jobs might not have been replaced at all. It is argued that one of the main reasons why foreign firms have decided to locate in Wales is because labour costs are lower than in competing regions, as well as their own countries. For instance, a typical weekly wage for an electronics worker in South Korea is £211. (Drinkwater 1997, 187)

The fact that newer FDI jobs are in lower paying industries also explains why US firms in Wales pay much better wages than

Japanese firms (Munday and Peel 1998, 61). When such 'industry effects' are controlled, differences in average pay between foreign-owned firms and the rest disappear and indeed foreign-owned firms paid higher wage increases during the 1989–92 downturn (Munday and Peel 1998, 62).

If FDI jobs are not as good as the ones that used to be available in the coal and steel industries, they are generally better than the jobs still available in non-FDI manufacturing in Wales. By 1992 the foreign-owned sector was paying significantly more, presumably because they hired more skilled workers (Munday and Peel 1998, 62). Nevertheless, as with non-FDI inward investment, FDI usually brings routine production jobs and no R&D facilities (Mainwaring 1996, 20; Roberts 1994). Although they may bring more R&D jobs to England, very few FDI firms bring R&D jobs to Wales which tends to get the production plants and not the national or international service centres set up by foreign-owned companies (Morris *et al.* 1993; Gripaios 1998, 40).

In 1996 a Mori survey showed that the forthcoming investment by the Korean company LG – which benefited from grants amounting to somewhere between £30,000 and £55,000 per promised job – had turned South East Wales into the best place in Britain to find work. The subsequent Asian financial crisis changed all this and raised anxieties about the security of all FDI employment in Wales. The pointers from previous studies are mixed, according to Munday and Peel (1998), who think foreign-owned firms in Wales did better in terms of employment during the UK recession of 1989–92: they reduced employment but not nearly as much as home-grown firms. Moreover, 'mean labour productivity levels were higher in the foreign-owned firms in both 1989 and 1992 and also grew faster over this period', their sales revenue was better, and their profits suffered less – starting off behind home-grown firms and finishing level (Munday and Peel, 1998, 72; but see Brand *et al.* 1998). It is, however, doubtful whether any of this helps us to predict how foreign-owned firms will react to a crisis *outside* the UK (Munday and Peel 1998, 50).

The service sector

The private service sector provides jobs for 34 per cent of men and 37 per cent of women in Wales (Lovering 1999a, 51n). Service-sector jobs as a proportion of Welsh employment grew from 58 per cent in 1980 to just under 70 per cent in 1995 (Brand *et al.* 1998, 49) and between 1985 and 1995 most new jobs were created by the service sector, with much the biggest contribution coming from banking, insurance and finance (Lovering 1996, 10). There were some signs that service-sector growth had slowed in the mid-1990s (Drinkwater 1998, 226), but the real problem was that the new service-sector jobs that were being created were of the wrong type (*Welsh Economic Review* 1997).

Far too many Welsh service-sector firms are in businesses like catering[4] and not enough in finance and other services, meaning that Wales has been strong in sectors which are declining and missing out (in comparison to the rest of the UK) where expansion has occurred (Blackaby *et al.* 1996, 231–2). Even where Wales has acquired jobs in financial services, for example, they are the poorer-quality jobs in the sector. Typically, Wales gains direct-line insurance brokers and financial product telesales workers but loses regional bank headquarters (Gripaios 1998, 43–4; also see Brand *et al.* 1998) while the higher-paying service-sector non-manual jobs are created on the other side of the Severn (Gripaios 1998):

> Wales has, compared to the UK average, an economy dominated by relatively slow growth sectors, and remains under-specialised in the fastest growing sectors of the UK economy . . . A Welsh economy more orientated towards Financial Services *of an average UK quality*, would . . . have grown significantly faster. (Brand *et al.* 1998, 51)

In 1989 9 per cent of total Welsh employment was accounted for by tourism, but a lot of the businesses in this sector were not very profitable. Nearly half of the 21,000 non-agricultural businesses in rural Wales are in tourism or related sectors but, as with agriculture, the small scale of many Welsh enterprises appears to be a problem. In rural Wales the future development of tourism is thought to be valuable mainly because of the contribution it will make to farm incomes (Blackaby *et al.* 1996, 283).

All the problems with the manufacturing sector in Wales seem to reappear when we consider private services. Where manufacturing has too much routine assembly, services has call centres: 'The current drive to attracting call centres is an example of the problem, in seeking to attract a narrow functional activity whose long term employment prospects are poor because of technological changes' (Brand *et al.* 1998, 52). In general, the service-sector jobs that Wales gets are not the most productive, or well paid. As Lovering (1999a, 32) explains, 'earnings in the private-sector dominated Finance and Distribution industries are between 81% and 86% of the UK average'. Moreover, as Brand *et al.* (1998, 53) explain, 'what is more surprising has been the relatively low contribution[5] made by many of the new service sector jobs in Wales, reflecting relatively poor occupational structures and low value-addition'. In Wales, non-manual wages are depressed by the absence of high-paying professions and the excess of routine sales workers and the like (Blackaby *et al.* 1996, 243).

The Public Sector

The dependent status of the Welsh economy used to be signified by the large numbers of jobs in the nationalized coal mining and steel industries for Welsh men, but now: 'Wales has replaced its dependency on Coal and Steel with a Public Sector dependency. This inherent structural weakness will continue to undermine Wales's prospects in the new regional competitive arena. Public sector jobs inevitably make relatively low contributions to GDP' (Brand *et al.* 1998, 53). Lovering also highlights this phenomenon, commenting that

> The public-spending-dominated employment categories of Public Administration and Defence, Health, Social Services and Education account for a higher proportion of both GDP and employment in Wales than in any mainland UK region. In the last decade and a half these sectors created twenty-two times as many jobs as the manufacturing sector. In no other UK region was the public sector the greatest contributor to job creation. (Lovering 1999a, 31)

This job growth was more than twice the *gross* gain in jobs from FDI, and twenty-two times the net contribution to employment of manufacturing industry, over the same period (Lovering 1999b, 3). The increased significance of public-sector services has been accompanied by another change: in contrast to the days of mass employment in coal and steel, now the public sector provides jobs for *women*. These jobs are the most important reason why, by the end of 1996, female employees outnumbered male employees in Wales (male employees outnumber female employees in all the regions of the UK except Wales, South West England and Scotland – Drinkwater 1998, 226). According to Lovering (1999a, 51n), 48 per cent of all women in employment in Wales, and 23 per cent of all men, are employed in the public sector. These jobs keep Welsh earnings higher than they would otherwise be: 'Welsh average earnings in education, social services and health are 95 per cent of the UK average (albeit a low average, linked to the fact that these overwhelmingly employ women)' (Lovering 1999a, 32). While these jobs may require higher skill levels than some private-sector jobs, the public sector is no better at spending money on R&D in Wales than the private sector (Blackaby *et al.* 1996, 229).

Growth and Prosperity

For a brief period in the early 1990s unemployment was actually lower in Wales than in the UK as a whole, although by 1996 the Welsh rate once more exceeded the UK rate just as it had throughout the 1980s. The standard way of measuring unemployment may, however, be particularly misleading in Wales (because of the way the numbers in 'invalidity, government training and other forms of involuntary nonwork move in sympathy with reductions in opportunity' (Mackay, 1999, 67)). A measure of 'real unemployment' which takes this into account produces a rate 7 percentage points higher than the equivalent UK count (Mackay 1999, 67). In comparison with the rest of the UK, Wales has had no special problem with *long-term* unemployment (according to official figures from the Department of Employment: Blackaby *et al.* 1996, 244) although it has often had especially high rates of redundancies (*Welsh Economic Review* 1998). The main difference between Wales and the rest of the UK can be found in 'economic activity rates', meaning the proportion of the total population in employment or self-employment.

In Wales these rates are as low as in the most deprived parts of big cities in England and Scotland and lower than other parts of the UK (Lovering 1999a, 34–5; Gripaios 1998, 34). In fact the gap between Welsh activity rates and those in the rest of the UK is increasing (Mainwaring 1996). This fact has a great deal to do with the dependence of the Welsh economy on poor-quality jobs brought into Wales from elsewhere:

> The issue of [job] quality is also illustrated by persistently low Welsh activity rates, where people may be choosing not to enter the job market because of poor pay and limited career opportunities . . . Relatively low activity rates may therefore be as much a consequence of low GDP per head as a cause. (Brand *et al.* 1998, 51)

Low activity rates rather than high unemployment rates explain why social security benefits make up a much higher proportion of incomes in Wales than elsewhere in the UK (Blackaby *et al.* 1996, 220). The proportion of Welsh household income coming from benefits fell significantly in 1996 but Wales was still 'the only UK region where wages and salaries constitute less than 60% of gross weekly household income' (*Welsh Economic Review* 1997, 35).

All other things being equal, activity rates will increase if the number of jobs grows. The number of employees in employment in Wales grew at nearly twice the UK rate between 1981 and 1991, and fell only a little in the recession of the early 1990s, but the growth in employment between 1993 and 1996 was less than half that of the UK (Gripaios 1998, 34). In the mid-1990s female employment continued to grow, first in part-time jobs, latterly in full-time jobs, but male employment in Wales fell (Drinkwater 1998, 226; *Welsh Economic Review* 1998). Mackay shows how weak job creation in Wales leads people into forms of inactivity that do not appear in government unemployment counts. According to Mackay '[t]here is a process of detachment and withdrawal from the working population which is highly sensitive to variations in opportunity' (Mackay 1999, 67), and this helps to explain why such unemployment counts do not fully reflect low economic activity rates in Wales.

As we know, there was also reason to be concerned about the sorts of jobs being created when employment increased. In 1979 the level of pay in Wales was *above* the Great Britain average for males and females in manual jobs (and not very far below the average for non-manual workers of both sexes) but throughout the 1980s there was a steady decline in the relative level of Welsh pay (*Welsh Economic Review* 1997, 31). Wales entered the 1980s near the *top* of the regional UK pay league and entered the 1990s near the *bottom* (Morris 1996). There was some evidence of a recovery in the 1990s with slight improvements (but not for females in manual jobs) vis-à-vis the rest of the UK (Blackaby *et al.* 1996, 258) and general Welsh average earnings now run at about 95 per cent of those found in England and Scotland (*Welsh Economic Review* 1997, 31).

By 1997 Welsh manual workers' earnings (especially for men) had risen to something like average UK levels once more but 'the gap between earnings in non-manual sectors for males and females show few signs of change through time' (*Welsh Economic Review* 1998, 14). Over the longer term, pay for Welsh manual workers (which was once *higher* in Wales) has got closer to average UK levels while at the same time, the gap between manual and non-manual pay has increased, making the effect of low levels of non-manual pay on Welsh incomes much more telling (Drinkwater 1998, 236).

The poor quality of the jobs created in Wales in recent times accounts for the widening income gap between Wales and the rest of Britain (Mainwaring 1996, 22; Blackaby *et al.* 1993). In the mid-1990s male earnings in Wales were 89 per cent of the Great Britain average (97 per cent for manual and 88 for non-manual males) (Blackaby *et al.* 1996, 255). In 1997 104,000 workers in Wales earned less than £3 an hour (*Welsh Economic Review* 1997). Although the position is a little bit better for women, non-manual males in Wales have the lowest earnings in Great Britain (Blackaby *et al.* 1996, 255):

> Compared with the other regions, Wales has traditionally had lower earnings in non-manual occupations, and in the service sector in particular. As these sectors account for an ever larger proportion of the workforce, it is not surprising that relative earnings in Wales are on a downward trend . . . Welsh earnings in non-manual occupations have continued to deteriorate compared to the rest of the country. (Drinkwater 1998, 226)

Manual earnings in manufacturing have improved in the 1990s and from the foregoing it is clear that much of the responsibility for low pay lies with private employers in the service sector, especially those that employ men in non-manual jobs (Blackaby *et al.* 1996, 256).

Throughout the 1980s and 1990s wage *inequalities* within Wales increased (Blackaby *et al.* 1996, 263; Drinkwater 1998, 236–7). There is also a growing gap between more prosperous households with more than one earner and those households with no wage earners at all. By the late 1980s the proportion of non-pension households which had no wage earner was twice the UK level (Mackay 1999, 66). There is a regional element in such inequalities and the east of Wales, which has experienced much faster economic growth, is generally much more prosperous than the west. (Blackaby *et al.* 1996, 220).

Unemployment rates strongly illustrate the east/west divide within Wales (Blackaby *et al.* 1996, 250) as do comparisons of earnings (Blackaby *et al.* 1996, 259). Cardiff is a particularly good example of the relative success of east Wales. Between 1965 and 1994, nearly a quarter of all retail development in Wales took place in central Cardiff (Guy 1995, 164). It was predicted to be the fastest-growing conurbation in the British Isles in the 1990s and set to become a major business and financial services centre (Blackaby *et al.* 1996, 223). Gripaios (1998, 45) shows how Cardiff has benefited from a different sort of investment in financial services compared to the rest of Wales: twenty of the twenty-three main financial services suppliers and all five of the top 100 UK (excluding London) law firms working in Wales are located there. All the annual statistical profiles show Cardiff (together with smaller centres like Hay on Wye or Cowbridge) becoming increasingly differentiated from other Welsh towns and cities and, in fact, becoming rather more like the south of England in terms of earnings[6] and house prices and productivity (Drinkwater 1997, 172; Brand *et al.* 1998, 50).

The conventional way to measure the productivity of a population is in terms of Gross Domestic Product per head. This measure shows how much people are producing and earning for their country.[7] Wales has very low figures for GDP per head, but in part this results from the low activity rates of the Welsh population. With fewer people contributing to production, average output is bound to be lower. In what follows we should therefore bear in mind that if we count only those people in employment then Welsh GDP moves closer to UK levels, although it still remains some 9 points below this average (Brand *et al.* 1998, 51). In fact in Welsh *manufacturing* high levels of investment have kept GDP per *employee* above UK levels for some time (Morgan and Price 1996, 95).

Nevertheless, GDP per *head* in Wales is much lower than in the UK as a whole – lower than any other standard region. There was a slow but steady improvement between 1987 and 1992 but this did not continue into the mid-1990s as some commentators had hoped (Blackaby *et al.* 1996, 294). The 1993–5 Regional Accounts showed Welsh GDP at between 83.7 and 89.4 per cent of UK levels (Blackaby *et al.* 1996, 298; Drinkwater 1998, 221). The Welsh share of UK GDP in 1995 was actually lower than it had been in 1986 (Lovering 1999a, 32). GDP per head in Wales relative to the rest of the UK actually declined in the mid-1990s (1995–6) and the gap between Wales and the very poorest region, Northern Ireland, was narrowing (Drinkwater 1998, 220).[8] Wales was expected to lag behind UK growth in GDP again in 1997 and by early 1998 the rate of growth in real GDP for Wales was expected to decline in 1998 and in 1999 even without taking the effects of the Asian crisis into account (*Welsh Economic Review* 1998, 4).

If Welsh manufacturing is not to blame for low Welsh GDP, the service sector certainly is:

> Public sector jobs inevitably make relatively low contributions to GDP: what is more surprising has been the relatively low contribution made by many of the new service sector jobs in Wales, reflecting relatively poor occupational structures and low value-addition. (Brand *et al.* 1998, 53; also see Dunford 1996)

Wales's low GDP per head is partly the result of low productivity but it is worth noting that the profit share of GDP is especially high in Wales – twice that of South East England (Lovering 1999a, 18).

Conclusions

Brand *et al.* think that the low levels of GDP are a good proxy for everything that is fundamentally wrong with the Welsh economy and observe that 'the regional economy entered the mid-1990s as it had the mid 1980s, as the poorest region of the UK mainland in terms of personal economic well-being' (1998, 50). They conclude that 'Wales looks set to enter the new century firmly fixed at the bottom of the British prosperity league' (Brand *et al.* 1997, 59). John Lovering thinks that: 'Within mainland Britain Wales is now the most unsuccessful of all regions, if success is defined as the ability to provide its population with jobs and good incomes' (1999a, 34). Ross Mackay concludes his most recent article in this way: 'Comparing Wales with the UK, opportunity to work and earnings in work moved strongly against Wales in the 1980s. Even with substantial inward investment, Wales remains a low wage and low opportunity economy in the 1990s' (1999, 73).

Such comments show that the fundamental nature of the Welsh economy has changed very little since its condition fifty years ago when thousands of steel jobs were brought to south Wales to make up for the shortfall in domestic employment. The difference is that in the days of the Steel Company of Wales, the jobs that were brought to Wales paid relatively high wages (Fevre 1989). The steel industry is still a rare example of high levels of investment even now. In the rest of Welsh industry (with the partial exception of some foreign-owned firms, especially from the United States) investment levels, skill levels and pay levels are all low. Indeed they are so low that many Welsh people remain economically inactive, so further depressing GDP. It is hard to see how this vicious circle can be escaped without some fundamental change in the nature of the Welsh economy which will allow it to create enough jobs to escape dependence on imported jobs and government subsidies.

Notes

1. Wales has also received a great deal of financial assistance from the European Union (Blackaby *et al.* 1996, 285; *Welsh Economic Review* 1998).
2. They were a particularly important source of new jobs in the north and west – and this part of Wales seems to fare better when it appears to be seen as a component of a regional economy which straddles the Welsh/English border.
3. This was particularly likely to happen with FDI by North American-owned firms.
4. 39% of all workers in employment are concentrated in selling, catering and personal service, clerical and transport (Blackaby *et al.* 1996, 241).
5. To GDP – see note 7 below.
6. Although note that average weekly earnings in Cardiff are on a par with those of the affluent manufacturing workers of Flint and Neath-Port Talbot (*Welsh Economic Review* 1998, 15). Remember, also, that people commute to Cardiff from the rest of south and east Wales.
7. There are two ways to count Gross Domestic Product: the 'expenditure method' (in which you add up consumer spending, government spending, investment spending, net stock changes and net exports) and the 'income method' (adding

up income from employment and self-employment, gross trading profits and surpluses, and rent, and take away stock appreciation).

8. The same Regional Accounts also show that personal disposable income in Wales varied between 83.3 and 90.5% of the UK average (see Blackaby *et al.* 1996, 298; Drinkwater, 1998, 221).

References

Atkinson, J. (1997). 'Where is inward investment going?', *Welsh Economic Review,* 10/1, 6–9.

Blackaby, D. H., Murphy, P. D. and Thomas, D. E. L. (1993). 'The widening wage gap in Wales', *Welsh Economic Review*, 6, 40–9.

Blackaby, D., Murphy, P., O'Leary, N. and Thomas, E. (1996). 'Wales: an economic survey', *Contemporary Wales*, 8, 213–304.

Brand, S., Bryan, J., Hill, S., Munday, M. and Roberts, A. (1997). 'Differences in Welsh and UK GDP per head', *Welsh Economic Review*, 10/1, 54-9.

Brand, S., Bryan, J., Hill, S., Munday, M. and Roberts, A. (1998). ' "An Economic Strategy for Wales": response to the Welsh Office consultation document', *Welsh Economic Review*, 10/2, 49–54.

Drinkwater, S. (1997). 'The Welsh economy: a statistical profile', *Contemporary Wales*, 9, 171–90.

Drinkwater, S. (1998). 'The Welsh economy: a statistical profile', *Contemporary Wales*, 10, 219–47.

Dunford, M. (1996). 'Disparities in employment, productivity and output in the EU: the roles of labour market governance and welfare regime', *Regional Studies*, 30, 339–57.

Fevre, R. (1989). *Wales is Closed* (Nottingham: Spokesman).

Gripaios, P. (1998). 'The Welsh economy: an outside perspective', *Contemporary Wales*, 10, 32–49.

Guy, C. M. (1995). 'Retail development in Wales', *Contemporary Wales*, 8, 161–81.

Lovering, J. (1996). 'New myths of the Welsh economy', *Planet*, 116, 6–16.

Lovering, J. (1997). 'Making mountains out of molehills?', *Welsh Economic Review*, 10/1, 14–16.

Lovering, J. (1999a). 'Celebrating globalization and misreading the Welsh economy: the "new regionalism" ', *Contemporary Wales*, 11, 12–60.

Lovering, J. (1999b). 'Theory led by policy: the inadequacies of "the new regionalism" (illustrated from the case of Wales)', *International Journal of Urban and Regional Research* (June).

Mackay, R. (1999). 'Wales and north Wales: the nature of regeneration', *Contemporary Wales*, 11, 61–74.

Mainwaring, L. (1996). 'Catching up and falling behind: south-east Asia and Wales', *Contemporary Wales*, 8, 9–28.

Midmore, P., Hughes, G. and Bateman, D. (1994). 'Agriculture and the rural economy: problems, policies and prospects', *Contemporary Wales*, 6, 9–32.

Morgan, B. (1997). 'Yes, inward investment works, but . . . ', *Welsh Economic Review*, 10/1, 17–20.

Morgan, K. and Price, A. (1996). 'The state of the Welsh economy', *Planet*, 117, 94–5.

Morgan, K. O. (1981). *Rebirth of a Nation: Wales 1880–1980* (Oxford and Cardiff: Clarendon Press and University of Wales Press).

Morris, J. (1996). "McJobbing a region: industrial restructuring and the widening socio-economic divide in Wales', in R. Turner (ed.), *The British Economy in Transition* (London: Routledge).

Morris, J., Munday, M. and Wilkinson, B. (1993). *Working for the Japanese: The Economic and Social Consequences of Japanese Investment in Wales* (London: Athlone Press).

Munday, M. and Peel, M. (1998). 'The comparative performance of foreign-owned and domestic manufacturing firms during recession: some descriptive evidence from Wales', *Contemporary Wales*, 10, 50–80.

Roberts A. (1994). 'The causes and consequences of inward investment: the Welsh experience', *Contemporary Wales*, 6, 73–86.

Williams, K. (1997). 'Wales in a spin', *Planet*, 120, 31–4.

5 The Rural Dimension

GRAHAM DAY

Introduction

Passing through mid-Wales recently on a return visit, a leading authority on rural sociology exclaimed 'Time stands still in rural Wales'. This momentary aberration from a normally critical awareness is very revealing; it shows that even the experts among us can be taken in by appearances and illusions, because the reality of rural Wales in recent years has been one of rapid and unsettling social and economic change, rather than stability. Yet the extent of these changes is not always widely perceived.

In fact, as we approach the new millennium, there are signs of crisis in rural Wales. Welsh farmers have been involved in scuffles and protests over the importing of food from Ireland and Europe, the falling prices of Welsh agricultural produce and the profits made by supermarket chains when the same produce reaches the consumer. Some farmers have been forced to sell off part of their land in order to stay in business, so threatening their long-term survival. At the same time, there has been an orchestrated campaign, supported by prominent Welsh celebrities including actors (Sir Anthony Hopkins) and pop stars (the Stereophonics; the Alarm), to raise money to buy agricultural land on Snowdon, for the nation. Friends of the Earth and EarthFirst! have been organizing protests against the extension of the A55 north Wales expressway across Anglesey (Ynys Môn) and there have been various local protests, such as that around Brewery Fields in Bangor, to prevent development occurring on sites of special scientific interest (SSSIs) and areas of environmental significance.

These incidents signal a number of important themes relevant to the rural dimension of modern Wales – the gap between image and reality; the clash between alternative meanings of the countryside and of 'rurality'; and the changing balance between the different social groups and interests that engage with rural issues.

'Truly Rural' Wales

Although the particular issues confronting rural Wales at the present time may be new, the sense of crisis and uncertainty is not. Indeed, there has been among social commentators a long-standing preoccupation with the troubled condition of the Welsh countryside, which reflects difficult long-term alterations in the nature of Welsh rural society. Sociologists and human geographers have brought a series of changing perspectives to bear to make sense of this transformation, and have produced a number of illuminating interpretations of the way in which it has developed.

Like rural areas in other countries, the Welsh countryside occupies a special place in the imagination. Often it has been referred to as the 'Welsh heartland', the very centre of what is distinctively Welsh, and therefore as a repository of essential values and patterns of social organization (Gruffudd 1994). These features are identified usually with the special nature of the Welsh rural community and there is a strong tradition of research and analysis dealing with this, dating back to the work of Alwyn Rees and his associates at the University of Wales, Aberystwyth, during the 1940s and 1950s (see Rees 1996; Davies and Rees 1960; and for a fuller discussion of their work, Day 1998).

In a series of studies of particular small rural communities, such as Llanfihangel-yng-Ngwynfa, Tregaron and Aberdaron they produced a remarkably coherent account of the nature of traditional Welsh rural life, and also a warning that it was under serious threat. As well as providing an influential insight into rural Wales, their work played an important part in establishing the image of 'truly rural' social organization for British sociology as a whole, offering a kind of baseline against which subsequent change could be assessed (Frankenberg 1966).

The aspects of life which they identified as 'truly rural' in relation to Wales included: the centrality of agriculture, and a way of life that was adapted to the demands of the natural environment in Wales, a relatively poor and marginal upland region; the social integration of the rural community, which revolved around the social networks of family and kinship, of chapel, and of co-operation in farming; and the linguistic and cultural values of Welshness, such as a non-materialistic ethos and a lack of concern with questions of class and social division. The picture they painted was of quite a homogeneous society, unified by these common threads of identity, language, religion and a strong sense of local belonging, into a 'community of communities', that had deep roots into the past. Alwyn Rees stressed the continuity between the rural society he observed, and a much older, tribal, pattern of Welsh life.

Subsequently, the underlying theoretical framework employed by this group of researchers has been seen as reflecting a kind of implicit functionalist emphasis on social consensus and order that may have underestimated the divisions and contradictions within the society which was described. However, Rees and his collaborators were more acutely conscious of the extent to which these values and traditions were being challenged from outside, by the forces of modernization, especially the impact of urban society and the spread of English influences and values, which threatened to destroy Welshness, including the Welsh language. They regarded the Welsh rural community as the bulwark for the defence of these key values and social patterns, and argued that it had to be protected from the changes which were undermining it, if necessary by sealing it off from external influences. Yet their intervention was powerless to halt the mounting pressures for change which led to a period of severe depopulation and rural decline.

The Modernization of Rural Wales

The years up to and following the Second World War saw the steady replacement of labour on the land by technology and capital. Farm incomes, especially in the more marginal rural areas, remained low relative to what could be earned elsewhere. The declining opportunities provided by Welsh agriculture resulted in large numbers of people migrating from the Welsh countryside, mostly while young, leaving behind a decaying social fabric and an ageing population. This increased the costs of providing essential services for the rural population, and put at risk the ability of Welsh rural society to reproduce itself and its characteristic ways of life. Membership of the chapels and the numbers enrolled in rural schools both fell sharply as the population could no longer sustain its basic institutions.

From the 1960s onward, in response to local and political pressure, there has been government action to try to assist rural Wales to move towards a new, and more prosperous, economic and social condition. The main instrument for achieving this was the creation of rural development agencies, principally the Development Board for Rural Wales (DBRW), which were charged with the task of economic recovery. Side by side with the extensive support provided to farming via British and then European agricultural policies, a separate strand of regional policy encouraged measures to bring alternative employment, especially in small manufacturing industry, into rural Wales. This was done by the provision of improved infrastructure, such as better roads and communications, purpose-built factories and workshops available at low rents, and other subsidies to employers. The intention was that by opening up rural Wales and reducing its relative isolation from major markets, inward investment could be attracted to make good the weaknesses in the indigenous economy, and give it a more balanced and modern profile. In response, firms moved to rural Wales from the more congested, and more costly, parts of urban Britain, and provided new sources of employment for the rural population.

The development agencies have provided consistently optimistic statements of the number of jobs they were able to create by pursuing these policies. Along with new jobs, the industrialization of rural Wales implied new demands for housing, and new sources of income and spending power. One of the tasks the agencies faced was to reposition rural Wales in a kind of marketing exercise, presenting it to potential investors not as a declining region of old-fashioned communities and quaint types of behaviour, but as a desirable place to live and work, with excellent scenery and environment, and a high quality of life. For example, the Development Board tried to 'brand' rural Wales as 'the British Business Park', proposing that it was possible to combine up-to-date business activity with all the advantages of life in the countryside. This appealed to a growing sentiment among sections of the British population that they would like to participate in the 'rural idyll' (Newby 1979), but if possible without sacrificing the benefits of urban living. Obviously, however, attributing this meaning to the Welsh countryside competed to some extent with other existing meanings, such as the conception of rural Wales as essentially centred on farming and more traditional rural activities, or as the focus of a peculiarly Welsh (and non-urban) way of life.

Initially at least the development strategy met with local opposition from farmers and small employers who feared that it would drive up wages, and take away their sources of labour. Other local people were unenthusiastic about factory work, and about having industry on their doorsteps, which might spoil their own appreciation of a rural environment. In fact, much of the new development tended to be concentrated spatially, particularly around Newtown and Welshpool in Powys, and to a lesser extent in a number of other key rural centres – it was a belief of the development agencies that prosperity would spread out from such growth centres to the rest of the rural area.

There has always been an undercurrent of scepticism from those who have viewed the claims made on behalf of this strategy with suspicion. To begin with, there was much talk of 'branch plants' – that is, of the location in rural Wales of subordinate elements in companies which would fail to establish themselves locally and which would be liable to pull out again when things got tough, as dictated by their headquarters outside Wales. Certainly there was a continuous turnover of businesses, with closures having to be offset against new openings, and the expected numbers of new jobs often failed to materialize. Some critics argued that in this respect rural Wales had to be placed in the context of other dependent and peripheral regions, both in Europe and elsewhere, which suffered by being exposed to only the least rewarding, and least reliable, kinds of development. These included large-scale projects with limited impact upon local job creation, such as nuclear power stations. Two were located in rural Wales, at Wylfa and Trawsfynydd; much of the benefit went to people from outside the region, including construction workers who temporarily swelled the local labour force (Williams 1980).

More recently, rural Wales has been categorized as still holding a 'clientalist' position among rural areas, that is, as being heavily reliant for its economic existence upon state support and welfare payments. This distinguishes it from other rural areas which have enjoyed contrasting fortunes, as preserved, contested or paternalistic regions (Marsden 1998). In other words, after more than three decades of sustained development effort, it is questionable whether rural Wales has managed to secure an independent basis for economic survival. The fear is that this renders it vulnerable to any change in state policies, especially calculations as to whether the cost of this kind of support is too great, or politically unacceptable. Its withdrawal could leave the area exposed to similar kinds of decline as were taking place in the early 1960s.

Economic and Social Restructuring

Despite these reservations, a fundamental shift has been achieved in the employment profile in rural Wales. The proportion of the population engaged in or reliant upon agriculture and associated activities has fallen dramatically, although by comparison to average UK figures it remains substantial, and therefore rural Wales still has much to lose from any further decline in the fortunes of its farmers. The share of the population involved in manufacturing has grown, but continues to be only a small fraction of the total numbers employed. As elsewhere in Britain today, the vast majority of jobs in rural Wales are to be found in the various branches of the service sector – the public sector (government, education, health and welfare), retailing and the leisure industries, such as hotels and catering.

As indicated by Gareth Rees, these movements in the underlying economic structure were bound to have far-reaching social consequences for rural Wales:

> Changes in rural employment structures are central to any understanding of the reality of rural social life. On the one hand they reflect profound shifts in the nature and organization of capitalist production . . . On the other, employment changes themselves have resulted in radical developments in terms of rural class structures, gender divisions, the forms of political conflict occurring in rural areas and indeed of the complex processes by which 'rural cultures' are produced and reproduced. (Rees 1984)

This statement represents an expression of the 'restructuring' approach which became influential in British regional sociology during the 1980s. It aims to locate the specific changes taking place in rural Wales within a broader analysis of the general processes of economic and social change operating throughout Britain at the time. In these terms, much of what was happening in the Welsh countryside could be explained by forces and pressures emanating from outside, as the British economy was reorganized and restructured. The particular contribution of the various state policies and development agencies previously described can be understood better when related to these wider economic and social circumstances.

Advocates of the restructuring approach argued that the logic of capitalist development requires periodic alterations in prevailing economic conditions. Government, and the state, played its part in assisting (and at terms moderating) the workings of the private sector and the market. Hence the changes that have been referred to as taking place in rural Wales cannot be wholly understood as the outcome of deliberate and planned state intervention, or conscious strategies, but represent the often unintended effect of the combination of many decisions made by various private interests, especially the investment decisions of firms, and by numerous other agencies. This makes it extremely difficult to estimate precisely how effective policies have been, because it is so hard to disentangle their effects from what might have happened anyway. For example, help given to businesses to make rural Wales a more profitable place to invest – which included advertising the fact, held out as an explicit enticement, that wages were low and labour likely to be well behaved – may only have encouraged them to implement relocation decisions which were already made (see Day *et al.* 1989).

Where rural Wales probably did benefit was in having a development agency, backed by the Welsh Office, which was especially dedicated to advancing the interests of its region, and to persuading 'footloose' industry to locate in Wales rather than elsewhere. This gave it an edge over other competitor regions. Even within Wales, there were complaints that the geographical boundaries set for the operations of the DBRW left out some rural districts which were just as deserving of assistance as those inside them. It fell to the Welsh Development Agency (WDA) to look after these excluded areas, but with less extensive powers to act on social grounds.

If we follow through some of the implications of the changes already outlined, we find that inevitably they result in a major shake up of most, if not all, Welsh rural communities. Thus, industrialization brought in significant numbers of people from outside as 'key workers' possessing the skills and experience required by the jobs they were to fill, and which the local population, to begin with at least, could not supply. This was especially true at managerial, professional and technical levels, so that among the incomers were some who tended to have advantages over locals with regard to authority at work, income, and career prospects. Their arrival in turn led to housing developments, including so-called 'executive housing', designed to accommodate such new social and class groupings. This helped tip the balance locally between insiders and outsiders, locals and others, working and middle class, and gave rise to a whole series of interactions being played out as these different groups adjusted to one another (Day and Murdoch 1993). As would be expected, the incomers were predominantly English, adding another 'ethnic' and linguistic dimension to the encounters which took place.

Such changes were not exclusively the result of new employment patterns. Given the pervading attractiveness of rural locations for many people in Britain, rural Wales is widely perceived as among the more desirable places to live. Whenever people have the ability to act on their preferences, they may opt to move towards such places. In recent years, there has been significant inward movement, as part of a wider trend of 'counter-urbanization' that has affected all rural locations. This first came to prominence as an issue surrounding second-home ownership, when people who could afford it began to purchase housing left vacant by rural depopulation. In parts of rural Wales, the ownership of whole streets and even villages passed to outsiders, who were absent for much of the time, leading to intense resentment among some locals. Subsequently this trend took a different form, with the inward migration of large numbers of new residents, including retired people, those with assets released from sales of housing in the better off parts of Britain such as the South East, and others who were taking the opportunity to drop out of urban life and conditions. At the peak of this movement, there were estimates putting the total numbers of people moving into and out of rural Wales as high as a million, leading to very large population shifts at local level (Day 1989). While this helped increase the total numbers living in rural Wales, the inflow often concealed a continuing exodus of young and local people who were still unable to find work locally, or, increasingly, unable to match the rising prices of local housing. New demands began to be heard for 'affordable' housing and for controls to be put on the availability of housing to outsiders. Rural space became contested space.

Uneven Development and Social Fragmentation

A leading theme of the restructuring framework was that economic and social development tends to occur in a highly uneven way: gains made in one place, or by one group, are often related directly to losses occurring elsewhere. Such uneven development has been experienced within rural Wales, both geographically and socially. The result is a much more fragmented and diverse situation than appears to have existed in the past.

In spatial terms, the exceptional growth witnessed in Powys, particularly around Newtown, has contributed towards a definite east–west split. Greater success has been achieved in attracting and creating new jobs and new types of employment down the eastern side of the country, which is explicable partly in terms of closeness and ease of access to urban centres and English markets. Travelling westwards, for example along the A55 in north Wales, one meets fewer signs of a vibrant economy. Summing up the peripheral economy of Gwynedd and north Wales, Williams and Morris (1996, 37) describe it as marked by:

> the high level of long term unemployment and the associated depreciation of skills, the relatively small population size . . . , the high rate of out-migration of the more talented young people, the relatively high proportion of older people in the demographic structure, the lower female activity rate, the lack of dynamism in the economic structure, the high incidence of part-time employment and its relationship to pluriactivity, and the evidence of an exaggerated seasonality in employment.

Many of these attributes of relative deprivation and disadvantage pertain to other parts of rural Wales as well. Despite the hard work and achievements of development agencies, many of the jobs which have been brought to the region provide only limited opportunities. Wage levels and career structures suffer from the typically small size of local businesses. The contemporary economy is disjointed and fragmentary, and the labour market functions accordingly, with many workers experiencing limited scope for movement between jobs, or into secure positions. The jobs on offer include large proportions of part-time, seasonal or casual work, requiring relatively low skill and offering little career progression. This is true of work in the service sector as well as in manufacturing; there is a dearth of real quality employment. The recent penetration of rural Wales by major supermarket chains, for instance, implies the replacement of local shops and small family concerns with new, part-time, employment.

Consequently, wage levels are low. Average earnings in rural Wales for both men and women lag about 20 per cent or more behind those earned in Wales and Britain as a whole. Indeed, the situation has worsened over time: in Gwynedd, for example, male earnings fell from 91 per cent of the British figure in 1981 to only 79 per cent by 1996. It probably comes as no surprise to learn that many of these low-paid and low-skilled jobs are done by women: as in the rest of Britain, the labour market in rural Wales has been feminized, but at the cost of women undertaking much of the least rewarding, least secure, work. Indeed, the availability of a pool of under-employed female labour was probably among the attractions which brought jobs to rural Wales.

Conversely, there are fewer highly paid professional and managerial posts, and fewer jobs in the most advanced sectors of the economy, such as financial services, than would be found in other parts of Wales, and so a relatively weak presence of some of the more dynamic fractions of the middle class. Like all generalizations, this has to be qualified in detail – since there are significant clusters of such employees in places like Aberystwyth, Carmarthen, Lampeter and Bangor, where they are connected to institutions of higher education, or government and administration. It is important to remember that places in rural Wales are not all alike; there are very significant local variations in economic and social structure, which have a significant impact on social behaviour and relationships.

Agriculture and the Farming Community

The state of agriculture in Wales gives further cause for concern. Welsh farming consists mainly of small family farms raising livestock; 80 per cent of the land qualifies for Less Favoured Area payments, and farm incomes are low. The farming community has been battered by a succession of shocks, such as the introduction of milk quotas and the BSE crisis, and is still under very serious pressure (IWA 1998). Reform of the Common Agricultural Policy, the main benefits of which have gone in any case to the larger cereal farmers outside Wales, is likely to result in the further withdrawal of support, or its transfer from agricultural production towards environmental and possibly social goals – such as the maintenance of rural communities. The future looks quite bleak, with further anticipations of job losses in farming.

Yet farmers and their families continue to be a key element in the social framework of Welsh rural life (Day and Murdoch 1993). Indeed, the common definition of rural Wales largely coincides with an area consisting of the old counties of Dyfed, Gwynedd and Powys which is in receipt of European Objective 5B support, justified in terms of its high level of dependence upon a declining agricultural sector. But although farm families may still exert a great deal of influence over such local institutions as community councils and village hall committees, there has been a significant weakening of their power nationally. After all, most people in rural Wales today have only rather tenuous connections to agriculture, and as has been evident elsewhere in rural Britain, there are many rural dwellers now for whom the realities of farming, including its smells and noises, are alien, or even objectionable. One indication of the changing alignments of power and interests which flow from this is the recent effort to redefine the map of Wales in such a way as to cut across the rural/urban divide, to bring together the deprived communities of rural west Wales with the south Wales Valleys as worthy of EU Objective 1 support, on grounds of poor economic performance. The acceptance of this ploy in Brussels would loosen further the ties between the fate of rural Wales and the agricultural economy. The DBRW has also been merged into the new 'economic powerhouse' in Cardiff, with consequent loss of its specifically rural policy focus.

At present the survival of Welsh family farming relies heavily on the extent to which family members tolerate working long hours for exceptionally low returns, and on their readiness to combine various limited income sources through their 'pluriactivity'. It is impossible to imagine the Welsh countryside without a thriving farming community, but it also clear that the terms on which the industry survives will have to change. Moves are taking place to create a more environmentally friendly agriculture, with greater emphasis on organic production and food quality, partly in order to combat the growing power of the food industry and super-markets, and it is likely that farmers, especially in marginal areas like Wales, will be rewarded increasingly for their work as custodians of the landscape and environment. However, it follows that they will also be under pressure to accommodate other competing interests and social meanings attached to the countryside – such as its accessibility to those who wish to use it as a leisure and recreational resource, its maintenance as a place of scenic and landscape interest and its 'heritage' value. There are anxieties that this may reduce farmers from productive business people to glorified rural museum keepers. An example of an effective accommodation is the income now earned by some Welsh farmers from wind turbines positioned on their land, but this itself highlights the clash between differing conceptions of appropriate development in the countryside. What is evident is that, unlike the earlier generation of researchers, social scientists can no longer assume that the fate of rural Wales is bound up primarily, or even exclusively, with the interests of farmers and landowners.

Social and Cultural Diversity

The picture of rural Wales we have been developing is of a society which is far more diverse and fractured – economically, socially and culturally – than it was in the past. Within its population we encounter a wider range of values, attitudes and experiences. This is a central thrust of the most thorough recent investigation of social life in the region, the 'rural lifestyles' project of Paul Cloke and his colleagues (Cloke *et al.* 1997). Using information derived from in-depth investigations in four localities, they provide a detailed account of the plurality of ways of living which now coexist within the region, and show how, despite living in close proximity, different population segments may have very little mutual awareness or comprehension. This emerges clearly in relation to a key finding, which caused a good deal of controversy and even some resistance to the publication of the findings, the reality across rural Wales of poverty and deprivation, and the associated phenomena of marginality and social exclusion.

Given what has been said already about the presence of a low-wage, low-skill economy, this should not come as a surprise, especially when we add into the equation the high proportion of elderly and retired, pensioner, households within the population; but the calculation that roughly a quarter of the households in rural Wales are close to or at the poverty line has dismayed many, although it is not out of line with evidence for other parts of Britain. Rural poverty tends to be grossly under-reported, and does not fit romantic images of a rural idyll. Because poor households in rural areas, like their better-off counterparts, tend to be dispersed and do not form large and visible concentrations as they might in more urban settings, they are easily overlooked. Hence, even the majority of those studied did not contemplate the existence of poverty in their locality. Nevertheless, not only do Cloke *et al.* produce persuasive evidence of poverty, there are also mounting indications of associated problems such as drug taking, youth disaffection, crime and delinquency in small rural communities which show that, beneath the surface, all is not entirely well.

There has been greater awareness of linguistic divisions in the Welsh countryside; it is impossible to ignore the fact that neighbours may be using different languages. Traditionally, the stronghold of the Welsh language has lain in the most pressurized parts of rural Wales, the north and west, and within the farming community. The new social mixture resulting from inward migration has made the battle to maintain the language a continuous one, but there has been remarkable success, and with the backing of the Welsh Language Act and the preservation of Welsh-language schooling in the rural counties, the decay of the language seems to have been stemmed. Although all Welsh rural communities are now linguistically divided, Welsh-speaking continues to be a vital part of country life, and the worst fears of anglicization have not been realized. The interplay between the two language communities clearly adds to the social and cultural complexity of contemporary rural Wales, while the maintenance of Welsh upholds some of the continuities which were emphasized by the early generation of social researchers. Welsh nationalism draws some of its greatest strengths from rural Wales.

Conclusion

This chapter opened by indicating some of the symptoms of change and disturbance in rural Wales today. Throughout rural Wales, there is now visible evidence of economic recovery and new development, with refurbished towns and villages, the restoration and 'gentrification' of previously abandoned housing, and redundant chapels and schools, and the spread of numerous (albeit small) speculative housing developments catering to an expanding rural population. Many parts of rural Wales, and many sections of the rural population, appear to have done well for themselves, and have managed to secure that uniquely valued combination of comfortable material standards with environmentally attractive and healthy conditions of living which constitutes the contemporary 'rural idyll'. At the same time, there is also ample evidence of genuine poverty and insecurity, not least among the farm population. Like other rural areas, the Welsh countryside has become much more the stamping ground of the middle classes, or the new, socially assertive, 'service class', and a large proportion of these have English backgrounds, and behave in ways which are novel to the region, and sometimes disconcerting to established residents. This includes showing a lack of sensitivity towards local language and culture. The direction and purpose of rural society is much more contested than in the past.

Contrary to what was feared widely in the 1960s, the period since has not seen the total decline – let alone collapse – of the economic basis of the countryside, but its reconfiguration, and with it a reshaping of the accompanying social organization. Recent years have seen the emergence of new policy directions, and alternative development strategies, endorsed for example in the recent government White Paper *A Working Countryside for Wales* (1996), where stress is laid upon the importance of 'sustainable communities' and new routes to economic and social development involving greater participation and 'bottom up' self-reliance. It is hoped that these will overcome some of the limitations of earlier strategies. Whether or not this is the case, both the reality and the myths of rural Wales will continue to play an important part in the development of Wales and its distinctive national identity.

References

Cloke, P., Goodwin, M. and Milbourne, P. (1997). *Rural Wales: Community and Marginalization* (Cardiff: University of Wales Press).

Davis, E. and Rees, A. D. (1960). *Welsh Rural Communities* (Cardiff: University of Wales Press).

Day, G. (1989). 'A million on the move? Population change and rural Wales', *Contemporary Wales*, 3, 139–62.

Day, G. (1998). 'A community of communities? Similarity and difference in Welsh rural community studies', *Economic and Social Review*, 29, 3, 233–57.

Day, G. and Murdoch, J. (1993). 'Locality and community: coming to terms with place', *Sociological Review*, 41/1, 82–111.

Day, G., Rees, G. and Murdoch, J. (1989). 'Social change, rural localities, and the state: the restructuring of rural Wales', *Journal of Rural Studies*, 5/3, 227–44.

Frankenberg, R. (1966). *Communities in Britain* (Harmondsworth: Penguin).

Gruffudd, P. (1994). 'Tradition, modernity and the countryside: the imaginary geography of rural Wales', *Contemporary Wales*, 6, 33–48.

IWA (1998) *Rural Wales and the Agricultural Crisis – A Report*, Discussion Paper 4 (Cardiff: Institute of Welsh Affairs).

Marsden, T. (1998). 'New rural territories: regulating the differentiated rural spaces', *Journal of Rural Studies*, 14/1, 107–18.

Newby, H. (1979) *Green and Pleasant Land: Social Change in Rural England* (London: Hutchinson).

Rees, A. D. (1996). *Life in a Welsh Countryside: A Social Study of Llanfihangel yng Ngwynfa* (Cardiff: University of Wales Press).

Rees, G. (1984). 'Rural regions in national and international economies', in T. Bradley and P. Lowe (eds.), *Locality and Rurality* (Norwich: Geo Books).

Welsh Office (1996). *A Working Countryside for Wales* (Cardiff: Welsh Office).

Williams, G. (1980) 'Industrialization, inequality and deprivation in rural Wales', in G. Rees and T. Rees (eds.), *Poverty and Social Inequality in Wales* (London: Croom Helm).

Williams, G. and Morris, D. (1995). *Peripheral Economic Structure, Labour Market and Skills. Report of the TARGED Labour Market Supply Survey* (Bangor: Research Centre Wales).

6 The Welsh Language Today

JOHN AITCHISON and HAROLD CARTER

Introduction

An appropriate starting-point for a consideration of the state of the Welsh language today is the 1991 population census, the most recent enumeration and the last of the twentieth century. At that date the returns indicated that in Wales some 508,098 (18.6 per cent of the population aged three and over) were able to speak Welsh. In terms of regional distribution, the broad pattern (Figure 6.1) is remarkably similar to that recorded in all previous censuses. Still in evidence, for instance, is the contrast between a Welsh-speaking north and west, once called Y Fro Gymraeg, and the anglicized south and east – a division that had been characteristic from the very first census (1891), and indeed for a very long period before that (Jenkins 1998a, b; Pryce, 1978). While the apparent resilience of the language heartland is notable, it is evident from a closer examination of the statistics that over more recent decades it has weakened in strength and experienced considerable spatial fragmentation. Thus, whereas at the 1961 Census the greater part of the area still included communities (parishes) where over 80 per cent spoke Welsh, by 1991 these had been reduced to a very thin scatter (Aitchison and Carter 1994).

While the situation in the traditional heartland is an issue of some concern for the long-term sustainability of the language, it has to be set against contrary trends that suggest a new dynamism in other parts of Wales. Paradoxically, it is in those areas of prior anglicization – the marcher lands, both to east and south, and especially the south-eastern section about Cardiff – that a linguistic resurgence is most in evidence. Although in statistical terms it has

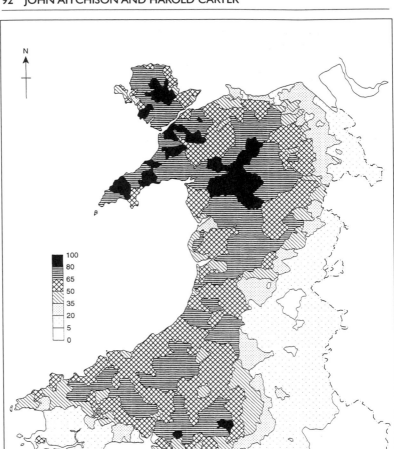

Figure 6.1. Percentage of population able to speak Welsh, 1991.

not fully compensated for the decline elsewhere, the increase in numbers of Welsh-speakers in these regions of growth has helped considerably to reduce the rate of loss at a national level. Thus, whereas numbers nationally fell by 17 per cent between 1961 and 1971, the equivalent percentage for 1981–91 was only 1.4 per cent. The processes that have underpinned this particular linguistic shift have been articulated elsewhere (Aitchison and Carter 1987, 1997), and do not warrant lengthy exegesis here. Suffice it to say that between 1961 and 1991 socio-economic restructuring in the areas concerned had significant and unexpected consequences for the language. Thus, the process of deindustrialization, and the expansion of employment in services, resulted in the emergence in these regions of a new bourgeoisie, largely educated in the University and the colleges of Wales, and with a substantial and influential Welsh-speaking element. That element could set the agenda for public discussion and so keep the language issue to the fore. Effective and proactive backing came from Cymdeithas yr Iaith Gymraeg, the Welsh Language Society. Indeed, many early members of the Society became the later bourgeois protagonists. One of the main demands of the Welsh-speakers was for more Welsh-language or bilingual education, and the success both of the general movement for revitalization and of the specific campaigns for Welsh schools is reflected in the very substantial increases of Welsh-speaking in the younger age groups between 1981 and 1991 (Table 6.1).

Table 6.1. *Numbers of Welsh-speakers aged 3–15 (1981 base)*

	1981	1991	% Change 1981–1991
Clwyd	13796	18167	31.7
Dyfed	23163	25811	11.4
Gwent	1921	3490	81.7
Gwynedd	28785	27889	−3.1
Mid Glamorgan	8906	14604	64.0
Powys	3284	5463	66.4
South Glamorgan	5152	7690	49.3
West Glamorgan	6064	8719	43.8
Wales	91071	111833	22.8

From this very brief review it is apparent that an anomalous situation has arisen in regard to the condition of the language. On the one hand, the situation in the heartland remains problematic, as negative demographic trends (notably the in-migration of non-Welsh speakers) continue to assert themselves. On the other hand, nation-wide, the major losses of the decades after the Second World War have been greatly reduced and increases have occurred in critical emerging areas and amongst crucial sections of the population. Given these dual tendencies, two quite different interpretations of the status and future of the language have come to dominate the debate.

The Language: The Fight has been Won

For some commentators and analysts the fight for the language has, to all intents and purposes, been won. Thus,

> Mewn teitl bras ar dudalen flaen y Western Mail ym mis chwefror eleni [1998] cyhoeddwyd yn ddewr 'Language war is over'. Mae Prys Edwards yn mynnu bod protestwyr iaith bellach yn greaduriaid prin iawn – yn wir, eu bod wedi diflannu mwy neu lai wedi'r Gymraeg ennill ei phlwyf yn y byd . . . (Phillips 1998, 13)
>
> In banner headlines the front page of the Western Mail in February of this year bravely proclaimed 'Language war is over'. Prys Edwards declared that language protesters were now an endangered species – indeed that they had largely disappeared since Welsh had won its place in the world . . .

Perhaps the most direct evidence for such a view comes from the Welsh Language Board's commissioned attitude survey. It revealed that 84 per cent of Welsh-speakers and 68 per cent of non-Welsh-speakers agreed with the Board's declared aim of enabling the language to become self-sustaining and to serve as a medium of communication in Wales, whilst 96 per cent of Welsh-speakers and 94 per cent of non-Welsh-speakers agreed that the numbers of Welsh-speakers should be increased. Some 94 per cent of Welsh-speakers and 80 per cent of non-Welsh-speakers agreed that opportunities to use the language should be provided, whilst 92 per cent and 77 per cent respectively agreed that Welsh should be strengthened as a community language (Welsh Language Board 1996a, 2–3).

Other formal evidence comes from a survey of the minority language groups of the European Union (European Commission, 1996). Seven main variables were used to measure and ordinate the condition of lesser used languages. These were: the family role in language-group production; the role of the community; the role of education; the value for social mobility – that is social prestige; the relevance of culture; the legitimization of language use; the institutionalization of language use. The weightings adopted in such scaling procedures are inevitably open to debate, but in this particular survey Welsh is ranked eleventh out of the forty-eight languages considered and is assigned to cluster B of which the authors write.

> Two of the language groups – Basque and Welsh – are similar in many respects. They are both languages which have considerable linguistic distance from the respective dominant language, and they have a similar degree of language density and a comparable number of speakers . . . They are also integrated into the mainstream of economic diversification, even if the entire population of speakers are differentially integrated into that process. The rapid process of economic change and the associated process on migration has had a profound impact upon the respective languages, but it has also stimulated action that has led to innovative developments by reference to the production of the languages which is the *sine qua non* of survival under such conditions. (European Commission 1996, 36)

The implication from the attitude data cited above, and partly confirmed by the scaling of the language amongst the minority languages of Europe, is that a consensus has been reached over the language's role and status. This same view reinforces the argument that the debate concerning the language has now been depoliticized. No longer is it an issue in the political field, for major divergences of opinion as to its role and status have gradually been eliminated. The opponents, like the active protagonists, are now limited in number and can be viewed as isolated individuals.

Fundamental to the affirmation of this particular perspective on the language is the Welsh Language Act of 1993. It was the culmination of a series of enquiries and legislation over the whole period of agitation for the language in the second half of the century. Its purpose is clearly stated:

> An Act to establish a Board having the function of promoting and facilitating the use of the Welsh Language, to provide for the preparation by public bodies of schemes giving effect to the principle that in the conduct of public business and the administration of justice in Wales the English and Welsh languages should be treated on a basis of equality . . . (Welsh Language Act 1993, 2)

The prime purpose, therefore, was the establishment of a 'body corporate to be known as Bwrdd yr Iaith Gymraeg or the Welsh Language Board', which was to be provided with the necessary finance to make grants and loans to further language interests.

The various parts of the Act can be briefly summarized. Part 2 enacts that every public body in Wales must prepare a scheme to demonstrate how it would give 'effect so far as is both appropriate in the circumstances and reasonably practicable, to the principle that in the conduct of public business and the administration of justice in Wales the English and Welsh languages should be treated on a basis of equality' (Welsh Language Act, 3). To help those bodies concerned in the preparation of such schemes the Welsh Language Board published a document *Welsh Language Schemes: Their preparation and Approval in Accordance with the Welsh Language Act* (1996b). There it is adumbrated that the basic principle of equality is to be achieved by offering the public in Wales the right to choose which language to use in their dealings with organizations, by recognizing that members of the public can express their views and needs better in their preferred language, by recognizing that enabling the public to use their preferred language is a matter of good practice, not a concession, and that denying them the right to use their preferred language could place members of the public at a real disadvantage (Welsh Language Board 1996b, 8). A large number of these schemes have been prepared, put out for public consultation and approved by the Board. The bodies range from local authorities to the Environment Agency, and from the Office for National Statistics to the Benefit Agency. Although not applicable to the private sector, many organizations in that sector have responded to the spirit of the Act.

Part 3 of the Act is headed 'miscellaneous' but deals largely with the use of Welsh in legal proceedings. The Welsh Courts Act of 1942, the Welsh Language Act of 1967 and the Administration of Justice Act of 1977 are all accordingly repealed. The fundamental statement of the 1993 Act is that, 'In any legal proceedings in Wales the Welsh language may be spoken by any party, witness or other person who desires to use it . . . and any necessary provision for interpretation shall be made accordingly.' The Lord Chancellor, now calling himself the Lord Chancellor of England and Wales, has subsequently informally reinforced this condition especially in relation to the provision of Welsh-speaking judges (*Western Mail*, 17 October 1998). In addition, in this section powers are set out to provide Welsh names for statutory bodies and to prescribe the availability of forms in Welsh. There are also provisions for the appropriate use of Welsh by industrial and provident societies, by credit unions, by charities and by companies. There is little doubt that the Act, as far as is possible through the means of government, gives a full measure of equality to Welsh.

Moreover in three crucial fields, education, publication and the media, substantial progress is manifest. In 1996 there were 449 primary schools out of a total of 1,681 where Welsh was the sole or primary medium of education, and a further ninety-five where Welsh was used as a medium for part of the curriculum. Together, these constituted 32.2 per cent of all primary schools. Furthermore, there were forty-nine secondary schools which were Welsh-speaking schools as defined by section 354(b) of the Education Act 1996. In addition, a whole range of schemes have been provided for adults to learn Welsh, by the University of Wales, by colleges, by local authorities and by organizations such as Cyd. The numbers of books published in Welsh have grown steadily. The total for 1975 was 308; for 1997 it was 636. Significantly, of the latter 63 per cent were books for children or young adults (Cyngor Llyfrau Cymraeg 1998). Finally, the establishment of S4C has provided a television channel where Welsh has to be used during the peak viewing hours. Along with Radio Cymru, it ensures that Welsh homes are not necessarily subject to a constant stream of English penetrating to the hearth, the ultimate point of language maintenance and reproduction.

The positive effect of all these developments is reflected in the census by a steady decrease in the rate of loss of Welsh-speakers. Thus, in the second half of the century decadal losses in percentages have been 8.2 (1951–61), 17.3 (1961–71), 6.3 (1971–81) and 1.4 (1981–91). This clear improvement has been accompanied by a substantial growth in Welsh-speaking amongst the young, as evidenced in Table 6.1. Furthermore, in spite of fears that the language is likely to be lost when the young leave school, the 1991 Census shows a retention of the language in the succeeding age group. Thus, the proportion speaking Welsh in the fifteen-to-twenty-four age group rose from 14.9 per cent in 1981 to 17.1 per cent in 1991.

The case for the view that the fight for the language has been won can be stated quite succinctly. Attitudes which were once antagonistic to the language and its propagation have been reversed, for support is now almost universal; all the domains of language use, which were lost from the Act of Union onwards, have been reclaimed; and finally, all this is evidenced in the data of the 1991 Census which suggest that a turnaround of historic proportions is nigh.

The Language: Problems Remain

Perversely, the opposing view, that the struggle to ensure the future of the language cannot be regarded as over, and that the language crisis still remains, can also draw upon supporting evidence from recent censuses and parallel surveys. It is argued, for instance, that a fundamental basis of a language's vitality is the number and proportion of the population who are brought up with it as their mother tongue, rather than as a second language. The census does not yield insights into such matters but a Welsh Office survey in 1992 revealed that only 56 per cent of Welsh-speakers regarded Welsh as their mother tongue. More disconcertingly, the figure for those aged between three and fifteen was only 27 per cent. Although this particular survey returned a slightly higher proportion claiming to be Welsh-speakers than the formal census (21.5 as against the 18.6 per cent), only 13.4 per cent regarded themselves as fluent. Again, data from the primary schools show that in 1996/7 only 6.4 per cent of the pupils came from homes where Welsh was spoken (Government Statistical Service 1998). Census data on household composition (Government Statistical Service 1994, table 5) reveal that households where all of the adults and dependent children spoke Welsh numbered only 27,513 out of a total of 1,111,689 – a mere 2.5 per cent. Households where all the dependent children spoke Welsh, regardless of the ability of the adults, numbered 66,201 – some 6 per cent. However, there were 762,898 households without dependent children and if they are subtracted, so that the figures are calculated only for households with children, then the percentages rise to 8 per cent and 19 per cent, respectively. Even so, examination of the more detailed bases of Welsh speech begin to raise unease over immediate assumptions from the simple census enumeration. This is compounded when the areas of decrease are scrutinized, for these are revealed as those parts of the north and west which have been the traditional heartland of the language, where Welsh has been the mother tongue, and which provided the reservoir of speakers for the growth areas of the south and east. This has been largely due to patterns of population movement, the out-migration of Welsh-speakers and the in-migration of population from outside Wales.

Out-migration has been no more than the continuation of the process of depopulation which has characterized rural Wales since the last quarter of the nineteenth century. The overlay of recent inward migration has made it much less apparent, but it still remains. The job opportunities for highly trained young people are limited and although it cannot be argued that emigration is language specific, nevertheless there is inevitably a drawing off of young, active Welsh-speakers. But the compensation, which has produced increases in the populations of the rural counties of the north and west, is largely of English monoglots. In the last quarter of the twentieth century, the process of counter-urbanization (rural retreating) has characterized the whole of the western world, and has led to the movement of people to the small towns and the countryside, seeking there alternative lifestyles. At the extreme it has given rise to communities such as Tipi Valley near Llandeilo and the eco-village of Brithdir Mawr near Newport in Pembrokeshire. But away from those extremes good numbers of people from England have moved to rural Wales attracted not only by the countryside itself, but by a different and less stressful way of life. The impact of these movements can be seen in Table 6.2 which sets out data from the migration table of the *1991 Census Welsh Language* (Government Statistical Service 1994). If the rural counties are examined it is apparent that in all cases the percentage of the in-migrants able to speak Welsh was considerably below the proportion speaking Welsh in the county. Thus in Gwynedd where 58.8 per cent of the population spoke Welsh, only 21.1 per cent of those coming into the county did so. Moreover, these are crude county figures and the impact on those areas where there were high proportions of Welsh-speakers have been all the greater. The data also show that although there were greater numbers of Welsh-speakers moving in, there was also a very considerable reciprocal flow outward. A table showing migration by language only became

Table 6.2. Welsh-speakers: in-migration and out-migration*

County	% resident population able to speak Welsh	% of in-migrants able to speak Welsh	% of Welsh-speaking in-migrants from outside Wales	Total number of in-migrants able to speak Welsh	Total number of out-migrants able to speak Welsh**
Clwyd	18.1	9.8	55.1	889	370
Dyfed	43.1	16.5	51.7	1416	691
Gwent	2.4	3.3	42.9	233	158
Gwynedd	58.8	21.1	63.3	1327	581
Mid Glamorgan	8.4	7.3	37.4	553	373
Powys	20.0	12.0	49.3	477	202
South Glamorgan	6.5	7.7	37.1	876	495
West Glamorgan	14.9	11.4	34.2	695	429
Wales	**18.9**	**10.8**	**48.9**	**6466**	**3299**

*Movements of residents within counties have been excluded from this tabulation.

**These figures do not include Welsh-speakers who had addresses in Wales a year before the census, but who subsequently moved out of Wales. To an indeterminate degree therefore they are an underestimate of the number of Welsh-speaking out-migrants.

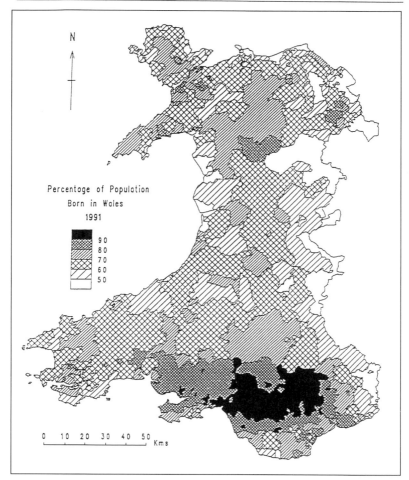

Figure 6.2. Percentage of population born in Wales, 1991.

available at the 1991 Census and it is worth observing that the decade 1981–91 was not the greatest period of counter-urbanization. Perhaps the most convincing evidence of the impact of immigration over recent decades is provided by the map of the percentage of the population born in Wales (Figure 6.2). As might be expected, the border regions show low proportions of Welsh-born, but so do significant parts of Ceredigion, Gwynedd and Conwy – the clear consequence of immigration. As long as these characteristics and trends are manifest in the heartland of the

Welsh language then it could be argued that the future of the language is far from assured.

It is for this reason that the central theme of agitation by Cymdeithas yr Iaith Gymraeg has been for legislation to prevent the purchase of property in Wales by in-migrants. It is epitomized in the slogan 'Nid yw Cymru ar werth', or 'Wales is not for sale'. The solution has been sought in the development of planning regulation. As a result of pressure by language activists the Welsh Office responded in 1988 by issuing Circular 53/88 entitled 'The Welsh Language: Development Plans and Planning Control'. It stated that, 'where the use of Welsh is part of the social fabric of a community, it is obviously appropriate to take this into consideration when drawing up land-use policies expressed in structure and local plans'. But the circular offered no guidelines as to how the recommendations were to be applied in practice and as a result attempts to restrict the sale of housing, through the use of what are termed Section 106 (Local Needs) Agreements, were consistently overturned by the Welsh Office on the grounds that they interfered with individual liberties and could undermine economic development. Discussions with local authorities led the Welsh Office in 1994 to intimate that the local authorities might identify settlements which could be regarded as 'culturally sensitive' where specific regulations could apply. No definition of 'culturally sensitive' has been agreed. But, following the principle, Ceredigion started with a draconian definition of areas deemed to be culturally sensitive in its draft local plan. Thus, new housing was to be restricted to people either born in the county or who had lived within a distance of twenty-five miles for at least five years. This was to apply to all areas where over 50 per cent of the population spoke Welsh. There were some exceptions, however, essentially the towns and suburbs. These radical policies were substantially revised and greatly modified in the final local plan (Ceredigion County Council 1998) where proposals in the consultation draft outlined above were deleted (p. 3) and a more general statement substituted. That statement simply reads that 'Proposals for development which can be demonstrated to be beneficial to the needs and interests of the Welsh language will be supported' (p. 33, para. 6.6), and that 'every encouragement should be given to the development of facilities and opportunities which specifically strengthen or promote the interests of the Welsh language'. It continues, 'This policy should not however be interpreted as justifying development which would not normally be acceptable. Proposals should still conform to other planning policies contained in the plan' (p. 34). Because of criticism of Circular 53/88, a revised draft was circulated by the Welsh Office in 1998 under the title 'The Welsh Language: Unitary Development Plans and Planning Control'.

But there remains a further problem. Much of the public discussion concerning the state of the language is based on the proportions of the population able to speak Welsh, both nationally and at local levels; equally significant, however, are the absolute numbers of speakers. If analysis focuses on this dimension then other patterns and trends emerge. Significantly, it is the areas with the largest numbers of Welsh-speakers – east Carmarthenshire, Swansea and Neath and Port Talbot – that have recorded the greatest absolute losses over recent times. The situation in the former county of West Glamorgan illustrates this. Here, between 1961 and 1991 numbers of speakers fell from approximately 76,000 to 51,500 – a reduction of some 31 per cent. Whereas in Wales as whole the fall in the number of Welsh-speakers for the decade 1981–91 was 1.4 per cent, for West Glamorgan it was a massive 11.4 per cent. Given this, it is hardly surprising that one of the areas chosen by the Welsh Language Board for its community research project should have been the Gwendraeth and Aman Valleys (Williams and Evans 1997), and that these were also among the sample sites selected by Mentrau Iaith or Language Enterprise Initiatives to reinvigorate Welsh as a community language. This is not the place for an extended discussion of the success of Mentrau Iaith – indeed that will not be possible for some years. But the crucial conclusion that arises from any discussion of the distribution of the language and changes in its distribution is that the two main core areas for the language – the traditional rural heartland with its relatively high proportions of Welsh-speakers, and the old industrial regions of south-west Wales with high numbers of Welsh-speakers – are both experiencing problems.

It could of course be argued that the fight for the language should be mainly concerned with its status. Whether or not the success of that fight ensures language survival and growth is another and a different problem, for whatever the status of the language it is the people's use of it which will determine its future well-being.

However, even within that limited context, the extent of success is open to question. Certainly the results of an attitude survey can be considered as meaningless. Many questioned will agree that the language should be supported for that has now become politically correct. But what that means in real terms of active backing and the willingness to ascribe priority in the allocation of resources is another matter. Again, it is possible to contend that much of what has been achieved in the Welsh Language Act is little more than tokenism writ large and that the Welsh-language schemes are cosmetic. That has certainly been the view of Cymdeithas yr Iaith which has 'accused the Welsh Language Board of providing a policy of "skin deep bilingualism" which would fail to establish the language as a normal feature of daily . . . life' (*Western Mail*, 2 October 1998). It is difficult to make any firm judgement on these issues other than to comment that doubts over the impact which the Language Act will have are certainly widespread. However, there are more fundamental bases for concern over the future and these are best discussed in relation to the Welsh Assembly. The idea that the language has been depoliticized is clearly untenable. The language will always be a competitor for resources and the distribution of scarce resources amongst competing interests is the very core of politics. This task will devolve to the Assembly.

Welsh and the Welsh Assembly

Much of the emotional attachment to the language derives from its role as the key constituent of Welsh ethnic identity. Both ethnic identity and the relation of language to it have been the subject of extensive review. At its most direct it is contended that 'the language spoken by somebody and his or her identity as a speaker of this language are inseparable. This is surely a piece of know-ledge as old as human speech itself. Language acts are acts of identity' (Tabouret-Keller 1997, 315). But perhaps some modification of that absolute statement is needed. Joshua A. Fishman, maybe the most widely respected writer on the subject, begins with but then modifies the same view:

> That there should be some link between language and ethnicity is obvious, since the major symbolic system of the human species must be

associated with the perceived dimensions of human aggregation. If people group themselves . . . into differently speaking collectivities . . . then their languages become both symbolic of as well as a basis for that grouping. However, just as ethnicity itself is perspectival and situational, and therefore variable in saliency, so the link between language and ethnicity is also variable. For some (and in some historical and situational contexts) language is the prime indicator and expression of their own and another's ethnicity, for others, language is both merely marginal and optional (i.e. detachable) vis-à-vis their ethnicity (and that of 'others' as well). (Fishman 1997, 329–30)

Briefly, therefore, although language is fundamentally linked to ethnicity it is not necessarily the only conditioning factor.

Fishman draws attention to 'some historical contexts' and it is in such a context, and for very specific historical reasons, that the Welsh language became the main ethnic signifier. This was because Wales never had a true political unity due to its very early assimilation by England, certainly two centuries before Scotland and Ireland became part of a 'united kingdom'. For that reason Wales never developed the institutional characteristics of a nation-state. Such as there were, a separate legal system for example, were snuffed out by the Act of Union of 1536 and the Act of Great Sessions of 1543. Since there were no institutions then, identity gathered about the clear remaining symbol, the one carrier of the myths, symbols and values of a people, and that was language. But the twentieth century has seen a process of the re-establishment of national institutions. During the second half of the nineteenth century and the early part of the twentieth century a University of Wales, a National Library and a National Museum were founded. The second half of the twentieth century has seen the creation of the Welsh Office and a Secretary of State. The Welsh Assembly, with a First Secretary, is a major step forward. Through these institutions, and other developments such as the progress of national sports teams, especially in rugby and soccer, a sense of identity has been built which is not immediately tied to language. Indeed, there are certainly some who see the possibility of building on this basis and eliminating what is seen as the divisive issue of language. The *Western Mail* on 28 January 1997 reported a characteristic attack by Professor Christie Davies of the Social Affairs Unit in an article titled 'Loyalty Misplaced' in which he called for the 'euthanasia of an already-dying language and the immediate removal of bilingual signs'. In Fishman's terms quoted above, language becomes merely marginal and optional in an *ethnie* reliant on other bases. It is here that the main problematic arises in relation to the Assembly, for to many it represents a major step in the progress to separate identity and as such pushes the language aside as the prime and only signifier. Indeed it is argued that the Assembly, however small the majority in its favour, unites whereas the language divides. It is only necessary to turn to a Celtic neighbour to derive a parallel. Dylan Phillips in pointing to the dangers inherent in the establishment of the Assembly quotes the Professor of Geography at University College Galway, Breandan Mac Aodha:

> by foolishly presuming that the establishment of an Irish State ensured the preservation of Irish culture, the League left the State with no effective critic, with no permanent prodder of its conscience. So it was that the Gaeltacht was allowed to wither away without any protest and the dedication of the State to its Gaelic ethos was permitted to become in large measure a dead letter. (Phillips 1998, 24)

The problem is likely to be even more acute when the Assembly has to decide on priorities as to its spending and the willingness of members to give relative importance to the language alongside calls for expenditure on the whole gamut of urgent social needs. It is in this context that Phillips (1998) wrote his pamphlet – *Pa ddiben protestio bellach?* (What need to protest further?). The need is apparent from the above discussion.

Linguistic Degeneration or Regeneration?

There is one additional matter relating to the language which is not within the competence of the present authors but which does demand mention, and that is change within the language itself. There are many studies devoted to what is called the death of language, or more circumspectly, language contact and language degeneration. Many of these aspects can be directly related to contemporary Welsh. Thus Craig writes, a category of speakers most typical of the situation of language death is that of the 'semi-speakers', defined by Dorian as imperfect speakers with very partial command of the receptive skills required to speak it, but almost perfect command of the skills required to understand it. (1997, 259)

Such a condition, though measured on a different basis, that of the ability to read and write as well as to speak, is undoubtedly characteristic of Welsh where in the 1991 Census although 508,098 claimed to speak the language only 369,609 returned an ability to speak, read and write it. This is not illiteracy in its conventional meaning but indicative of 'semi-speakers' noted above. The only reservation which needs to be made is that 'semi-speakers' could be equally characteristic of language growth, that is of the ability to speak before the competence to write, for example, is acquired. But other features of language degeneration can apparently be identified in Welsh. Amongst those usually set out (Craig 1997, 261–64) are: loss of registers, lexical loss (where the loss of native lexicon is accompanied by replacement from the dominant language), loss in phonology (where modification of pronunciation occurs), loss in morphology (where insecurity develops over structures) and loss in syntax. Of these, whereas loss of registers was at one time a characteristic of Welsh, where the language was used for informal communication as against English for formal contacts, that has largely been reversed by the language movement. Loss of phonology has not occurred. But all the other features have. Lexical loss, with a widespread use of English words, is widely marked. So is loss in morphology where, for example, the gender of words is often unrealized and mutations are certainly insecure. Numbers have always been complex in Welsh and now simplified forms are almost universally used. Loss in syntax is apparent too, especially where morphological tense is dropped in favour of periphrastic forms, and where the more esoteric forms of the verb are simply ignored. Internal vowel changes are abandoned (*Cenwch* – *canwch*, for example). All this comes to a head in the nature of the language used in popular television programmes such as *Heno* on S4C where the modifications outlined above are accepted, much to the chagrin of language purists. But there is one important reservation which must be made. All these features are seen as evidence of language degeneration, but they can equally be seen as evidence of regeneration as learners struggle to bring their language up to standard. Certainly, the one point which needs to be stressed is that the language is not static but changing, and that change can be seen as much as evidence of vitality as of decay. It is also likely that the Welsh of the twenty-first century will be a somewhat different language from that even of the recent past.

Conclusion

A conclusion as to the contemporary condition of the Welsh language must be derived from the contradictory trends which have been outlined. In formal terms it can be asserted that the fight for the language has been successful. The status is the equal of English and all the domains of use lost over the centuries have been reclaimed, most importantly that of education. The catastrophic decreases in the number of speakers that characterized the period after the Second World War have been reined back, and there have been significant gains amongst the young. On the other hand, there are manifest problems in the threat to the language in its traditional heartland, especially as a consequence of in-migration, and the proportion for whom Welsh is the mother tongue is dangerously low. In addition the greatest absolute losses have been in those areas where the largest numbers of Welsh-speakers are to be found. Moreover, the emergence of an ethnic identity made more explicit and surer by the rise of specific Welsh institutions and devolved governmental responsibility, remove the significance of the language as the sole symbol of Welshness. Most certainly the language is in a far healthier state than could possibly have been envisaged some thirty years ago, but the future is far from assured.

References

Aitchison, J. W. and Carter, H. (1987). 'The Welsh language in Cardiff: a quiet revolution', *Transactions of the Institute of British Geographers*, NS 12, 482–92.
Aitchison, J. W. and Carter, H. (1994). *A Geography of the Welsh Language* (Cardiff: University of Wales Press).
Aitchison, J. W. and Carter, H. (1997). 'Language reproduction: reflections on the Welsh example', *Area*, 29, 7–66.

Ceredigion County Council (1998). *Ceredigion Local Plan*, vol. 1. *Written Statement* (Aberaeron: Ceredigion County Council).

Craig, C. G. (1997). 'Language contact and language degeneration', in F. Coulmas (ed.), *The Handbook of Sociolinguistics* (Oxford: Blackwell), 257–70.

Cyngor Llyfrau Cymru (1998). *Dadansoddiad o Lyfrau Cymraeg 1972–1997* (Aberystwyth: C.Ll.C.).

European Commission (1996). *The Production and Reproduction of the Minority Language Groups in the European Union* (Luxembourg: Office for Official Publications of the European Union Communities).

Fishman, J. A. (1997). 'Language and ethnicity: the view from within', in F. Coulmas (ed.), *The Handbook of Sociolinguistics* (Oxford: Blackwell).

Government Statistical Service (1994). *1991 Census Welsh Language* (London: HMSO).

Government Statistical Service (1998). *Statistics of Education and Training in Wales: Schools 1998* (Cardiff: Welsh Office).

Jenkins, G. H. (ed.) (1998a). *A Welsh Language before the Industrial Revolution* (Cardiff: University of Wales Press).

Jenkins, G. H. (ed.) (1998b). *Language and Community in the Nineteenth Century* (Cardiff: University of Wales Press).

Phillips, D. (1998). *Pa ddiben protestio bellach?* (Tal-y-bont: Y Lolfa).

Pryce, W. T. R. (1978). 'Welsh and English in Wales: a spatial analysis based on the linguistic affiliations of parochial communities', *Transactions of the Honourable Society of Cymmrodorion*, 229–61.

Tabouret-Keller, A. (1997). 'Language and identity', in F. Coulmas (ed.), *The Handbook of Sociolinguistics* (Oxford: Blackwell), 315–26.

Welsh Language Board (1996a). *A Strategy for the Welsh Language* (Cardiff: Welsh Language Board).

Welsh Language Board (1996b). *Welsh Language Schemes: Their Preparation and Approval in Accordance with the Welsh Language Act 1993* (Cardiff: Welsh Language Board).

Williams C. H. and Evans, J. (1997). *The Community Research Project* (Cardiff: Welsh Language Board).

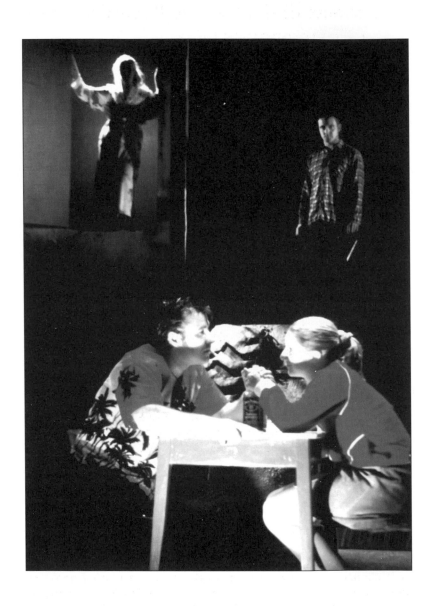

7 Aspects of the Live and Recorded Arts in Contemporary Wales

STEVE BLANDFORD

'The only sexy thing about Wales used to be the sheep, but that's all changed.' Nina Dempsey on how the Taffia dragged Cymru out of the pits.

> (By-line on an article entitled 'To Dai For' in *Frank (Another Women's Magazine)*, September 1997)

Newport, the new Seattle . . .

> (*The New York Times*, cited by Brian Logan, *Guardian*, 15 February 1997)

Beneath the puns, clichés and damnings-with-faint-praise in articles typified by the above quotations, are there grounds for asserting that there is currently a minor Welsh cultural renaissance that is genuinely shaking perceptions of the country, both in the rest of the UK and internationally? This chapter will attempt to chronicle some of the recent developments in Welsh popular music, theatre, film and television drama and assess how far they have indeed managed to bring what Peter Morgan has called a 'degree of cool and confidence to the national debate' (Morgan 1997, 39).

Pop Music

If somebody had said ten years ago that a Welsh band's single would enter the charts at number one with a title taken from an Aneurin Bevan speech and lyrics about the Spanish Civil War then their chances of being taken seriously would have rated about as highly as those of say . . . a Welshman becoming Prime Minister. The Manic Street Preachers' *This is My Truth Tell Me Yours* not only did this, but the album of the same title also remained for some weeks in the top ten of the album charts and went on to win the 1999 'Brit' award. Perhaps more significantly nobody is hugely surprised. The Manics, Catatonia, the Super Furry Animals, the Stereophonics, Gorki's Zygotic Mynci and others have arguably taken Welsh music beyond patronizing novelty-value status to the point where it is has become internationally recognized as making a significant contribution to contemporary music in ways that distinguish it from the general mass of the British rock and pop scene.

Back in October 1996 *Rolling Stone* magazine asserted that 'the most exciting and innovative scene in the UK is now happening far beyond the borders of the insular Brit-pop community – in Wales' (Wiederhorn 1996), and in August 1998 the normally insular *Washington Post* featured a lengthy article on Catatonia's rise from Welsh-language novelty at Breton festivals to Mercury Prize nominees and album chart-toppers across Europe with *International Velvet* (Jenkins 1998). These are just two of the many examples of increasingly prestigious international coverage and, whilst the pursuit of the good opinions of smart American papers is probably far from most of the bands' agendas, it does illustrate the extent to which they are making a powerful contribution to a new identity for Wales which is clearly being linked in commentators' minds to the political changes under way in Wales. (The *Post* article makes specific reference to Catatonia's voting habits and the precise nature of their 'nationalism'.)

So what kind of contribution is it that Wales is getting from its rock musicians? To begin with I think it is important to stress that it is a diverse one. Many of the bands have things in common, to be sure, but they represent such a broad range of musical styles and influences that it would be crass to try and group them too closely. Many would say the most important thing that they collectively give to Wales's identity is simply youth itself. To a culture used to seeing itself represented abroad as the land of Harry Secombe, Shirley Bassey, Tom Jones or even Max Boyce, the success of Catatonia and the Manic Street Preachers is, to say the least, an injection of energy.

There is clearly more to it than this, though. If we start with the bands' sense of place we do certainly get varying degrees of reference to their sense of Welshness, but crucially it is far from being the principal thing that governs their work. For some this means a new freedom to laugh at your own culture and yourself rather than always being on the defensive. The chorus to Catatonia's *International Velvet* is '*Everyday when I wake up / I thank the Lord I'm Welsh*', whilst the Welsh verses 'are actually saying what a sleepy little nation Wales is, how we need a good kick in the backside sometimes to get anything done. So we're sort of poking fun at ourselves in the Welsh language part' (quoted in Jenkins 1998). As far as the Super Furry Animals are concerned:

> 'There's always been good music in Wales' says the singer, Gruff Rhys. But before, the ones who made it did it by having no relevance to anything, like The Darling Buds. I don't feel anything in common with the other Welsh bands – we're all from different parts of the country, . . . I suppose the one thing we're all fighting against is this romanticised, comedy view of Wales.

And later in the same article, Rhys still more explicitly explains: 'We're introducing people to different kinds of heroes . . . who maybe don't live in that clichéd leeks and rugby view of Wales' (quoted in Forrest 1996).

What is perhaps most refreshing and interesting, though, is that the bands' own heroes are so diverse, so that one relatively tight and outmoded vision of Welsh popular culture is not simply being replaced by another. Whilst the more self-consciously 'political' Manic Street Preachers included the following dedication on the cover of *Everything Must Go*: 'Inspiration – Tower Colliery, Cynon Valley, South Wales', the Super Furry Animals have a close association with Howard Marks, whose fame rests on once being 'the most wanted drug smuggler in the world'. Different models of liberation perhaps, but undoubtedly both new versions of Wales that retain interesting and unpredictable roots in what they seek to leave behind.

Some mention must here be made of the role that Welsh language has played in the current music scene. For many the bottom line would be well summarized by Peter Morgan (1997, 39): 'Recording in Welsh, performing in Welsh, Gorky's and the Super Furries have enlarged the sense of what is possible, of what one world finds of interest in another.' The importance of the implicit stance taken on the language by some of the new Welsh bands (for example, the Super Furry Animals have a clause in their contract with Creation that allows them to record in Welsh) is that it is yet another dimension to the way that the culture is moving forward. They refuse to render the language invisible, even in an industry as dominated by English as the music business; but nor is it an entrenched purist position. Instead bilingualism becomes a layer of complexity in a culture, to be embraced as richness (as it is in a lot of Europe) with a life in contemporary art forms, rather than the subject of divisions.

It would be easy to overestimate the importance of Wales's possessing a lively popular music scene in the 1990s; the list of prominent bands is a little larger than those that there has been space to mention here, but the numbers are still comparatively small. On the other hand, of the three art forms under discussion here it is rock and pop music that has delivered not only the largest audiences for a new Welsh culture, but also arguably the greatest diversity. The picture that emerges therefore is not just a dimension of Brit-pop, but of bands emerging from a culture genuinely interested in forging new identities in ways that actually have some meaning for young audiences.

> Political shifts have cultural roots: the role of Scottish bands in helping to define a modern Scots identity has often been mentioned . . . For the moment, it seems as if that energy and confidence is working through Welsh music. Goodness me, perhaps it's finally cool to be Welsh . . . (Morgan 1997, 39)

Theatre

In the context of the audiences being reached by popular music and film, arguably what Wales lacks most in the area of theatre, especially around the largest centres of population in the south, is a natural home for both new writing and intelligent revivals of modern and classical drama. Made In Wales, set up in the early 1980s to foster new Welsh writing for the theatre, has made often noble attempts to occupy some of this territory, whilst Theatr Clwyd in the north has had periods of success under imaginative directors. The current director of Made In Wales has secured working space and, like his predecessor, has tried hard to find new voices, particularly in under-represented areas of the community, but if Made In Wales could run its workshops, new writing festivals and special production projects in Cardiff in the context of their being something like the West Yorkshire Playhouse, then it would be able to flourish more easily.

So much then for what Welsh theatre lacks. It is arguable that what it has possessed over the last two decades is much more remarkable. In terms of small-scale (in some cases not so small) experimental theatre Wales has often been at the very forefront of work in the UK and in certain ways of Europe as well. For most people Brith Gof have been at the very heart of this 'movement' in Welsh theatre in the 1980s and 1990s and it is worth starting a consideration of this body of work with a statement by Mike Pearson, its central figure since the company was founded:

> The aim of Brith Gof is to develop a new, vibrant and distinctive theatre tradition in Wales, one which is relevant and responsive to the perceptions, experience, aspirations and concerns of a minority culture and a small nation and which is more than just a pale reflection of English theatre convention. (Quoted in Adams 1996, 55)

Pearson's statement was made at a conference in Barcelona and his vision is clearly that of a Welsh culture drawing strength from positioning itself alongside that of Catalunya and other marginalized aspirant 'nations' across Europe and beyond.

Although the company has produced a very varied body of work, in the end though it is perhaps for two principal reasons that Brith Gof's work will be seen as crucial to recent Welsh theatre; the first is the use of unconventional spaces to make theatre and second is their contribution to theoretical debates, not only about Welsh theatre, but about performance in an international context. On the question of using non-traditional spaces Mike Pearson has said:

> Wales has only a limited range of theatre auditoria. Experimental theatre has always sought other venues. This is not solely the result of expediency, but challenges the notion that the auditorium is a neutral vessel of representation. Seeing it rather as the spatial machine of a dominant discourse which distances spectators from spectacle and literally 'keeps them in their place' in the dark, sitting in rows, discouraging of eye contact and interaction. It dismisses the stage as a field ploughed to exhaustion. (Pearson 1997, 94–5)

The overall project of 'site-specific' theatre to which Brith Gof has made such an important contribution has then a fundamentally subversive purpose. It finds a natural home in a culture that has consistently needed to keep alive questions about where power genuinely resides.

It is possible to see this dimension of Brith Gof's work as using theatre as a means to set up new relationships between its audience and its own history (one thinks for example of their stunning production of *Haern* (1992) in The Old Iron Foundry, Tredegar). Very often a Brith Gof audience has had to make an actual 'journey' to view a performance beyond simply that of going to a theatre; typically an audience would be transported *en masse* to an inaccessible location. This heightens the sense of an exploration or investigation, forcing us to confront the bleak reality of a disused Rover car plant after the 1980s had finished with it and to explore its 'meaning' in ways that go beyond naturalist representation.

Beyond this distinctive Welsh take on the notion of 'site-specific' theatre Brith Gof, along with the Centre for Performance Research (with which it has had key overlaps of personnel), has also been central to the country's powerful contribution to theoretical debates about the nature of performance and of theatre itself. This is not the context in which to explore the work fostered by these companies in depth, but it is important to record not only the invitations to Brith Gof to perform throughout Europe, particularly in contexts where theatre is seen as a key focus of debate around marginalized identities, but also the ability of the Centre for Performance Research to attract practitioners of international standing to their frequent conferences, workshops and retreats. Their contribution to the field of performance research is undoubtedly of international quality.

Frequently lumped together with Brith Gof as representing Welsh experimental theatre's predominant 'physical' nature is Swansea's Volcano Theatre. The two companies are of course radically different, not only in the way they make theatre but in their perceived relationship to Wales. Paul Davies, the company's joint artistic director, put it like this:

Volcano is a national and international touring theatre company . . . Their work has not focused on 'the problem of Welshness' . . . One consequence of this is that it might be said that Volcano has made little impact within the Principality. Nevertheless the work has been widely seen outside of Wales, in Hong Kong, Greece, Spain, Macedonia, Germany, Montenegro, France, Italy, Russia, Holland . . . (Davies 1997, 163)

I am not sure whether 'little impact within the Principality' is quite right, but certainly Volcano's agenda has rarely if ever explicitly been about Wales. This of course has made them absolutely key to the projection of a young and vital Welsh theatre scene.

Their concerns have been about retaining a sense of theatre's political importance whilst seeking to expand what that can mean. For Volcano this has often meant controversial interventions into debates on sexual politics and questions of masculine and feminine identities. They have also brilliantly confused those who use the 'physical theatre' tag too easily and lazily by devoting a lot of work to exploring text-based theatre traditions. In this they can hardly be accused of shying away from the big challenges as they have taken on both Ibsen (*How to Live*) and Chekhov (*Vagina Dentata*).

As implied above, Volcano's contribution to Welsh cultural identity has been to avoid discussing it and instead choose to stand as living proof that there is exciting radical theatre made in Wales. In doing this they have managed to put a kind of Welsh identity on the menu not only at places like the Riverside Studios, but right across Europe.

It is clearly significant that the names of both Fiction Factory (formerly Y Cwmni) and its founder and leading practitioner Ed Thomas are connected with all three sections of this chapter. It is arguable that Thomas has made one of the most significant contributions of any individual to the current reputation of contemporary Welsh theatre and film and he has constantly used the work of Welsh rock and pop musicians as 'soundtracks' in both media.

Unlike Volcano, Fiction Factory's work for the theatre has often been centrally concerned with a contemporary Welsh identity. Indeed for David Adams it is entirely what Thomas the writer is about:

Virtually everything Thomas writes addresses itself to the problem of cultural identity and he echoes Gwyn Alf's ideas about an invented

Wales. His first major play, *House of America*, was a metaphor for Wales' reliance on myth and tradition, its low self-esteem, its apparent need to tell lies about itself, its dependence on American culture. It's an amazing piece of theatre, possibly the best play to have come out of Wales . . . (Adams 1996, 52)

Even if the kind of judgement that Adams makes in the last line will always provoke debate, few can deny that *House of America* in its several incarnations has made a major impact on the way that Welsh drama is viewed both inside and outside Wales. Thomas has spoken a number of times of how the BBC mistook the play for another social-realist piece about drugs, mine closures and incest in the Valleys when he and Marc Evans (the director of the film version) took it to them as a potential project. As is now widely recognized, what Thomas has done is take this kind of con-temporary mythology and radically rework it in ways that owe much more to a notion of a theatre of dream and fantasy than one of social realism.

The work of Thomas and Fiction Factory for film and television is discussed elsewhere in the chapter, but the power of their work for theatre in not only *House of America* but *Flowers of the Dead Red Sea, East from the Gantry, Song from a Forgotten City* and *Gas Station Angel* has brought it closer to that most elusive of all prizes: a theatre that is interested in experimentation, in form, in asking difficult questions of the culture from which it springs, but which also manages to reach out and create new theatre audiences, even if only on a modest scale.

In such a brief account it is inevitable that more is left out than has been included. In the very generalized area of 'experimental theatre' is the work of Man Act whose powerful, physical explorations of, in particular, contemporary masculine identity earned them a prestigious Barclays New Stages award. Alma Theatre, nurtured on a shoestring by a group of women graduates from the Aberystwyth drama department, still survives producing witty and intelligent work that continually surprises in its variety; Hijinx Theatre manages to combine a commitment to touring to community and non-traditional venues with real theatrical ambition. Earthfall is frequently labelled as a 'dance' company, but is close to producing physical theatre, often in combination with other media. Above all perhaps there is the work of Geoff Moore at Moving Being, which is now confined to short-term projects, but which has been such a source of inspiration for so many of those mentioned here.

Dalier Sylw have done much to keep alive a tradition of new theatre writing in Welsh by regularly staging the work of those who have had to turn mainly to TV and film for their opportunities: Gareth Miles, Sion Eirian, Meic Povey. A whole host of small companies maintain a strong tradition of educational theatre in Wales that so often defies the patronizing pigeonhole of 'Theatre in Education': Cardiff's Theatre Iolo, Porth's Spectacle Theatre, Theatr Powys and Aberystwyth's Arad Goch have all used (variously) strong new writing, bilingualism and physical experimentation in ways that link them firmly with the contemporary Welsh defiance of convention in theatre practice.

Sadly, though, the future of theatre-making in Wales may be all about fragility. A row still simmers about an Arts Council decision to reduce the status of the funding that even Brith Gof receives and there is much pessimism about more wide-ranging funding proposals that will further reduce the number of companies that receive the revenue funding that provides at least some kind of stability. Whilst it may always have lacked a solid middle ground, the recent history of theatre in Wales has hardly been dull; at the time of writing many of the sources of energy and vitality are in danger of being obliterated and the confidence of practitioners so severely eroded that a recent influential report was able to state: 'One of the concerns that a smaller country must have about its cultural life is that it is possible to allow practice to decline beyond the minimum level of sustainability . . . I'm afraid to say that Welsh theatre is close to this line' (Clarke 1998, 6–7). If David Clarke is right then it is clearly scandalous that a recent history such as the one outlined above be allowed to be thrown away; for the moment let us hope that the closing words of his report will end up being the keynote for the future of Welsh theatre and that this chapter will not end up being a contribution to an extended obituary notice: 'Look at the work of many artists working and showing their work all over Wales and it is easy to have one's faith refreshed. Let us carry it through to action' (Clarke 1998, 16).

Film

In the area of film and television fictions it is inevitable that comparisons are always made with Scotland and with both sides of the Irish border. Whilst Scotland and the Republic of Ireland have made a powerful impact in terms of both film and television drama in the last two decades, Wales (until very recently) has lagged behind. One large-scale contributory factor has clearly been the massive dependence of the UK film industry on Channel 4 and Wales's very different relationship to this source of funding because of the existence of S4C.

Ironically the first 'Film on Four' season did contain a powerful and politically controversial film from Wales's most consistent director over the period, Karl Francis, but *Giro City* (1982) proved to be a false dawn. In terms of feature-film funding over the next decade Channel 4 virtually ignored Wales to the point where Francis asked the Commission for Racial Equality to initiate a prosecution against the channel. The attitude was (and arguably still is) that Wales has S4C so it has no right to expect funding from a channel that serves hardly any of its population.

What all this adds up to is that at a crucial time for the development of the overall British film industry, a time when Film on Four and Channel 4's Department of Independent Film and Video were both building substantial records of achievement, there was a total absence of Welsh projects.

It is important here of course to say that S4C has played a crucial part in getting some fine work in Welsh made. Perhaps the most significant achievement politically was the shortlisting of Paul Turner's *Hedd Wynn* for the 1993 Best Foreign Language Academy Award, but S4C's support was crucial to the building of a substantial body of work by Endaf Emlyn (*Un Nos Ola Leuad/One Full Moon*, 1991; *Gadael Lenin/Leaving Lenin*, 1993; and *Y Mapiwr/The Making of Maps*, 1995) as well as work by Steve Gough (*Elenya*, 1991), Karl Francis himself (*Milwr Bychan/Boy Soldier*, 1986), Stephen Bayly (*Rhosyn a Rhith/Coming Up Roses*, 1986) and Ceri Sherlock (*Dafydd*, 1993, *Branwen*, 1994, *Cameleon*, 1996).

Inevitably though there is a huge difference in scale relative to Channel 4's achievement. This is partly because the Welsh fourth channel was set up with an entirely different remit which did not include the same commitment to innovation or the encouragement to tackle difficult or sensitive subjects. At present S4C is attempting to increase its presence as a source of feature-film funding, but during an important period it was unable to exert the kind of influence that might have given Welsh film-makers the opportunities that their Scottish counterparts have had.

If we are looking for the causes of the scarcity of telling Welsh images during the last twenty years we must also examine the records of the major English-language broadcasters in Wales. For long periods during the late 1980s and 1990s both BBC Wales and HTV struggled to maintain any consistent output in fiction at all.

The BBC drama department in Llandaf has suffered from numerous changes of senior personnel, from being ignored and patronized by London at a time of huge internal change to the organization and most of all from a failure to establish a clear policy that would have encouraged young writers and directors from Wales. There is strong evidence that during the 1990s there was so little confidence in Welsh drama output that even when a series or single drama was commissioned from Wales there were attempts to minimize its 'Welshness'. This included the casting of non-Welsh leads such as Kevin Whately (*Trip Trap*), Dawn French (*Tender Loving Care*) and Alan Bates (*Oliver's Travels*), the use of non-Welsh directors on anything likely to be given a strong network presence and even, according to the original author, the watering down of any sense of 'place' on the promising detective series *Harper and Iles*.

Partly as a result of the appalling financial crisis caused by the Thatcher administration's decision to auction the regional franchises, HTV has operated on a shoestring drama budget for a long time. Much of this has been absorbed in well-intentioned, but rarely inspiring, exercises such as filming the Sherman Theatre's season of lunchtime short dramas for later broadcast and it has gone through a period of hardly generating any of its own drama at all.

At the time of writing there are more promising signs from both broadcasters. BBC Drama in Cardiff is now headed by Pedr James who has directing credits which include major achievements such as *Our Friends in the North* to his name; there are schemes to attract and nurture new writers, an increased staff of script editors and producers has been recruited and there appears to be a determination to up the rate of commissions and the Welsh presence on network. HTV also has a new head, an experienced independent producer Peter Edwards, who has initiated a soap opera project set in Merthyr and also begun to commission relatively prestigious single dramas, some of which might get their chance of a cinema release. However, the failure to establish a real culture of producing film fictions, especially at a time when the British film industry as a whole was struggling back to a kind of life, has undoubtedly been damaging.

What, then, are the small, but significant achievements of the current industry in Wales? To date it is little more than three feature films in English released (*House of America, Twin Town, Darklands*), with more in the pipeline; a powerful and innovative range of short films (particularly the PICS collaboration between BBC Wales and the Welsh Film Council); the establishment of a number of individual talents with distinctive voices that are being heard outside Wales – Ed Thomas, Marc Evans, Ceri Sherlock and Endaf Emlyn and to an extent Julian Richards, Justin Kerrigan and Sara Sugarman. There is also, of course, an internationally significant animation industry that resulted in 1998 and 1999 Oscar nominations for Joanna Quinn, with a body of mainstream work which embraces both Super Ted and animated Shakespeare.

What is perhaps more important is the *kind* of work that is currently being produced and the way that it tends to fit loosely into the type of image presented by rock and pop music and some aspects of contemporary theatre. At the time of writing, the contemporary film industry is represented in the wider public consciousness primarily by the three films released in 1997, *House of America, Twin Town* and to a lesser extent *Darklands*, though some would make a justifiable case for the equal significance of the work in Welsh of Endaf Emlyn and Ceri Sherlock, whilst Karl Francis's most recent work, *Streetlife*, was controversially consigned to television despite being conceived for feature release.

House of America, whilst depicting a family in the most dire circumstances, still manages to suggest a Welsh capacity to imagine, to dream and to reinvent itself. Throughout the various versions of the stage play and film Thomas has never seemed quite sure how much to condemn his doomed central characters for basing their whole lives on a Kerouac-inspired vision of the American dream. As audience of the film we are also never sure whether we are seeing just a distorted vision of the upper Swansea valley or a wholly mythic landscape upon which is being played out a nightmare metaphor for contemporary south Wales. Above all, the film is full of oddities that leave us groping for any sense of reality. For example, in a film that is so much about how our hopes and dreams are defined by an all-enveloping American sensibility, it is a brilliant reversal to have commissioned a soundtrack by John Cale. It turns out that Cale, one of the founder members of the hugely influential Velvet Underground, collaborator with people like Lou Reed and Andy Warhol, was born and bred in south Wales.

With its hip soundtrack that mixes Cale's original score with Tom Jones, Pulp, the Manic Street Preachers, Catatonia and Primal Scream, *House of America* is the epitome of what many hope will be an emergent Welsh culture. Still concerned with identity, but in wholly different ways, it is young, literate and intelligently ironic. Its Dutch co-producers, its French cinematographers (who also worked on the acclaimed *La Haine* in 1995) and its central concern with American impact on minority cultures all mark it out as representative of a Wales that remains interested in its past, but which recognizes the possibilities in a much more self-confident future that will see the country repositioning itself in Europe and beyond.

The question of whether *Twin Town* was 'good for Wales' has been hotly contested, even amongst those who are passionate supporters of a Welsh film industry. Its backing by the *Trainspotting* production team of Andrew Macdonald and Danny Boyle inevitably drew comparisons with the latter and many concluded that Wales was being treated to a second-rate version that simply sought to cash in on *Trainspotting*'s success: 'The shocking thing is that for all *Twin Town*'s determination to borrow from *Trainspotting*, it has so signally failed to capture the essence of the earlier film' (Thompson 1997, 54). *Twin Town* also incurred the wrath of a number of self-styled guardians of Wales's image, including the tourist board and the clergy. The latter were rather comically concerned that the film would lead to 'a series of copycat poodle beheadings' – a reaction surely more likely to encourage a comic-book view of Wales than anything that *Twin Town* was likely to achieve. The film clearly did not have the same kind of ambition as *House of America*, either in formal terms or in relation to an understanding of contemporary Wales. It does however share with that film a kind of up-beat irreverent confidence that allows it to ignore most of the obvious ways to 'be Welsh' or, better still, to laugh at them from within.

The third film that there is space to consider as representative of the current film 'industry' is Julian Richards's *Darklands*. It is the closest of the three to being a popular genre piece, but also the one to get the least widespread distribution. It is heavily based on a British cult horror film of the 1970s, *The Wicker Man*, and bravely uses this unlikely vehicle to try to combine a consideration of a quasi-fascist version of Welsh nationalism, a detective story set in Port Talbot and paganism. At times the film's very low budget clearly shows, but we again have a film that dares to take risks both aesthetically and politically. It refuses to be confined by an old Welsh agenda, but like the other two has a strong sense of recent history. The director has often been one of those bemoaning the lack of opportunity for monoglot English-speaking young directors in Wales and he did clearly see his film as being a small part of a contemporary debate over post-devolution identity: ' "My film's not primarily political," Richards says now. "But the Devolution vote proved that Wales remains a deeply divided country and part of my agenda was to say that, in Wales, English language culture has a right to exist equally." ' (Berry 1997, 3). Nothing particularly remarkable about this perhaps: what is striking is that Richards should choose to attempt such an intervention through a horror piece capable of winning a major prize at a Portuguese fantasy film festival.

If these three films and the establishment of reputations for Ed Thomas and Marc Evans (his film *Towards the Light*, a drama based on the Tower colliery story, was trailed by the *Observer* as 'set to do for South Wales Miners what *The Full Monty* did for Sheffield steel workers') are the most tangible outcomes of a new film revival there looks like being more to come. Out of the short-film initiatives previously mentioned are emerging young directors with either feature débuts forthcoming or at least enough critical attention to give hope that one is not far away: a group of women (interestingly, given the traditional view of Welsh culture) led by Sara Sugarman, Margaret Constantas and Philippa Cousins are among those who have had genuinely interesting work recognized so far, and as this volume goes to press, Justin Kerrigan's *Human*

Traffic is being released. The early reviews suggest a positive reaction and, despite being funded from Ireland rather than Wales, the film gives us images of Cardiff that may be some of the most important to date in revising the way that the world sees the Welsh.

The Welsh International Film Festival was held in Cardiff for the first time in 1998, controversially moving from its home in Aberystwyth with the express intention of raising its profile; a Media Agency for Wales, operating inevitably out of Cardiff Bay, had the specific aim of championing 'the development of film, television and new media in Wales to its full potential', and there is talk yet again of the establishment of a Welsh Film School. A fragile culture is clearly established and it has already thrown up individual talents that are trying to redefine what is possible when working in Wales. The hope must now be that it can last and that the next decade will see film and television fictions become an important part of a much wider project to 'reinvent' Wales.

References

Adams, D. (1996). *Stage Welsh* (Llandysul: Gomer).

Berry, D. (1997). 'Darkman', *Orson* (November).

Clarke, D. (1998). *The State of the Arts* (Cardiff: Institute of Welsh Affairs).

Davies, P. (1997). 'Physical theatre and its discontents', in A. M. Taylor (ed.), *Staging Wales: Welsh Theatre and its Discontents* (Cardiff: University of Wales Press).

Forrest, E. (1996). 'Leek jokes: just say no . . .', *Independent* (6 December).

Jenkins, M. (1998). 'Welsh band Catatonia: internationalists abroad', *The Washington Post* (9 August).

Morgan, P. (1997). 'My patio's on fire', *Planet*, 125.

Pearson, M. (1997). 'Special worlds, secret maps: a poetics of performance', in A. M. Taylor (ed.), *Staging Wales: Welsh Theatre 1979–1997* (Cardiff: University of Wales Press).

Thompson, B. (1997). 'Twin Town', *Sight and Sound*, 7/4 (April).

Wiederhorn, J. (1996). 'Wales a go-go', *Rolling Stone*, 17 October 1996.

8 The Media in Wales

STUART ALLAN and TOM O'MALLEY

What is BBC Wales for? It is there to serve the nation of Wales in all its diversity, and with united purpose. It is there to reflect, and enrich the life of the Nation, to draw its strength and purpose from the community but at the same time to put back into the community the richness and variety it perceives and reflects; to be reporter and patron at one and the same time. It should continue to provide the debating chamber for democracy, the platform for artistic achievement, and the repository for historic archives. It is there to speak of Wales and things Welsh with authenticity and authority to the United Kingdom as a whole. Above all, it is there to provide enchanting programmes of relevance to be enjoyed and appreciated by all those who choose to listen and watch wherever they are.

(Geraint Stanley Jones (1990, 160), former Managing Director of BBC Regional Broadcasting)

Introduction

To the extent that one can safely generalize about the variety of existing examinations of the mass media in Wales, we think it fair to suggest that many of these analyses share a distinguishing feature. That is to say, they generally impose – either explicitly or, more typically, implicitly – a sharp conceptual division between the media and the larger society within which they operate. Studies tend to focus on the media themselves, so as to ask questions regarding how they affect Welsh society (the findings usually make for grim reading). Or they centre on Welsh society in order to explore how it affects the media ('the Welsh public gets the media it deserves'). In both instances, the respective sides of this relationship are usually treated as being relatively exclusive or independent from one another.

A key aim of this chapter is to render problematic this media–society dichotomy from a sociological perspective. We want to suggest that the invocation of such a dichotomy is placing severe limits on what sorts of questions can be asked about the media in Wales. Should the media be removed, in analytical terms, from the cultural, economic and political contexts within which they operate, we run the risk of exaggerating their power and influence. At the same time, any enquiry into how a society is 'made and remade in every individual mind', to use Raymond Williams's (1958) apt turn of phrase, needs to account in one way or another for the efficacy of the media. In our view, then, this media–society dichotomy needs to be transcended so that we may better grapple with all of the messy complexities, and troublesome contradictions, which otherwise tend to be neatly swept under the conceptual carpet.

It is with this concern in mind that this chapter outlines, first, a broad set of issues regarding the role the media play in the construction of Welsh identity. At stake is the need better to understand how these different media institutions are shaping the projection of contending discourses of Welshness across the 'public sphere'. Secondly, the chapter proceeds to explore the development in Wales of the newspaper, radio and television industries, respectively, from a sociological vantage point. Special attention will be given to considering how they are each regulated by the state (an emphasis is placed on the impact of London-based decisions on the Welsh context), the changing dynamics of their ownership patterns and the extent to which their content encourages forms of active citizenship by their audiences. Finally, the chapter will conclude by posing several questions for future sociological enquiry.

The 'Debating Chamber for Democracy'

Before turning to examine the mass media in relation to debates about the construction of Welsh identity, it is important briefly to clarify a number of conceptual issues pertinent to sociological enquiries of this type. The term 'mass media', for our purposes here at least, refers primarily to newspapers, radio and television (terrestrial, cable and satellite). Allow us quickly to add, however, that a more thorough analysis than this one would need to stretch to include other forms of mass communication such as film, books, magazines, advertizements, videos, CDs and the Internet. Our decision to confine this discussion to these three types of media institution is due to our perception that they are amongst the most salient and influential sites for the formation and articulation of 'public opinion' in Wales. That is to say, each of these media, in highly varied, interconnected and sometimes contradictory ways, makes a decisive contribution to the mass circulation of ideas, viewpoints and beliefs which members of the public hold about the pressing issues of the day. Indeed, for many people their very sense of Wales as a distinct nation, with its own traditions, customs and rituals, is largely derived from the content of these media (see also Curtis 1986; Hannan 1990; Humphreys 1995; Smith 1998; Stead 1995).

Some sociologists have found the notion of a 'public sphere' to be useful when thinking about the media as arenas for public debate and discussion in modern societies. The writings of the German sociologist Jurgen Habermas (1989, 1992) have proved to be invaluable in this regard. Very briefly, it is Habermas's contention that under ideal conditions the public sphere serves as a discursive space situated between the realm of the state, on the one side, and the economic domain, on the other, for public deliberations over social issues. In his words, the public sphere represents a space for 'rational-critical debate' amongst citizens, one where 'a time consuming process of mutual enlightenment' may take place 'for the "general interest" on the basis of which alone a rational agreement between publicly competing opinions could freely be reached' (1989, 195; see also Allan 1997). This normative conception of an open and free relation of communication, where people can engage in discussion about the conduct of political life as equals, throws into sharp relief many of the factors which constrain public debate today.

Of particular concern in Wales are the respective roles the English- and Welsh-language media play within the public sphere. To what extent, we may proceed to ask, do these media institutions succeed in fulfilling the ideal of 'rational-critical debate' envisaged by Habermas? More specifically, do they ensure that a pluralistic range of voices is heard on social issues as they affect the people of Wales, and that governmental and corporate bodies are held publicly accountable for their actions? In looking for answers to questions such as these, it is necessary to identify how media representations of public life, and thereby 'public opinion', shape the ways citizens participate in decision-making processes. Many sociologists have argued that these media representations have a crucial influence on how people regard the very legitimacy of the political and economic processes and structures which make up Welsh society. It follows, then, that we need to examine the political implications associated with how public debate is structured throughout society in a way which avoids being limited to the partisan disputes indicative of parliamentary democracy.

Accordingly, we want to suggest that it is advantageous to broaden our conception of what counts as 'public opinion' so as to address people's everyday experiences of life in Wales. This is not to deny that important insights can be gained by scrutinizing the impact the media have on how people choose which political party to support at election time, or which way to vote in a referendum. Rather, it is to propose that the complex ways in which people relate to media representations of Wales on a day-to-day basis are equally deserving of sociological enquiry (see also Allan and Thompson, 1999). It is at this ostensibly mundane level of the everyday, where people negotiate the meaningfulness of these representations for their own lives, that the factors constraining the capacity of the media to serve as forums for public debate assume a profound political significance. We are thus seeking to disrupt the very 'common sense' of contending discourses of Welsh identity as they are inflected in and by the media in order to begin to discern the cultural, economic and political relations which underpin them.

As Kevin Williams (1997, 24) observes, the 'power to define Welshness has been at the centre of the debate about the role of the media in Welsh society'. Questions of identity, far from being abstract, esoteric concerns, matter at a concrete level. He argues that the kinds of everyday problems confronting the people of Wales − such as unemployment, rural depopulation, poverty, substance abuse, education provision, housing, environmental degradation and daily subsistence costs − are inextricably caught up in the cultural dynamics of media representation (see also Adamson 1998; Rees 1998). In his words:

Often discussion of our national and cultural identity is made without reference to the quality of the daily life of many of our fellow women and men. It neglects the real problems that exist in the streets and fields of Wales. But the importance of the mass media is the crucial role they play in how we make sense of these problems and understand our plight and that of our fellow citizens. (Williams 1997, 5)

Consequently, Williams maintains, much greater attention needs to be directed to the ways in which media institutions project a sense of Welsh identity in relation to these types of social problems. Indeed, in his view, 'the media are the main means by which Wales represents itself to the outside world as well as defining what it is to be Welsh to the people who live in Wales' (1997, 5).

It is this question of how, and to what extent, the media affirm, transform and contest discourses of Welshness across the terrain of the public sphere which underlies the remaining sections of this chapter. We shall attempt to situate a range of different media institutions in relation to ongoing debates about the role they play in constructing Welsh identities. As we shall see, of particular significance in sociological terms is the potential each of these respective media possesses for contributing to the realization of a truly democratic public sphere in Wales.

Newspapers

Today a wide range of newspapers is being published across Wales, although their ownership is steadily being concentrated into an ever smaller number of hands. Newspapers do not receive a direct subsidy by the state, although they do benefit through such forms of assistance as preferred postal rates and the absence of value-added tax. The financial success of a newspaper is thus contingent upon its daily circulation and the purchase of space on its pages by advertisers.

Regulation
The newspaper press in Wales is subject to the same legal frame-work which governs the industry in the rest of the UK. This means that the press is constrained by, amongst other factors, the libel laws, official secrecy laws and those laws protecting minors and the

victims of some crimes from being named in the press. The content of newspapers is decided by journalists, editors and proprietors, many of whom would insist that they are simply providing the public with what it wants to read. Needless to say, the 'letters to the editor' section in many newspapers in Wales routinely provides evidence to the contrary.

Since 1945, there have been repeated attempts to provide members of the public with adequate protection from the excesses of the press. Initiatives have often focused on the need to ensure a legal 'right of reply', as well as laws to protect individuals from unjustified invasions of their privacy (O'Malley 1998). These efforts have largely failed, however, primarily because of the general reluctance amongst politicians to be seen to be passing laws which unduly restrict the 'freedom of the press'. As a result, the industry has its own body, the Press Complaints Commission, which enforces 'codes of practice' and deals with complaints about the press from the public. There is no specific Welsh dimension to the PCC's activities. Similarly, it is important to note that in the case of public inquiries into the press, such as those mounted by the 1947–9, 1961–2 and 1974–7 Royal Commissions on news-papers, Wales has been treated as part of the UK industry on all matters relating to the law and to the regulation of standards.

Ownership

Historical examinations of the newspaper press in Wales suggest that from the 1890s onwards there has been a reduction in the number of titles being published as well as a growing concentration of ownership. These developments broadly mirror the trends indicative of the newspaper industry in the UK as a whole. Between 1920 and 1960 there was a dramatic decline in the number of English-language titles (131 to 101) and Welsh-language titles (twenty-one to eight) being published in Wales. Overall, as Aled Jones (1993, 209) points out, 'the proportion of Welsh-language titles fell from 17% in 1914 to 8% in 1960'. The economic logic underpinning the growing concentration of ownership accelerated in the 1920s, largely due to the rising prominence of companies committed to intertwining their newspaper interests throughout Wales and England. If most of these companies were English in origin, one exception was Allied Newspapers owned by the Berry brothers from Merthyr Tydfil. Having made their fortune in

London, where they already owned such major titles as *The Sunday Times* and the *Financial Times*, in 1928 the brothers proceeded to purchase titles such as the *Cardiff Times* and the *South Wales Daily News* (the latter eventually incorporated into the previously acquired *Western Mail*).

An overview of the situation in early 1999 indicates that the most influential of the major owners of newspapers in Wales is Trinity International Holdings. Trinity became the largest regional paper publisher in Britain with its purchase of Thomson Regional Newspapers for £327.5 million in November 1995. It publishes several major titles, including the *Western Mail*, the *South Wales Echo, Wales on Sunday* and, significantly because of its extensive readership in north Wales, the Welsh edition ('speaking up for Wales') of the *Liverpool Daily Post and Echo*. All in all, Trinity controls 120 titles (daily, weekly or monthly; paid or 'free') which include the following in Wales: *Abergele Visitor; Bangor and Caernarfon Chronicle; Bangor Mail; Bridgend and Ogwr Post; Caernarfon Herald; Cardiff Post; Cynon Valley Leader; Glamorgan Gazette; Gwent Gazette; Llandudno Advertiser; Neath and Port Talbot Guardian; North Wales Weekly News; Pontypridd and Llantrisant Observer; Rhondda Leader; Rhyl and Prestatyn Visitor; The Chronicle; Vale Post;* and *Yr Herald*.

Following the same pattern of increasing concentration, United News and Media – owners of the London-based the *Express*, the *Express on Sunday* and the *Daily Star* – sold its holdings in United Provincial Newspapers in February 1998. One portion of its titles went to the venture capital firm Candover, owners of Regional Independent Media (publishers of the *North Gwent Campaign* and the *South Wales Guardian*), for £360 million. A second group of titles was sold to Southnews, based in Harrow, Middlesex, for £47.5 million. Southnews, which owns a total of thirty-two titles altogether, publishes a number of papers in Wales: *Chepstow News; Cwmbran and Pontypool News; Monmouthshire and Abergavenny News; Newport News; Rhondda Campaign;* and the *Western Telegraph* in Pembrokeshire.

Other prominent newspaper groups in Wales include:

- Northcliffe Newspapers Group, which controls: *Burry Port Star; Carmarthen Citizen; Carmarthen Journal; Llanelli Star; South Wales Evening Post;* and *Swansea Herald of Wales,* amongst others. Overall control of the group rests with London-based Associated Newspapers, publishers of the *Daily Mail* and *Mail on Sunday*.

- North Wales Newspapers, based in Flintshire, which controls: *Anglesey Chronicle*; *Denbighshire Free Press*; *Flintshire Leader*; *North Wales Chronicle*; *Rhyl/Prestatyn Journal*; *The Pioneer*; *Wrexham Evening Leader*; and *Y Cymro*, amongst others.
- Southern Newspapers, based in Southampton, which controls: *Barry and District News*; *Blackwood and Risca News*; *Cardigan Advertiser*; *Cwmbran Free Press*; *Merthyr Campaign*; *Newport Free Express*; *Penarth Times*; *Pontypool and District Press*; *Pontypridd Campaign*; and *South Wales Argus*, amongst others.
- Tindle Newspapers, based in Chester, which controls: *Abergavenny Chronicle*; *Barry Gem*; *Cowbridge Gem*; *Fishguard County Echo*; *Glamorgan Gem*; *Llantwit Major Gem*; *Monmouthshire Beacon*; and *Tenby Observer*, amongst others.

Readership

While some UK national newspapers occasionally produce Welsh editions, notably the *Mirror*, London-based titles have a high readership in Wales (as was similarly the case in the nineteenth century: see also O'Malley *et al.* 1997). Figures for 1995 show that the *Sun* had the highest take up in Welsh households, with 22.5 per cent reading it; followed by the *Mirror* (12.5 per cent) and the *Daily Mail* (9.8 per cent). The *Western Mail* and the *Daily Post* each had a share of 6 per cent. During the same year, only 13 per cent of all newspapers sold in Wales were actually produced in Wales (Mackay and Powell 1997, 15; Williams 1997, 9). Little appears to have changed since Ian Hume's (1983, 231) observation, made in the mid-1980s, that 'there is little in the English language press – particularly the weeklies – which offers any support to the idea that Wales is a distinct nation'. Indeed, Hugh Mackay and Anthony Powell (1997, 11) go even further, contending that 'it is fair to say that, in terms of newspaper sales, Wales is less cohesive than Yorkshire (with *The Yorkshire Post*)'.

The *Western Mail*, founded by the third marquis of Bute on 1 May 1869, continues to claim for itself the unique status of being 'the national newspaper of Wales'. From its early days the paper steadily moved to the centre of Welsh political life, particularly after it expanded its operations to north Wales in 1922. Today, the title succeeds in delivering a more 'upmarket' readership (that is, a higher proportion of managerial and professional readers) than any other paper produced in Wales. It is evidently the case, as many commentators have suggested, that it is the interests of these relatively affluent readers which guide the newspaper's editorial policy on Welsh affairs. The newspaper recurrently appears to be out of step with the political views of the majority of the Welsh people. This point was amply demonstrated during the 1997 general election as the pro-Conservative *Western Mail* looked on as every constituency across Wales rejected the Conservative candidate at the ballot-box.

Broadcasting

Public-service broadcasting

Since its inception in 1922, broadcasting in Britain has been subject to regulations governing ownership, content and finance. At stake, first, was the formal recognition of the electro-magnetic spectrum as a scarce public resource, and as such deserving of careful regulation. Secondly, politicians and civil servants were fearful of the possible influence broadcasting might have on public opinion, and so moved to ensure that it be regulated to maximize social benefits while, at the same time, minimizing any potential for 'social unrest'.

Within this context the BBC was forced at a very early stage to acknowledge the status of Wales as a distinct nation with its own traditions and aspirations. As the BBC network slowly began to stretch across Britain, a Cardiff station began broadcasting in February 1923. Not surprisingly, however, the high degree of (London-based) centralization in BBC services led to protests from political and cultural figures in Wales. Centralized control was judged by these people to be inhibiting the development of a distinctively Welsh orientation to the service. In 1935 the protesters achieved an agreement to establish a separate BBC Wales Region (Jones 1993, 231–4). As John Davies (1994) has argued, this was a significant moment for the development of Welsh broadcasting and other aspects of Welsh life:

In the history of BBC broadcasting in Wales, the importance of the victory won in sound radio in the mid-1930s can scarcely be exaggerated. All the subsequent recognition of Wales in the field of broadcasting (and, it could be argued in other fields also) stemmed from that victory. (Davies 1994, 205)

It is thus possible to see in this victory the basis for a public-service ethos which continues to inform the institutions with which we are familiar today, such as BBC Radio Cymru, BBC Radio Wales, BBC Wales TV, Harlech TV (HTV) Wales and the bilingual (Welsh and English) S4C.

In sharp contrast with the newspaper sector, then, the distinctiveness of Wales has been recognized in the way broadcasting has been organized in the UK. Under this system, television and radio services have been structured so that they are potentially available to all members of society. Moreover, these services – whether funded by licence fee, like the BBC, or by spot advertising and sponsorship, like HTV Wales or Red Dragon FM Radio – are obliged to provide high-quality programming designed to inform, educate and entertain.

The British Broadcasting Corporation (BBC)

The BBC is established by Royal Charter – a legal instrument which is in effect created by the government. The BBC's board of governors is appointed by the government and has, traditionally, included a Welsh member to represent Welsh interests. It also has a Broadcasting Council for Wales, which is appointed, not elected, to oversee Welsh interests. The BBC provides radio services for Wales, notably BBC Radio Wales and Radio Cymru, as well as its UK-wide services, Radios 1, 2, 3, 4 and 5. It provides a Welsh regional service on television with specific programmes, mainly news and features, being produced for BBC1 and BBC2 Wales. The BBC is thus essentially a London-based organization with a Welsh section.

Commercial radio

The Radio Authority, a body established under the 1990 Broadcasting Act, is responsible for regulating and licensing commercially funded or 'independent' radio stations in the UK (Radio Authority, 1998). In the Welsh context this means it monitors stations such as

Ceredigion (based in Aberystwyth), Marcher Coast FM (Colwyn Bay), Marcher Gold (Wrexham), MFM (Wrexham), Radio Maldwyn (Powys), Red Dragon FM (Cardiff), Swansea Sound (Swansea), Touch AM (Cardiff) and Valleys Radio (Ebbw Vale), most of which transmit a schedule dominated by popular music.

Ownership patterns in commercial radio are becoming increasingly concentrated, with large companies – based outside Wales – having controlling interests. To take one example, Red Dragon FM, which broadcasts to south-east Wales, is owned by Emap. The radio division of Emap is only one part of a larger corporation which also owns three publishing divisions, two of which are based in England and one in France, and a publications distribution arm. In 1997 Emap was the second largest magazine publisher in Britain, holding a 13 per cent share of the market through such as titles as *Elle*, *FHM* and *New Woman* (Peak and Fisher 1998, 85).

Independent television and cable TV

The 1990 and the 1996 Broadcasting Acts are the main statutory instruments governing commercial broadcasting in the UK. The Independent Television Commission is empowered under this legislation to license commercial television, cable and satellite services in the UK (that is, non-licence-fee or non-government-funded); to regulate these services through its licences and codes of practice; and to ensure that a wide range of television services is available throughout the UK and that these services are of a high quality (ITC 1998).

The ITC licenses the main Welsh ITV contractor which is currently Harlech TV (HTV) Wales (its management structures are separate from HTV West, based in Bristol). The extent of the commitment to Welsh programming on HTV Wales in 1997 was eleven hours and thirty-four minutes per week out of a total of 168 hours broadcast. Significantly, then, only 6.85 per cent of HTV Wales's output was defined as Welsh by the ITC in that year: 94.4 per cent of these programmes were made in Wales, but the vast majority of them were either news (five hours twenty-seven minutes, or 47 per cent of all Welsh programming) or factual pro-gramming (two hours and eleven minutes, or 18.8 per cent). Much of the output was transmitted on Sunday afternoons, not a peak viewing time. Thus the bulk of HTV Wales's output was not in any meaningful sense Welsh; rather, it was largely indistinguishable from the material transmitted across the UK by other ITV contractors (ITC 1998, 84–5).

The ownership of a television company is a crucial factor in determining the orientation of its programming towards Wales. It may be reasonably assumed, in our view, that a Welsh-owned company is more likely to show a commitment to Welsh programming than one owned elsewhere. If this is the case, recent developments would suggest that the likelihood that commercial broadcasting in Wales will enhance its Welsh programming is receding, perhaps decisively so. The 1996 Broadcasting Act relaxed the rules on cross-ownership in the media, thereby allowing the larger ITV contractors to purchase smaller companies and, at the same time, newspaper companies to take a bigger stake in television companies. In Wales this led, in July 1997, to HTV being taken over by United News and Media, a company which controls (as noted above) several London-based newspapers as well as two other ITV companies in England: Anglia Television and Meridian Broadcasting (ITC 1998, 84–9).

CableTel, part of the NTL group of companies, is currently the only provider of cable television in Wales. The third largest franchise holder in the UK, its owners are based in the United States (as is also the case with Cable & Telecoms (C&T), Comcast Europe and Telewest Communications). The rapid expansion of cable television in Wales is mirroring the larger UK pattern, where about one in ten households relies on broadband cable for its television. The desirability of cable services being owned by companies outside of Britain, particularly now with the advent of digital television, is a matter of considerable debate amongst media commentators. One line of argument stresses the need for UK companies to merge in order to compete more effectively at a global level, while another maintains that a further concentration of ownership in the sector will necessarily lead to a narrowing of diversity within the media. In any case, the effect of these processes on the content of the Welsh media needs much more detailed attention than it has received to date (see also Allan *et al.* 1999; Williams 1997).

It is apparent that Welsh viewers have taken not only to cable television with great enthusiasm, but also to satellite television. Satellite television in Wales, as is the case elsewhere in the UK, is dominated by BSkyB. About 40 per cent of the company is owned by media baron Rupert Murdoch's News International. It is significant to note that in 1996 the share of all viewing taken by terrestrial television channels in Wales (BBC1, BBC2, ITV, Channel 4, Channel 5 and S4C) was 83 per cent, a figure which fell to 80 per cent in 1997. The main beneficiaries of this shift seem to have been the cable and satellite services. In 1992 cable and satellite services had been taken up in 15 per cent of Welsh homes, yet by December 1997 this figure had risen to 32 per cent of homes (S4C 1998, 32–4).

Sianel Pedwar Cymru (S4C)

The 1980 Broadcasting Act which established Channel Four declared that the Welsh fourth channel frequencies would be used by Sianel Pedwar Cymru or S4C. The decision was made in the aftermath of a bitter campaign of civil disobedience, one which saw thousands of viewers in Wales refusing to renew their licences while a small minority of others raided transmitters. Arguably the most effective intervention was that of Gwynfor Evans, then the sixty-eight-year-old president of Plaid Cymru, who threatened to begin a hunger strike as a form of protest. As the *Observer* newspaper argued at the time:

> In the shadows in Wales are figures who would turn to violence – Wales has gone a small but significant way down the road to terrorism in the past year. Attacks on TV transmitters and English-owned cottages, incendiary devices left here and there, the smell of violence at this month's National Eisteddfod: the threat of a 'fast to death' by Gwynfor Evans, Welsh nationalism's peaceful patriarch and mentor – all these are warning signs . . . Is it politic to let the allocation of a TV channel be used as a rallying point for romantics and bigots when it could be a gesture of goodwill instead? (Cited in Lambert, 1982, 111)

The protests had their desired effect. In September 1980 the government amended the arrangements for Welsh-language broadcasting in order to allow for the concentration of these programmes on a single channel to be instituted as the Welsh Fourth Channel Authority or Sianel Pedwar Cymru.

Initially set up for a trial period of three years, the new channel began broadcasting on 1 November 1982, one day before Channel

Four was launched. 'In S4C's first two months,' writes John Davies (1994, 379), '45 per cent of its Welsh-language transmissions were provided by the BBC, 36 per cent by HTV and 19 per cent by the independent producers.' Early viewing figures for S4C, while tiny in relation to the overall figures for television usage in Wales, were nevertheless sufficiently strong to demonstrate the appeal of Welsh-language programming.

Funding for S4C has been directly allotted by the Treasury since 1993. The channel provides about thirty hours of Welsh-language programmes a week, most of which are scheduled in prime viewing time (between 7 and 10 p.m.). About ten hours of this programming is produced by the BBC, with the remainder provided by HTV and various independent producers. As one might expect, S4C has played a vital role in stimulating the production of Welsh-language content. *Pobol y Cwm*, a daily 'soap opera', is regularly found to be the most popular programme amongst the channel's viewers. 'Just as other UK soap operas are positioned in localities with distinct though frequently contrived and romanticized discourses and dialects,' writes Alison Griffiths (1993, 10), 'so *Pobol y Cwm* is firmly situated in a region of Wales characterized by a specific linguistic mode and rural diegesis.' The cultural significance of this programme's representation of daily life in south-west Wales is apparent, she argues, in the pleasure with which viewers – especially young people – negotiate its projections of Welsh identity.

The number of people in Wales who view S4C remains small. In 1996, S4C attracted an 8.75 per cent share of all viewers across all hours of transmission, but in 1997 this fell to 8.5 per cent. On the plus side, S4C has attracted a growing number of viewers during its peak-time broadcasts: 5.9 per cent in 1996 to 6.1 per cent in 1997. In 1997, 19 per cent of Welsh speakers watched S4C in peak time (S4C 1998, 32–4). The experience of S4C, as a minority broadcaster promoting specialist material, mirrors developments in the cable and satellite sectors. S4C, having been founded within the context of public-service provision of services to all, may in the future survive on the strength of its ability to appeal to a segment of the market. Whether S4C could survive without continued support in the form of its current subsidy, however, is open to question.

Issues of regulation

With the arrival of cable and satellite broadcasting in the 1980s, and the desire of the Conservative governments of that time to increase commercial forces in broadcasting, laws were changed to reduce the degree to which broadcasters were obliged to meet public-service goals.

Under the terms of the 1990 Broadcasting Act, the ITV network (and with it Harlech TV Wales) has significant obligations to provide high-quality programming. At the same time, however, several of its obligations were modified by the Act so as to allow the network better to compete with the emerging cable and satellite services (which are not subject to extensive public-service programming requirements). As a result, since then there has existed a distinction between those broadcasters with a strong public-service remit, those with less of a remit and those – largely cable and satellite – with hardly any at all. In 1998, the new Labour government summarized the position thus:

> The Government will look to the BBC, Channel 4 and S4C to pursue their distinctive public-service remits as public corporations in the multi-channel, multi-service future. Channel 5 has a distinctive role, as does ITV as, in many respects, a public-service commercial broadcaster, with strong regional diversity. (HMSO 1998, 4.47)

Thus Wales remains an area where strong public-service requirements will continue to exist for BBC Wales and S4C, with Harlech TV (HTV) Wales having less of an obligation in this area.

Also in 1998, the Labour government embarked upon a process of consultation over the future of regulatory structures in UK broadcasting. It marked an important breach with the past by asserting that, due to technical change, there is likely to be less of a need for the kind of positive programming requirements – described above – that have governed broadcasting to date: 'Regulation should be the minimum necessary to achieve clearly defined policy objectives. The presumption that broadcasting and communications should be regulated should therefore in general be reversed' (HMSO 1998, para. 3.2.6). If this line of thinking is developed it raises questions about the extent to which there will remain a strong public-service broadcasting sector in Wales in the next century. As many media commentators have pointed out, the spread of commercial services undermines the case for the continuance, let alone the enhancement, of public-service broadcasting. The very existence of S4C, together with the BBC's Welsh services and Harlech's Welsh programming, are all contingent upon a key imperative: that is, they are based on the 'presumption that broadcasting and communications should be regulated'. A change in this policy, even a gradual one, has the potential dramatically to alter the media landscape in Wales.

Future Explorations

In assessing the urgent need further to develop a national media culture for Wales in the mid-1980s, Michelle Ryan (1986, 195) accentuated its status as 'an important site for debating and representing what a progressive Welsh identity could mean and it provides an opportunity for people themselves to participate in this process of deconstruction and reconstruction'. Today, as a new century approaches, this aspiration to enrich the opportunities for people to participate in the making of a national media culture continues to resonate throughout Wales. As we have seen, the routine, everyday forms and practices of the media are helping to set down the cultural rules by which the reality of Welshness is being interpreted in acutely influential ways. The means of access to the public sphere engendered and sustained by the media are as limited as they are politically charged. In bringing this discussion to a close, then, we wish to highlight a set of pressing issues which in our view deserve much more critical attention than they have typically received to date. Accordingly, briefly outlined below is a range of questions revolving around a specific aspect of the media construction of Welsh identity.

What does 'freedom of the press' mean in Wales today? Given that most definitions focus on the constraints placed by governments on the right to express ideas, opinions and information, what impact are the changing dynamics of media ownership (particularly with respect to the growing degree of concentration, conglomeration and globalization throughout the Welsh media sectors) having on these same 'freedoms'? Judgements about news content are increasingly being made on the basis of considerations of news as a saleable commodity, as opposed to giving priority to professional judgements about news quality or the integrity of the reporting (see also Allan 1999). The *Western Mail*, the leading newspaper in Wales, is struggling to build its readership at a time when newspaper reading in general, let alone the market for all-Wales news, is in a state of decline. Meanwhile *Wales on Sunday*, launched as a 'serious' broadsheet in 1989, was quickly forced to embrace human-interest, entertainment-driven content in a tabloid format in order to attract sufficient readers (and, just as importantly, enough advertisers).

Is the notion of a 'Welsh public sphere' viable and, if so, how can the media in Wales best fulfil their social responsibilities? Is it the case that only 'free markets' ensure diversity of expression and open public debate? Or, alternatively, are critics such as Habermas (1989) correct to argue that the commercialization of the media has virtually displaced 'rational-critical debate' into the realm of consumption, thereby transforming active citizens into indifferent consumers? In what ways will the media in Wales have to change in order to enhance civic participation in government, especially with regard to the new Welsh Assembly? The creation of the Assembly is likely to transform the processes whereby different organizations (ranging from volunteer associations, citizens' juries, conservation bodies to corporate institutions) relate to government officials, not least at the level of the lobby system. Precisely how the media report on constitutional change, and in so doing help to construct the parameters of public debate about devolution, will have far-reaching implications for popular definitions of the 'public interest'.

How best can media institutions in Wales go about improving the provision of Welsh-language content so as to boost audience figures, especially with respect to young people? Or, as Huw Jones (1998), the chief executive of S4C, asks:

> what will be the relevance of Welshness, a quarter century from now, to the generation which is growing up in the midst of these huge changes? What value will they place on a language which is ignored by all these television channels bar one? The answer will depend to a large extent on how successful we Welsh are at making effective use of those media which we have in our possession – in particular the National Assembly which gives us a democratic voice and the mass media which give broad expression to our culture. We have got hold of a microphone so that we

can be heard amidst the deafening noise of the world. The question now is – what have we got to say?

Perhaps one way forward is for broadcasters to make a greater effort to tap into the types of local issues being addressed by community newspapers, especially the Welsh-language *papurau bro*.

What about the needs of the monolingual, English-speaking Welsh people when it comes to media representations of Welsh identity? Talk of a televisual channel to complement S4C with English-language content concerning Wales has failed to secure sufficient interest amongst potential governmental or corporate backers. The relationship between Wales and the rest of Britain, to say nothing of its place within a 'Europe of the Regions', is very much open to negotiation; this is particularly so now that the imperatives of devolution are being played out. The types of narrow, conservative notions of Welsh nationalism often mobilized in discussions about media policy, as Michelle Ryan (1986, 195) points out, do not connect in a direct way with the majority of Welsh people's experience. 'What we need', she writes, 'is a cultural identity that defines Wales not as a one-nation monolith cloaked in bourgeois sentimentality, but forged from within new formations of class, gender, ethnicity and language.'

What strategies are required effectively to challenge the misrepresentation of Wales in the British media, particularly those which are London-based? Similarly, and in light of the current trends in media ownership discussed above, how best to enhance the development of a strong indigenous media? 'Mass media of our own', writes Kevin Williams (1997, 6), 'are not only important in combating the stereotyping of Welsh identity by others but also vital ingredients in the building of collective solidarity and understanding inside Wales, and addressing the problems that we face as a community.' Notwithstanding the value of these types of insights, however, would the state legislation necessary to construct a predominantly Welsh-owned media system be desirable, let alone practicable? Under the present system, the importance of state regulation for creating distinctively Welsh media institutions has long been recognized in broadcasting, but would similar measures be appropriate in, say, the newspaper industry?

What will be the impact of new media technologies, such as digital television (terrestrial, satellite and cable), on Welsh identities? For over two generations Welsh-language activists have focused on gaining influence over broadcasting on the grounds that access to these institutions would deliver a national audience to a nationalist agenda. As the attendant technology changes, so the assumption that television can continue to perform this crucial task of promoting Welsh identities becomes increasingly problematic. Public-service broadcasting, with its commitment to sustaining a forum for a richly diverse array of contending ideas, beliefs and viewpoints to circulate from across Wales, is incompatible with the ethos of 'the market' so readily endorsed by the digital companies (see also Allan *et al.* 1999). If critics are correct when they argue that digital means 'chewing-gum television', then how do we ensure that the drive to maximize revenue in this sector does not silence the distinctive cultural voices which make up the substance of Welsh identities?

Overall, then, this brief sketch of several particularly salient issues (located, as they are, amongst an array of other ones) illuminates some of the key features of the ongoing debates we have considered to be central to this chapter's agenda. In electing to conclude by outlining them in this rather provocative fashion, it has been our intention to help establish several possible points of departure for future sociological explorations of the media in Wales.

References

Adamson, D. (1998). 'Social segregation in a working class community: economic and social change in the South Wales Coalfield' (University of Glamorgan, Social Science Research Seminar, 28 October).

Allan, S. (1997). 'News and the public sphere: towards a history of objectivity and impartiality', in M. Bromley and T. O'Malley (eds.), *A Journalism Reader* (London: Routledge).

Allan, S. (1999). *News Culture* (Buckingham and Philadelphia: Open University Press).

Allan, S. and Thompson, A. (1999). 'The time–space of national memory', in K. Brehony and N. Rassool (eds.), *Nationalism Old and New* (London: Macmillan).

Allan, S., Thompson, A. and O'Malley, T. (1999). 'The futures of digital television in Wales', in S. Blandford (ed.), *Wales on Screen* (Bridgend: Seren).

Curtis, T. (ed.) (1986). *Wales: The Imagined Nation* (Bridgend: Poetry Wales Press).

Davies, J. (1994). *Broadcasting and the BBC in Wales* (Cardiff: University of Wales Press).

Griffiths, A. (1993). 'Pobol y Cwm: the construction of national and cultural identity in a Welsh-language soap opera', in P. Drummond, R. Paterson and J. Willis (eds.), *National Identity and Europe* (London: BFI).

Habermas, J. (1989). *The Structural Transformation of the Public Sphere*, trans. T. Burger with F. Lawrence (Cambridge, MA: MIT Press).

Habermas, J. (1992) 'Further reflections on the public sphere', in C. Calhoun (ed.), *Habermas and the Public Sphere* (Cambridge, MA: MIT Press, 1992).

Hannan, P. (ed.) (1990). *Wales in Vision: The People and Politics of Television* (Llandysul: Gomer, with the co-operation of BBC Cymru Wales).

HMSO (1998). *Regulating Communications: Approaching Convergence in the Information Age*, Cm. 4022 (London: HMSO).

Hume, I. (1983). 'The mass media in Wales: some preliminary explorations', in I. Hume and W. T. R. Pryce (eds.), *The Welsh and their Country* (Llandysul: Gomer).

Humphreys, R. (1995). 'Images of Wales', in T. Herbert and G. E. Jones (eds.), *Post-War Wales* (Cardiff: University of Wales Press).

ITC (1998). *Annual Report and Accounts 1997* (London: Independent Television Commission).

Jones, A. (1993). *Press, Politics and Society: A History of Journalism in Wales* (Cardiff: University of Wales Press)

Jones, G. S. (1990). 'A sense of place', in P. Hannan (ed.), *Wales in Vision: The People and Politics of Television* (Llandysul: Gomer, with the co-operation of BBC Cymru Wales).

Jones, H. (1998). 'The Sound and Moving Image Collection Lecture', National Library of Wales, Aberystwyth, 15 October.

Lambert, S. (1982). *Channel Four: Television with a Difference?* (London: BFI).

Mackay, H. and Powell, A. (1997). 'Wales and its media: production, consumption and regulation', *Contemporary Wales*, 9, 8–39.

O'Malley, T. (1998). 'Demanding accountability: the press, the Royal Commissions and the pressure for reform, 1945–77', in M. Bromley and H. Stephenson (eds.), *Sex, Lies and Democracy: The Press and the Public* (London: Longman).

O'Malley, T., Allan, S. and Thompson, A. (1997). ' "Tokens of antiquity": the newspaper press and the shaping of national identity in Wales, 1870–1900', *Studies in Newspaper and Periodical History*, 4, 127–52.

Peak, S. and Fisher, A. (eds.) (1998). *The Media Guide 1999* (London: Fourth Estate).

Radio Authority (1998). *Annual Report and Financial Statement of Accounts for the Year Ending 31 December 1997* (London: Radio Authority).

Rees, T. (1998). *More Equal than Others? 25 Years of Equal Opportunities in Wales* (Cardiff: BBC Cymru Wales).

Ryan, M. (1986). 'Blocking the channels: TV and film in Wales', in T. Curtis (ed.), *Wales: The Imagined Nation* (Bridgend: Poetry Wales Press).

S4C (1998). *S4C Annual Report 1997* (Cardiff: S4C).

Smith, J. (1998). *The Welsh Image* (Cardiff: Institute of Welsh Affairs, Gregynog Papers Series).

Stead, P. (1995). 'Popular culture', in T. Herbert and G. E. Jones (eds.), *Post-War Wales* (Cardiff: University of Wales Press).

Williams, K. (1997). *Shadows and Substance: The Development of a Media Policy for Wales* (Llandysul: Gomer).

Williams, R. (1958). 'Culture is ordinary', in R. Gable (ed.), *Resources of Hope* (London: Verso).

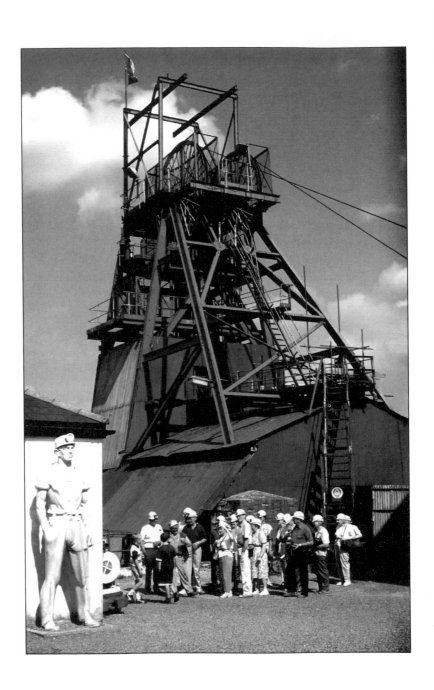

9   Heritage Tourism: A Mirror for Wales?

TERI BREWER

'Haverfordwest Railway – Imposing Demonstration' was the head-line in the *Illustrated London News* for 7 January 1854. Just three years after the Great Exhibition opened at the Crystal Palace in London, proofs of the Victorian 'March of Progress' were felt as far afield as west Wales when curious crowds turned up to watch an opening ceremony for the South Wales Railway Narberth Road Station in Haverfordwest.

The artist correspondent for the *News* sketched a biting satirical view of the scene – the illustration probably not a literal depiction of events, but a commentary on the possibilities of change brought about by new transportation networks. A passenger train is pulling out of the station. There on the platform a crowd mostly in modern dress clusters around banners wishing success to the railroad, all eyes forward, firmly glued on the future, the direction in which this train is clearly headed. On the opposite platform, the end of the line, a crowd of elderly ladies in the stovepipe hats, shawls and cloaks of a conventionalized Wales Past.[1]

This view looks back at the past as well as forward to anticipate the future. It raises questions already being asked at that time about the consequences of easy and affordable travel for Wales and anticipates questions that have perhaps become still more important since. But even more importantly the illustration records a time when tourism in Wales first became a popular activity, not just the privileged leisure of a monied few. In order to understand heritage tourism in Wales today we need to consider the position of tourism in the international economy in general and in Wales in particular.

The essence of tourism is the way the global interacts with the local
. . . mass tourism emphasizes a global scan for global (or at least
macro-regional) markets, while some forms of new tourism seek to
exploit the individuality of places. These global–local relationships are
not static but are subject to a variety of restructuring processes.
Attempts to make tourism more sustainable will be conditioned by the
very nature of these restructuring processes, but it is equally true that
the grand project of sustainable tourism will also be influenced by the
process of re-structuring.' (Hall and Lew 1998, 59)

In this chapter I will first look at the history of tourism as a form
of social, political and economic interaction in Wales and consider
why recent efforts have focused on encouragement of 'new
tourism' rather than mass-market provision. Heritage tourism in
particular has been a growth area for Wales, but it is one which
poses special problems to be solved in its development if it is to be
a sustainable form of tourism.

A Brief History of the Tourist in Wales

Tourism, in the modern sense, really only developed in Wales in the
late eighteenth century, when the combination of several factors
brought an increase in visitors. They focused initially on landscape,
secondarily on an antiquarian concern with the detritus of history
– the monuments and architecture of past times – and finally
shifted to a interest in the inhabitants, culture and language of
Wales.

Most tourism into Wales in the eighteenth century came from
other parts of the British Isles, and tended to focus on the parts of
Wales that were reasonably accessible for visitors travelling on
horseback or by public and private conveyance – in other words,
horse-drawn coaches. Accessibility and infrastructure (in terms of
graded and maintained roads, and inns) were required to attract
visitors in the past just as they are today.

Looking at published travellers' guides of the time it seems that
many came to see a romantic landscape, which is not surprising
given the taste for the romantic in literature and the arts during the
eighteenth century. Some came to follow up on their amateur
scientific interests in geology and botany. Published guides by these

early travellers, such as Thomas Pennant in 1778, are often what Richard Brinkley has termed 'picturesque accounts', travelogues which 'echo wonder at Wales as a strange country with wild scenery, rustic inhabitants and a strange language all as seen by educated gentlemen writing for the benefit of similar people in England' (Brinkley 1974).

Antiquarian studies were another popular pastime, and this gives us some clues to why Wales was initially such an interesting destination to many visitors. At a time when the advent of the industrial revolution, changes in agrarian practice and the spread of urban areas were all dramatic, Wales was one area of the British Isles relatively less affected by these changes. As a consequence, a tendency to think of Wales as a repository of physical evidence about pre-industrial history was already beginning to develop. This view would gradually be extended and projected upon people and customs as well as crags and ruins.

At the same time moves were afoot to improve and upgrade road networks, and the construction of tram roads and later railroads was initiated, making leisure travel into Wales easier and less expensive for visitors. A growing percentage of the population with some increase in discretionary income and the reshaping of work and leisure habits were beginning to lay the groundwork for a further development of leisure travel. But this would not really develop until the nineteenth-century construction of passenger railways and excursion steamers opened things up further.

Unrest in Europe in the period leading up to and for the duration of the Napoleonic Wars discouraged the traditional 'Grand Tour' of the continent as a way of finishing the education of wealthy young men and women. The taste for travel remained, however, and parts of Scotland, Ireland and Wales were the doubtful beneficiaries of tourism avoiding turmoil, inconvenience and possible danger.

During this same era, discussions about priorities and identity were also going on inside Wales, the extension of antiquarian concern to culture saw its parallel in the elaboration of the concept of the *gwerin* (folk, or people). In Welsh this term has been integral to a historical discourse on Welshness from the late eighteenth century onwards. A complex inter- and intra-cultural dialogue developed, in which those travelling English middle classes, Welsh villagers and gentry, industrialists and eventually other Europeans all joined. This resulted in a series of images and expectations being imposed on real people as well as the development of an ideological tool for the emergent European debates on nationalism.

Excellent studies have been written on informal portraiture and the human landscape defined by the development of tourism in Wales in about 1780–1880. Along with pictorial representations of Welsh identity, for sale in various forms (the postcard, souvenir print, etc.), and as illustration to travellers' guides, or illustrated magazines, the shifting ideological concept of a *gwerin* spawned a linked, if not parallel literary and iconographic portraiture. It can be argued that it was the aesthetic of a partially fictitious, literary, visualized, figurative and rather theatrical 'folk' which then informed and still informs the marketing of Welsh identities for external consumption, and indeed which stalks the urgent debates on regionalism in the European Union today, as well as British politics generally.

Beginning with the nineteenth-century writings of George Borrow and Augusta Hall, Lady Llanover, hurried on by the advent of passenger railways, the tour of Wales increased its emphasis on amateur ethnology. It is probable that the dissemination of literary portraiture did more to people Wales for travellers and tourists than was ever achieved by brochures. In 1828, the itinerant actor and sometime 'hack' writer Thomas Llewellyn Prichard published his most successful work. The tale of Twm Shon Catti, the Welsh Robin Hood, was aimed at an English market.

Prichard, who wrote many guidebooks to Wales as well as novels, was a quick man with a slogan, and prided himself on finding something distinctive as a selling point for any place he wrote about. 'Unless you've been everywhere, you haven't seen the lot' is supposed to have been his motto, and he sold Aberystwyth as the Naples of Wales, and Llandudno as 'The Queen of Welsh Watering Places'. Sloganeering and racy guidebooks, which thrilled with snippets of legend and bandit tales, but edified with details of spa developments and walking tours, gave the Victorian literature a different feel from the scholarly antiquarianism of the eighteenth-century guidebooks.

Heritage Tourism in Wales Today

Nearly 150 years on from that scene in Haverfordwest drawn by an artist, railways are nearly gone, but what they began incidentally in the opening of passenger travel was the seeding of an 'industry' which now moves towards domination of the Welsh economy. Travel and tourism was one of the growth industries of the 1980s. Not just in Wales but around the world, governments have realized that the development of cultural and environmental tourism offers possible assistance in solving the economic problems of some regions. This means that an activity which often developed in a fairly *ad hoc* way is now being re-examined on all sides. Governments consider the possibility of increased tax revenues from tourism as well as the possibility of net employment gains and general economic boost which tourism development might provide. Attention is given to encouraging new enterprises, regulating quality and looking at the possible types of tourism that might be developed in a given area. Is this region of interest primarily to independent travellers and small groups handled best by specialist operators? Is it possible to develop mass-market tourism? What does the region have to offer? Sun and sand? Landscapes? Wildlife? Nightlife? History and heritage?

Often it is only much later that consideration is given to some of the other, possibly less attractive, consequences of these developments. Encouragement of mass-market tourism often means that most of the profits will be made by the organizing tour operators in other countries, airlines and multinational corporations which can afford to develop large-scale hotels and resorts as speculations. The needs of the mass market may drive development more than the needs of the host country, and the social and environmental consequences to the host country may begin to outweigh the economic benefits of relatively low-paid service-industry jobs in a sector which can fluctuate dramatically as fashions in tourist travel change, or perceptions of a particular destination shift.

In Wales, the mass-market form of tourism has never really developed. The informal, small-scale and localized response to tourist interest was evaluated and resulted in the creation of a tourist board. In recent years tourism has been regarded as increasingly worthy of government attention, regulation and investment and promotion. Various experiments have been made with styles of advertising abroad, and the images which Wales wishes to promote for the purpose of tourism development have been carefully examined and hotly debated. Whatever other aspects of Wales are promoted, one of the most reliably interesting to tourists has been history and heritage, a modern presentation of many of the same aspects of Wales on which tourism here first focused.

Perhaps the most interesting aspect of twentieth-century tourism development is the establishment of fixed-site purpose-built heritage sites – not just museums, such as the famous Museum of Welsh Life at St Fagans near Cardiff which was founded as part of the larger European open-air museums movement in 1948, but also the interpretive centres linked to former industrial sites, slate quarries, coal mines, etc. What is remarkable about these new interpretive centres is that they are plainly aimed at both the visitor from abroad and the Welsh at home. These sites are increasingly supplemented by small-scale community-based local history and heritage projects which now have access to public and private funding, and more commercial or professional developments such as Celtica, a mixed display and research centre at Machynlleth.

This focus on heritage tourism though, is not just about bringing visitors' cash in and job creation, nor is it just about meta-phorically spinning gold from the straw of derelict post-industrial or post-agricultural landscapes and creating employment in side-lined communities. A revalued and revised representation of Wales continually affects the internal dialogues of identity, regionalism and nationalism. From community self-help projects to centrally mandated large-scale urban regeneration schemes, Wales has entered a distinctive period of increased reflection on the past in the hopes of creating opportunities for the future, and this process continues today.

In the title of this chapter the metaphor of a mirror is used to describe the role that tourism and the early development of heritage industries have played in Wales. In mirrors we see ourselves reflected, but it is important to understand the results of that experience. Having seen yourself reflected in the mirror, if the image did not match your mental picture of yourself, what do you do? You may act based on your reactions to the reflection, you change clothes, straighten your posture, you may put on make-up, comb your hair or even pull a face. You work to appear what you imagine yourself to be.

Historian Gwyn A. Williams and others have suggested that, as a nation, Wales is a creation of the collective imagination – an imagined nation. While he was making a serious point about institutionalized power and regional self-determination, it is worth reflecting on the idea of an imagined nation. To a certain extent, all nations, communities and regions are indeed imagined, dreams and ideas undergoing a process of realization into sought, imposed or accepted social institutions which become part of the means of bringing new social and cultural identities to life. Imagination, however, whether in originating or in rethinking cultural identities, combines together with a physical landscape, social facts, the facts of existing economies and other constraints. The combination of what can be imagined together with the limits of what is possible shapes a present and a future out of materials and events of the past.

Among the markers left in the landscape are signs of shifting power, such as Caerphilly Castle, the Roman gold mines at Pumsaint, a fortified manor house in north Wales; signs of social change – an abandoned farmhouse, a valley inundated to create a water reservoir for growing cities, a derelict dockland area or the archaeological remains of the industrial revolution. Some of these markers are interesting in architectural or scenic terms, most can lead us to an understanding of life in the past, of social change and of the elements available to us in constructing a future. These markers in the physical landscape are one aspect of our heritage, but there are parallels in our use of language, ideas, habits and customs, ways of knowing and thinking about the world also shot through with patterns and content that tell us individually and collectively where we have come from as well as who we are and where we are going.

Heritage is not just about sites and monuments, it includes forms of expressive culture and expert knowledge like Welsh fiddling, modern Welsh rock bands, Valleys choirs, language traditions, styles of public speaking influenced by traditions of chapel and eisteddfoddau, farm auctions, allotment gardening and local boxing rings, but also the skills of passing industries and occupations.

In the newly refurbished waterfront promenades of Cardiff and Swansea, in the subtle redesign of pedestrian spaces of Caerphilly, landscape architect Robert Camlann has presented Welsh communities with a physical embodiment of a philosophy about the past, and about issues of cultural heritage which have broad implications for thinking about history as capital as well as a basis for collective identity.

In a more informal way, local history groups or other community-based organizations apply for grants and are experimenting with the creation of heritage trails, corridors and tours as a way of presenting local knowledge about areas to a home audience as well as to outsiders, and to rethink the relationships between local communities and their landscape. Examples include the parish map project, the Taff Trail, the Bell Centre project, the Butetown arts and history group.

Re-enactors at Llancaiach Fawr and Penhow Castle make re-creations which allow schoolchildren to enter imaginatively into the past. The Museum of Welsh Life stages fairs, fêtes and festivals. Communities sponsor carnivals. The Rhondda Heritage Centre, Celtica, the Big Pit and the Museum of the Welsh Woollen Industry all work to engage the imagination of visitors through participation in interpretive acts, impromptu theatre and other audience-centred performance pieces.

Tourism Industry or Industries?

Tourism is sometimes described as though it were a monolithic industry involving a systematic and highly organized and co-ordinated production of goods and services by corporate activity. It is in fact aimed at a very particular kind of discretionary leisure spending in which the prospective market is diffuse, spread over many countries, hard to research and difficult to influence, despite attempts at targeted marketing. A tourist is 'a temporarily leisured person who voluntarily visits a place away from home for the purpose of experiencing a change' (Smith 1989, 1). Decisions about how to use free time or the act of spending free time in travel results in a potential demand for services – transport and facilities for travellers (including accommodation, meals, organized sights, guides, maps, books and other information resources) – which has encouraged the development of both informal and ad hoc or formal, planned, commercial and government-supported businesses to provide these facilities.

No monolithic industry exists, then, but a great many public and private interest groups influence and compete for attention and the money which tourism can bring to an area which is of interest to leisure travellers. Therefore, we should consider tourism as a discretionary activity which has become the basis of sometimes diffuse service-industry activities. Once we have made this distinction, it is easier to focus on areas of potential sociological interest.

A preliminary examination of tourism interests and their history in Wales shows the continual necessity to analyse the shifting characteristics, needs and interests of the tourists themselves, to look at a particular region's likely responses to those demands, to consider the consequences of meeting those demands: both economic impacts, but also human consequences such as the nature of likely interactions, the effect on local social structure and regional power relationships.

From the point of view of tourism planners in Wales today, then, there are perhaps two major categories of potential tourism: what could be called 'encapsulated tourism' offers a potentially very protected experience of travel abroad. Whether set up by mass-market package-tour operators, or with the assistance of custom itinerary specialists, private coaches, destination resorts and deluxe hotels offer tourists and travellers a low-risk experience with maximum control over quality, and coincidentally perhaps minimum personal contact with an unfamiliar way of life. This category is of course a broad one, taking in anything from expert-led small-scale specialist tours of destinations that it may be difficult for the independent traveller to arrange, involving the opportunity to have unusual experiences with expert guidance, to standard-itinerary passive sightseeing tours with prearranged accommodation in hotels of guaranteed standard.

The second primary category of tourism is that done by independent travellers who make their own arrangements – a group ranging from hostelling backpackers to those with relatively unlimited budgets who find some pleasure in travelling 'potluck' and maintaining flexibility, and, importantly, who are prepared to cope with risk themselves without much mediation.

The motivations of people in both groups can cover a very broad range. They may vary from curiosity to see different landscapes and lifeways, to historical, environmental-focused tourism, to tourism for its own sake, with countries to be ticked off on a list (the 'been there, done that' approach). Of these kinds of tourism, perhaps the most problematic and yet interesting from the perspective of a host country is environmental and heritage tourism. There are several reasons for this.

Travellers specifically interested in the special characteristics of a region's history or ecological landscapes are participating in a dialogue that has meaning to local people too. They are also more likely to support aspects of the local economy through entrance fees, purchase of locally made work, and because of their specialist interests they are more likely to seek out local expertise in interpreting heritage and landscapes. There is potentially more human interaction, and it is in this kind of tourism that UNESCO's criterion for supporting tourist development as a means of increasing cross-cultural human understanding can be achieved.

This all sounds rosy, but it is also in heritage and environmental tourism that there is greatest potential for conflicts between local and tourist perspectives. The two groups may in effect compete for power to influence priorities for preservation, interpretation and presentation. Whether or not this happens, residents and visitors can often feel some discomfort at the contrast between their views of Wales and tourists' tendency to romanticize the past or to be highly selective or partial in their views of a place, valuing difference, assuming that Wales has remained and will continue to remain unchanged.

Visitors to Wales, like tourists everywhere, are stepping out of the bonds of their daily lives, sometimes indulging in a form of temporary cultural flirtation – a holiday romance in fact, but the romance does not have to be with another person, it can be with a country, a region, a way of life.

> Romance is a form of insanity in which one projects onto another a response to needs unmet and ignores the reality of the other . . . needs unmet in [one's own] society for feeling connected to a group of people and experiencing a direct sensation of the physical environment lead one to romanticize [another way of life],

to adapt a comment made by anthropologist Janet Siskind (1973, 18).

Tourism and the businesses and industries it has provoked now make up the largest single sector of the world's economy, a situation that currently seems likely to continue according to most observers. It is therefore tempting to suppose that local initiatives which serve this market are likely to bring in an attractive slice of the $600 billion per year global pie to benefit local regions.

Of course it is not that simple. It is necessary to understand where the potential tourists for an area come from and who they are, what their interests might be, what their patterns of travel are and what is on offer that might interest them. Potential visitors need appropriate information and timely encouragement as well as reliable delivery of sites and services. These questions are addressed in tourism audits – surveys of facilities, attractions and resources often sponsored by local, regional or national government as part of regional economic planning. They also, however, require addressing in another respect. How much is the representation of culture to be based on outsider needs and views, how much is it to be based on needs within the country or region? Is heritage and history primarily an exploitable local resource or does it remain important to the heirs?

Defining Welsh Heritage

What is Welsh heritage then? How should we think about the past? What are the uses of the past? How far can we or should we use the relics and stories of the past as a primary source of cultural capital? Is there a danger that, by dwelling too much on or in the past, we undervalue our own times, ignoring present responsibilities, or fail to build a real future?

These questions and concerns are not exclusive to Wales. Many small nations, communities and regions in the world have been put under increased economic and social pressure by social and industrial change which has had the effect of peripheralizing or marginalizing them. When this happens, people will typically think about questions of identity and about their attachment to their communities and local history as conditions change, and in some cases make it difficult to sustain a way of life which many value.

These issues may be considered by individuals or discussed in families or at community level, but they will also be taken on board by local and national government which may consider solutions from a different perspective. In such cases, over the past fifty years particularly, one of the potential solutions to economic development, as we have seen, has been to assess and develop an area's potential for tourism. The questions asked at this level may well be different, and will mostly initially have to do with an analysis of existing infrastructure for economic development: transportation networks, the existence of appropriate housing or temporary accommodation, the assessment of exploitable environmental, cultural and human resources.

Heritage markers, taken out of the context of everyday life, continually shape the way visitors perceive Wales, whether as a land of daffodils, song and druids, as a contested frontier, pony-trekking, rock-climbing and rambling paradise, a Celtic Fringe, a wellspring of spirituality, a post-industrial landscape – to name just a few of the images of Wales promoted for tourism. Robert Nisbet (1976) pointed out the close connections between our sense of history, understanding of society and cultural landscapes in a way which suggests why it might be worthwhile to stop and consider these recombinant forms and some of the ways their relationship to one another have shifted or metamorphosed over the past several hundred years.

Epilogue

Back on the platform at Narberth Station in Haverfordwest, the unknown artist's work gives us an insight into the sociological imagination as it was developing during the mid-nineteenth century. What do I mean by the term 'sociological imagination'? In this instance the term is used to express the creative way in which people can take themes and ideas from the observation of the social landscape and fit notions from science to them as metaphors for explanation, trying to understand the relationship between a shifting order of things and the rapid change they observe around them. This mid-nineteenth-century sociological imagination was widespread in its experimental application of analogies and metaphors from one sphere of life to another: applications were essayed in poetry, fiction and painting as well as in writing history and social analysis.

What the artist could not have realized was how rapidly those railway carriages would be turned to a different purpose – bringing tourists in to Wales to see a vision of the past represented by those ladies. This was not the first railway to open in Wales by any means, in fact it marked the end of tramroads and railroads as a novelty if anything. With the end of the first half-century of development, the lines were down and the move to increase passenger travel as a supplement to the industrial carriage of raw materials and finished goods transported by rail and canal had begun. It was one thing to imagine all the possibilities that travel by rail brought to the people of Wales, it was another entirely to begin imagining how the potential attractions of leisure travel might attract visitors in ever greater numbers to Wales.

The glorious vision of growth and progress and the celebration of industry on view at the Crystal Palace would be juxtaposed, in the popular imagination, with another image of Wales as a place in which the processes of history were made apparent. Apparent in the dramatic geology and consequent scenery of the Welsh uplands, apparent in the survival of the Welsh language with its traditions of oratory and poetry, apparent in the daily life, housing and customs of the Welsh people themselves. Not as a timeless land, but a place where change and tradition are both viewed positively.

Notes

This chapter is based in part on two papers, 'The Selling of the Gwerin', presented at the American Folklore Society Conference 1994, in Milwaukee, Wisconsin, and on 'A Market for Folk', given at the AGM of the Folklore Society at Sheffield University in March 1996. It also reflects conversations with a number of people who share my long-term interest in the uses of the past. Particular thanks to David Adamson, Gwendolyn Leick, Elizabeth Coviello, Tecwyn Vaughan Jones, Meg Glaser, Glenn Jordan, and the community scholars of the Butetown Arts and History Project in Cardiff and the Bell Centre in Blaenllechau.

1. During the 1830s Charlotte Guest, Lady Llanover, popularized a revival of Welsh 'traditional' costume. Her watercolour sketches and writings on the subject were much discussed at the time and her essay on the subject won a prize at the 1834 Eisteddfod in Abergavenny. For further information see E. Hobsbawm and T. Ranger, *The Invention of Tradition* (Cambridge: Cambridge University Press, 1983).

References

Bassett, M. (1982). 'Formed stones', *Folklore and Fossils* (Cardiff: National Museum of Wales).

Bennet, G. (1994). 'Geologists and folklorists: cultural evolution and "the science of Folklore"', *Folklore*, 105, 25–38.

Brewer, T. (1995). *The Marketing of Tradition* (London: Hisarlik Press).

Brinkley, R. (1974). 'Welsh topographical literature 1770–1870', *The Local Historian*, 2, 7–13.

Buck, E. (1993). *Paradise Remade: The Politics of Culture and History in Hawaii* (Philadelphia: Temple University Press).

Carrog, E. (1991). 'The fragmented image', *New Welsh Review*, 15, 15–18.

Davies, J. (1993). *A History of Wales* (London: Penguin).

Evans, R. P. (1987). 'Thomas Pennant (1726–1798): "the father of Cambrian tourists"', *Welsh History Review*, 4/13, 395–417.

Ford, P. (1977). *The Mabinogi and Other Medieval Welsh Tales* (Berkeley: University of California).

Hall, M. and Lew, A. (1998). *Sustainable Tourism: A Geographical Perspective* (London: Longman).

Hechter, M. (1975). *Internal Colonialism: The Celtic Fringe in British National Development, 1536–1966* (Berkeley: University of California).

Hewison, R. (1987). *The Heritage Industry: Britain in a Climate of Decline* (London: Methuen).

Hughes, W. J. (1924). *Wales and the Welsh in English Literature from Shakespeare to Scott* (Wrexham: publisher unknown).

Jenkins, J. G. (1992). *Getting Yesterday Right: Interpreting the Heritage of Wales* (Cardiff: University of Wales Press).

Jones, N. (1993). *Living in Rural Wales* (Llandysul: Gomer).

Lord, P. (1995). *Words with Pictures: Welsh Images and Images of Wales in the Popular Press, 1640–1860* (Aberystwyth: Planet).

McLuhan, T. C. (1985). *Dreamtracks: The Railroad and the American Indian 1890–1930* (New York: Abrams).

Moore, D. (1976). *Wales in the Eighteenth Century* (Cardiff: University of Wales Press).

Morgan, P. (1986). 'The gwerin of Wales – myth and reality', *The Welsh and their Country* (Llandysul: Gomer).

Nisbet, R. (1976). *Sociology as an Art Form* (Oxford: Oxford University Press).

Owen-Jones, S. (1990). *Railways of Wales* (Cardiff: National Museum of Wales).

Parker, M. (1997). 'Wales: the rough guide', *Planet: The Welsh Internationalist*, 123, 7–11.

Siskind, J. (1973). *To Hunt in the Morning* (Oxford: Oxford University Press).

Smith, A. (1989). *Hosts and Guests: The Anthropology of Tourism* (Philadelphia: University of Pennsylvania Press).

Stockland, B. (1994). 'The role of the international exhibitions in the construction of national cultures in the nineteenth century', *Ethnologia Europaea*, 24, 33–44.

Trosset, C. (1993). *Welshness Performed: Welsh Concepts of Person and Society* (Tucson: University of Arizona Press).

Williams, D. (1955). *The Rebecca Riots* (Cardiff: University of Wales Press).

Williams, G. (1983). *Wales and the Past: A Consort of Voices* (Cardiff: National Museum of Wales).

Williams, G. (1994). 'Discourses on "nation" and "race"', *Contemporary Wales*, 6, 87–103.

Williams, G. A. (1985). *When Was Wales?* (London: Penguin).

10   A Decade of Youth Homelessness

SUSAN HUTSON

Introduction

In 1989 youth homelessness hit the headlines in the national press. One well-known image of the time was that of George Young, the then housing minister, stepping over rough sleepers as he left the opera in London. Through such pictures, the public became familiar with homelessness as a problem and youth homelessness came to symbolize what was wrong with western capitalist society (Hutson and Liddiard 1997). Although many of these pictures came from London, similar stories came from Cardiff, Swansea, Wrexham and other parts of Wales. In the press picture from Llanelli (Figure 10.1), a similar contrast is drawn – between the angelic face of Jason and the cold, hard bricks of his surroundings.

Behind this rise in youth homelessness lie important changes in the lives of young people in Wales that have been well documented by sociologists. Leonard (1980), looking at courtship and marriage in Swansea in the 1970s, gives us a picture of young people leaving school at sixteen, walking into employment, getting married in their late teens, leaving home and moving into their own homes. This was the time when the population had 'never had it so good' and when young people 'had money in their pockets'.

Routes into adulthood in the 1990s are substantially different for young people in Wales today. Sixteen-year-olds cannot find full-time jobs. Many stay on into further education. Young people expect to be dependent on their parents for longer. When young people do leave home, they are more likely to leave as single persons than on marriage. All these changes have occurred within a decade.

Some young people have been casualties of these changes. These are young people who do not have the support of their families. They are young people who come from a care background and young people who leave home early, at sixteen, because of family conflict. Many of these young people end up homeless and it is these young people, throughout Wales, with whom this chapter is concerned.

In 1989, I set out to answer the following questions in an all-Wales survey.[1] What has caused the increase in youth homelessness? Who becomes homeless? What are their experiences? Later research enabled me to evaluate the responses to homelessness by voluntary and statutory agencies.[2] In reviewing these findings, I will also consider if there is anything distinctive about youth homelessness in Wales and how it has changed over a decade.

What Causes Youth Homelessness?

What factors led to the increasing visibility of youth homelessness in the late 1980s – both in London and in Wales?

Unemployment

One crucial factor was the marked increase in youth unemployment during the 1980s. This arose from global changes with, initially, increasing oil prices and, later, competition in trade from countries with cheaper labour costs in the East. Throughout the UK, traditional industries collapsed. In Wales, the closing of the coal mines and the rationalization of the steel industry led to the loss of many jobs. Young people were disproportionally affected by these trends. Unskilled jobs, which had gone to early school-leavers with no qualifications, were the first to go. Nationally, the number of young people going straight from school into employment fell dramatically, from 53 per cent in 1976 to 15 per cent in 1986 (Jones and Wallace 1992).

A series of Youth Training Schemes, introduced from 1983, did little to improve the situation (Roberts 1997). Young people leaving school at sixteen could no longer gain a wage but had only a training allowance of £29.50 a week. Youth Training was unpopular with both young people and their parents who complained of 'slave labour' and 'shit jobs'. As the economy restructured, national unemployment rates dropped. However, some young people had little to gain from these economic changes. The new jobs in the retail and the service sectors tended to go to older women working part-time. The expansion of further education absorbed many school-leavers but to take advantage of this trend young people needed qualifications and parental support. Youth unemployment was, therefore, the main cause for the appearance of youth homelessness.

Welfare benefit cuts

A more direct trigger behind the increase in youth homelessness was the welfare cuts, in particular those of 1988. Sixteen- and seventeen-year-olds were no longer able to claim income support and the rate for those under twenty-five was reduced by nearly a quarter of that for older people. These cuts were part of wider public-spending cuts by a government concerned about welfare dependency. Young people were particularly targeted because of fears that a whole generation would leave home and live on benefit. The media fuelled this debate by reporting that young unemployed people were living in bed-and-breakfast accommodation in seaside towns, on the 'Costa del Dole' (Brynin 1987).

Young people were also targeted because it was assumed that their families could, and should, support them and so they could more easily live without welfare than other groups (Jones 1995). There is no doubt that most families did this. However, for those without family support, these benefit cuts meant that if young people were without work or training, sixteen/seventeen-year-olds had no income and young people aged eighteen to twenty-five had to live on £46 a week.

Young people and housing

Changes in the housing market have created further difficulties for young people who cannot live at home. Young single people have never been given access to council housing and are not in a position to take advantage of the government's encouragement of home ownership (Liddiard 1998). The private rented sector has been the main option for young people. This sector has seen a steady decline throughout this century as landlords have invested their money elsewhere. The situation of young people in the private rented sector deteriorated sharply from 1985, when those claiming rent benefits were required to move on every six weeks. Three years later, state payments for bonds and rent in advance were abolished and, in addition, full housing benefit was no longer paid in private rented properties. These moves escalated youth homelessness (Hutson and Liddiard 1991).

The impact of the 'six weeks rule' can be illustrated by the observations in 1989 of Richard, aged nineteen. He was exempt from the 'six weeks move-on rule' of 1985 because he was from care. From a bedsit in Port Talbot, he contrasts his own stability with the movement, and so homelessness, of his friends:

> . . . because, as I say, I've been here three years, I treat this like my own home. I mean, if I was moving like my mates are, just moving from one house to another – 'cos there's a law out there, isn't there – you're only allowed to stay in one place for six weeks or something – forget that. Then I'd be classed 'homeless' but, because I'm settled here, I've got no worries.

Who Became Homeless?

Thus, unemployment, the inadequacy of training and the withdrawal of benefits created problems for young people and, for some, destitution and homelessness. It was very clear that some young people were disproportionately affected by these trends – these were young people who did not have family support. The importance of family support was illustrated in a study of unemployed young people in Swansea and Port Talbot in the mid-1980s (Hutson and Jenkins 1989). It showed how parents compensated for the lack of work and supported their children financially and psychologically. It was families who were 'taking the strain' of economic change. However, not all children had this family support.

Care-leavers and homelessness

In the survey of homeless young people in Wales in 1990, 22 per cent came from care (Hutson and Liddiard 1991). This figure echoed other UK surveys where the proportion rose to 30–40 per cent (Strathdee 1992). Why is there a link between being in care and becoming homeless? Young people from care tend to take different routes through childhood and into adulthood (Baldwin 1998). Their earlier life often involves abuse that leaves them vulnerable to low esteem. Once in care, most experience instability in placements, often moving many times. Both these factors tend to disrupt their educational careers and leave care-leavers with a lack of school qualifications. A study in west Wales (Hutson 1995a) shows that care-leavers were disproportionately represented in truancy, school exclusion and 'special' education units. Moreover, young women from care are particularly likely to become pregnant at or before sixteen, thus cutting off their educational careers at that age.

Young people in care are more likely to be in contact with peers involved in crime or prostitution. Lack of money, exploitation and lack of family support can encourage young people from care to continue this lifestyle. Even more significant is the fact that most young people leave care at the earliest legal age – sixteen. Not only do many young people themselves want to be independent but there is pressure on social services to free up these costly placements. Care-leavers tend to be living independently nearly six years earlier than their contemporaries and so are particularly vulnerable to benefit restriction. One young man, from Cardiff, expressed in 1994 his view of being forced to leave at sixteen: 'I'd like to see people not being so anxious to get us out of care – to show us some consideration and to make sure we have somewhere to go.'

Young people leaving home because of conflict
The survey in Wales in 1989 showed that the young people who were leaving home and becoming homeless were leaving because of family conflict (Hutson and Liddiard 1994). This and other surveys show that young homeless people do not *choose* to leave home. Their accounts stress the suddenness of leaving. In 1989 a young man from Rhyl, aged sixteen, told of how the police picked him up at the train station and took him back to his family home: 'They knocked on the door and there was no answer . . . My parents said, "Come home but you haven't won. You're going in the morning".' A boy in Brecon in 1990 told how he came back one night and his parents, who had been talking to the police and found out that they could have thrown him out eight months earlier at the age of seventeen, told him 'to get your stuff in the morning'.

The sadness of family conflict was expressed in 1992 by a sixteen-year-old Asian boy in Cardiff. When the conflict between him and his mother became 'physical' he decided to leave. Asked how he felt, he said:

> In a way I was glad to get out. I do miss my mother, of course, because after living with someone – and my brother – for so long, you do miss them and nothing can change the fact that you are family. You can't pick your own family. At other times I do wish – especially on my birthday and at Christmas . . .

In some cases eviction from home was connected with new partners in the family or the disruption from parental relationship break-ups. As one eighteen-year-old young man said in 1989: 'because your parents have split up, you feel just: "Crumbs". If they've split up, you want to split up. I know that's how I thought – I just can't handle the arguing, you know what I mean.'

Eviction from the family at the age of sixteen put these young people at risk of homelessness in the same way as care-leavers. In the changing economic conditions, these young people lack the necessary emotional and financial family support. Young homeless people from Merthyr Tydfil, in 1995, knew well the importance of having such support (Hutson *et al.* 1995). When asked what advice they would give to other young homeless people, these views were expressed again and again: 'Stay home.' 'Stick it at home.' 'Stay home definitely.' 'Don't leave home – life's too hard away from home. Don't do it unless it's intolerable. Only leave if it's really bad.'

Where did Homeless Young People Live and What were their Experiences?

Sleeping on friends' floors

A decade of research into youth homelessness in Wales shows that young people always attempt to solve their own problems and the main way in which they do this is to turn to friends, relatives and even family. Most remain within the local area, using their own networks (Fitzpatrick and Clapham 1999). These young people are 'homeless' because their accommodation is neither stable nor secure. Staying with others is always temporary. One young man described it, in 1998, as: 'Oh, a night here, a night there, that's all.

It's just like I go there and say: "Can I stay tonight?" "Yea, sure like". But their parents didn't know – they just thought it was like them having a friend to stay the night.'

These young people are intruding on other people and are always liable to be evicted. It is difficult, in these circumstances, to get or maintain a job, or to train, and difficult to make or maintain relationships for themselves. As one young man from Cardiff explained in 1989: 'Like, if I were to go out tonight and meet a young lady . . . I mean, can you imagine me saying "Hi, I live in the Salvation Army"? Can you imagine what sort of impression that would give off?'

Sleeping rough

Rough sleeping has always been part of the youth homelessness problem in Wales. The first reports were of young people sleeping in 'pig sheds' in Mid Glamorgan in 1988 (Hutson and Liddiard 1991). A decade later 9 per cent of single homeless people, reporting as homeless to agencies in Rhondda Cynon Taff, had slept rough at some time. Those young people sleeping on friends' floors often slept rough – in a bus shelter, a car or a ditch – for a night or two following an eviction. Longer-term rough sleeping, of several weeks at a time, is more likely to occur later in a homelessness career when an individual has run through their social network or is too old or problematic to be accepted onto a project. Whether for a long or short period, the risks of rough sleeping are always there. An eighteen-year-old boy reported in 1989: 'In the nights, I'd be sitting there quietly and a few boys came out of the pub, drunk like, and they gave me a hard time, kicking hell out of me.'

Private rented accommodation

Even when young homeless people manage to secure private rented accommodation, its appalling standard, together with other problems, can lead to depression and often poor health. In a survey (Hutson *et al.* 1995), nearly half of the forty young people interviewed had been admitted to hospital since they left home one to two years previously. The most common reasons for being admitted to hospital were overdosing, mental breakdowns and accidents. The following remarks, from girls of sixteen and seventeen in Merthyr Tydfil, indicate a lack of hope linked with lack of decent housing (author's emphasis):

Every morning I look around and think 'O God'. *A better environment would make a big difference.*

When I get depressed, I just go out and get drunk with my mates. *Nothing really would help apart from getting a new life.*

Sometimes I'm feeling low. Sometimes I'm screaming. I have to get out. I go and talk to someone – nan, one of my friends. *If I have a pleasant place, a job and money.*

Instability, movement and poor health can create a vicious circle for young homeless people. Accounts show that these problems often start in early childhood. One of the most tragic situations I came across was of a young man of seventeen, living in appalling conditions in a boarded-up hotel near Pontypridd. He said, at the time of the interview: 'I'm in a room. There's nothing to see. Nothing to do. I'm suicidal. You can't walk out.'

He himself had been through a special school. He was lodging next to an experienced offender and said that the only thing that helped him to survive was to go out and offend. He said that if he had a decent flat, he would not be tempted because: 'I'd stay at home, watch the TV. If I had a decent place, I'd spend more time there. I would like to make it permanent.' Sadly, he never found this as he was severely disabled in an electrical accident a few months after the interview. Let us now consider the provision that has been built up in Wales over the last decade, which this young man failed to access.

The Responses to Youth Homelessness

The voluntary sector

It would be wrong to imagine that there was no response to the situation of youth homelessness in Wales. In many respects, there has been more innovation and good practice in relation to vulnerable young people than in any other part of the UK. Wales led the way in the 1980s with projects from voluntary agencies such as Barnardos in south Wales; National Children's Home and CASH (later Adref) in Mid Glamorgan; the Children's Society in Cardiff and Clwyd; SASH and Young Single Homelessness project in Swansea as well as NACRO in north Wales. Other projects housed specialist groups in Cardiff, such as Anastasia for young offenders, Triangle for gay young people and Network for those with challenging behaviour.

Most provision was in the form of housing with support projects that were set up in partnership with housing associations. During the decade, the type of accommodation offered changed – from hostels to shared houses and, more recently, to self-contained flats for young people. The availability of Special Needs Management Allowance funding, which was only available in a few areas outside Wales, encouraged the development of projects and Tai Cymru (or Housing for Wales) took an active interest (Tai Cymru 1991). A number of Foyers, where accommodation is linked with training, are opening in Wales. The work of NAYPIC (now Voices From Care), run by care-leavers, added to innovation in Wales. Big Issue began operating in Wales in 1994. The presence of sellers on the streets of the main cities as well as towns like Bangor and Aberystwyth keeps the homelessness issue visible.

The importance of good quality accommodation and support for young vulnerable people was seen again and again (Hutson 1997). This young woman had experienced care, rough sleeping and prostitution. She spoke of the difference that a new housing association flat had made to her life:

> It's a safe address. I'm trying to stay out of trouble. New people (round here) don't know anything. It's a fresh start . . . I've got a lot better. I've stopped hanging around with the crowd. The flat is more important. If my mother comes in, I don't want drugs, drink. It's connected with the flat. If you've got a place of your own, you want it to look smart. I want to keep myself smart. I'm eating properly.

Statutory agencies and young homeless people

The development of services was slower in the statutory sector. This was despite the passing of the Children Act (implemented in 1991) which increased the duties of the social services towards care-leavers up to the age of twenty-one and gave lesser responsibilities to 'children in need' up to eighteen. It was hoped that this Act would improve young people's access to housing from housing departments and support from social services. These services were to come either directly or through partnerships between these departments and the voluntary sector.

This Act did form an impetus for the development of services but progress was slow and concentrated in Cardiff, Swansea and Newport. Very few extra resources were made available by central government for local authorities to fulfil their extra responsibilities. Within social service departments, care-leavers fared badly in competition with the demands from child protection work. Joint working between social services and housing was hampered by disagreements over definitions of 'vulnerability' and 'children in need'. Housing departments within Wales still do not generally accept young single homeless people as being in priority need and so eligible for council housing (Hoffman 1996). In terms of provision, despite early promise, progress has been slow. Let us now consider whether or not youth homelessness has been distinctive in Wales.

Is Youth Homelessness in Wales Distinctive?

The headline coverage of youth homeless presented pictures – of London. In 1990 £15 million was made available by the government to clear the streets of London in what was called the Rough Sleepers' Initiative (Randall and Brown 1993). Only later did this Initiative extend to other major cities – in England. The Labour Party's current initiative on rough sleeping covers England and Scotland – but not Wales. The assumption made is that there is not a youth homelessness problem in Wales.

However, all the accounts of youth homelessness in this chapter come from Wales. Moreover, the problem results from global economic change and was triggered by national cuts in benefits. The young people particularly affected – care-leavers and those leaving family conflict – are distributed throughout the UK. Logically, youth homelessness is a problem in Wales just as in other areas. In fact high unemployment and poverty levels in parts of Wales would suggest it to be a particular issue. As with the causes, the responses to homelessness are shaped by national legislation. Housing departments work to the Housing (Homeless Persons) Act and social services work to the Children Act whether they be in Llandrindod Wells or Luton.

Just as there is an assumption, in London, that youth homelessness is less of a problem in Wales, so, within Wales, there is an assumption that youth homelessness is only a problem in Cardiff and the urban south-east. The presence of voluntary-sector provision here confirms this view by making it visible. Arguments about the strength of both the family and the community in rural areas are often given as reasons why youth homelessness is not an issue here. People with influence, such as councillors, can see no sign of rough sleeping and assume that the homeless drift to the cities (Hutson and Jones forthcoming). In reality, however, the same causes operate in rural areas and, in fact, the lack of property to rent and the high cost of rural housing exacerbate the situation there (Cloke *et al.* 1997).

What has Changed over the Decade?

Homelessness statistics

Has youth homelessness increased? There is always a difficulty in gaining accurate figures on youth homelessness as official numbers only cover those who register at housing departments. Published Welsh Office statistics show that homelessness enquiries rose from 11,245 in 1987 to 16,639, indicating that general homelessness has increased. Unpublished figures show that enquiries from single people under pensionable age have risen, over the same period, from 3,303 to 7,331. Against these figures for enquiries, the number of single people under twenty-five accepted as 'homeless' in Wales in 1996 (1,700) and 'in priority need' (309) are markedly low. These figures are not strictly comparable as the first deals with single people under pensionable age and the second with single people under twenty-five. This shows the difficulties in drawing conclusions from official statistics. However, surveys (Hutson 1993, 1994) indicate that the majority of single homeless people are currently under twenty-five and so the discrepancy between enquiries and acceptances is marked.

Moreover, as Figure 10.1 shows, while the number of enquiries from homeless families has declined since 1994, the number from single homeless people under pensionable age has remained steady. Single homeless enquiries have risen in proportion, from 29 per cent of the total in 1987 to 44 per cent in 1996. In the 1977 Housing (Homeless Persons) Act, local authorities were not required to house most single homeless people, in part because this demand was not visible at the time. The increase in young homeless people has changed this demand but the duties of local authorities remain

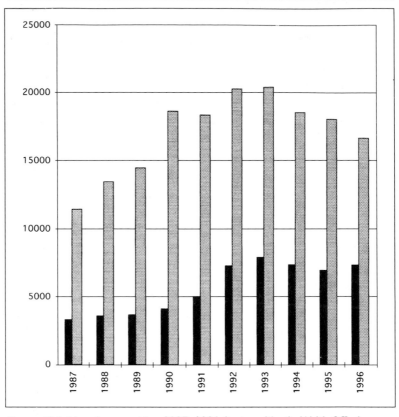

Figure 10.1. Homeless enquiries, 1987–1996 (prepared by the Welsh Office).

much the same. With dependent children, young people are much more likely to be seen as being 'in priority need' and so eligible for housing. Why should single-person status rule someone out of housing, particularly when young people are remaining single for longer? Sadly, restrictive policies by local authorities are often supported by people in local communities who do not wish to see young single homeless people housed next door to them (Hutson and Jones 1997).

The homeless experience

Accounts over a decade indicate that the experience of homelessness has changed little. Chris, in Rhyl, gave this account in 1989.

He had left home at sixteen because of conflict. He had stayed with a friend for a year, sleeping on the settee, but had been evicted when these friends moved to London. He had then moved in with his brother who had a flat with his girlfriend and young baby, again sleeping on the settee for six months. He then stayed with a mate but had had to leave here because of family trouble. When interviewed he was staying with his girlfriend's aunt. He said, of this period: 'It was rough – going to everyone else . . . They were fed up with me.'

Dave in Pontypridd gave this account in 1997. He had left care at sixteen. After six months back home, his mother evicted him. He went to his brother's house but was only able to camp in the garden. He was asked to leave and slept rough 'on the mountain'. He then went to stay with his father who sorted him out and found him a private rented flat – a 'dive' in town. After two months, he went back to his 'mam' who he felt had broken up a ten-year marriage by taking him in. After a few months, he returned to 'dossing' with mates. After meeting a girlfriend and spending two spells in hospital, they were both housed in a housing association flat. A year later, Dave at the age of twenty split up from his girlfriend and is homeless again.

These two accounts illustrate the constant movement, the lack of privacy or stability in these young men's lives. Both used family and friends although this accommodation did not last. Neither young man qualified for housing. Although Dave gained a housing association property after being in hospital, he lost this when he became single again.

Chris did not sleep rough and no informants from the 1989 survey were sleeping rough when interviewed (Hutson and Liddiard 1991). Dave had slept rough and one in five of those interviewed in the 1997 survey were sleeping rough when interviewed (Hutson and Jones 1997). Over a decade, noticeably less mention was made, in young peoples' accounts, of bed and breakfast or private rented flats. The private rented sector became even more out of reach to young people with changes to housing benefit in 1996 (Murphy 1998). In the survey when Chris was interviewed, 21 per cent were sixteen- and seventeen-year-olds. In the survey when Dave was interviewed 33 per cent were this age. Although it is difficult to compare surveys carried out in different places over time, they suggest an increase in the incidence of rough sleeping, a decline in the private rented sector for young people, and that homeless people are younger.

Homelessness and the New Deal

This decade has seen a change in political parties. The emphasis of the Labour Party on the need to tackle 'social exclusion' does acknowledge the multiple deprivation of those living in poor areas and such an approach should benefit young homeless people. However, the main route out of social exclusion is through work or training, whether for single mothers or for the young, long-term unemployed. These ladders, set up for the socially excluded to climb, are often out of the reach of young homeless people. New Deal training schemes, for example, often require written exams and regular attendance, which are not always achievable by young people without stable lives. Such young people – not sought by schools conscious of their league tables, nor sought by trainers conscious of their outcomes – often fail to reach the first rung into mainstream provision.

Moreover, housing is not generally built into the 'social exclusion' package – at least not for the young single person. Housing, generally, is not high on the political agenda. The focus of the 'homelessness Czar' is still to clear London streets. Unless youth homelessness is identified as an issue by the Welsh Assembly and the Welsh Office, the earlier Welsh initiatives in housing and support for young people will be lost.

Homelessness projects

I have outlined the expansion of housing and support projects – services of which people in Wales should be proud. However, the quality of these projects makes them relatively expensive. Moreover, as social services have increased their funding to voluntary schemes, it was inevitable that priority would be given to care-leavers. There are fewer places for young people made homeless from home. Other young people are excluded from projects because they are over eighteen or because they are seen as being likely to cause trouble in management terms – because of a drug problem or a history of violence. The irony of this was illustrated by a young man in north Wales who describes in 1989 his interview at a homelessness hostel:

So there I was, you know what I mean, I was homeless. I went to a homeless hostel and I was told I couldn't have a place in a homeless hostel! . . . You said that you didn't feel that I'd benefit from it! But if you're on the street, you've got nowhere to sleep right, how can you not benefit from a bed? I couldn't work that one out . . .

While we have good services for the vulnerable few, there is not yet an acknowledgement that homelessness is a problem for more ordinary young people. Nor is it acknowledged that homeless young people, like Chris or Dave, have friends or relatives who could themselves receive some support. Surveys suggest (Hutson *et al.* 1995) that many young homeless people are in touch with agencies – such as housing, social services and probation. All this means, however, is that young homeless people in Wales are not (usually) wrapped in blankets in the city centre but rather coming down from local neighbourhoods and making enquiries in local agency offices. These are young Welsh people wanting local housing close to friends and relatives.

Conclusions

In Wales today, as elsewhere in the UK, most young people stay at home until they are well into their twenties. They are able to mix further education with casual work because their parents give them both a roof over their heads and some financial support. However, a minority of young people need to leave home or care at sixteen. It is these young people who are at risk of homelessness. This can happen in London, Cardiff or Betws-y-coed. Improvements in the economy tend to leave these young people out, as do the Labour Party's initiatives on social exclusion. Young people without stable accommodation or parental support are often not in a position to take advantage of education and training which are the new passports to success. While there are special projects for young people, and Wales led the way in this positive response to youth homelessness, the state has progressively withdrawn state benefits from those under twenty-five and continues to exclude most young single people from council housing. These special projects are of high quality but are expensive and so only open to a few. While some young people need the special help they offer, others just need easier access – to income, to training and to jobs and houses. The homeless are simply young people, wanting to live in Wales, in their local area.

Notes

1. A survey of young homeless people in Wales was undertaken with Mark Liddiard and funded by the Joseph Rowntree Foundation (1989–91). Later surveys also inform this chapter, including work in Merthyr Tydfil with Jaqui Thomas and Margaret Sutton (1994), and in Taff Ely with Stuart Jones (1996–8).
2. This includes a project on leaving care in Wales (1992–5) and the evaluation of a young people's housing project (1993–6), both funded by the Welsh Office; a follow-on study of young people (1993–6) and an evaluation of a self-build scheme (1997–8), both funded by Barnardos. The latter was undertaken with Stuart Jones.

References

Baldwin, D. (1998). 'Growing up in and out of care: an ethnographic approach to young people's transitions to adulthood', unpublished Ph.D. (York: University of York).

Brynin, M. (1987).'Young homeless pressure groups, politics and the press', *Youth and Policy*, 20, 24–34.

Cloke, P., Goodwin, M. and Milbourne, P. (1997). *Rural Wales: Community and Marginalization* (Cardiff: University of Wales Press, 1997).

Fitzpatrick, S. and Clapham, D. (1999). 'Homelessness and young people', in S. Hutson and D. Clapham (eds.), *Homelessness: Public Policies and Private Troubles* (London: Cassell).

Hoffman, S. (1996). *Against the Odds: Youth Homelessness in Wales* (Swansea: Shelter Cymru).

Hutson, S. (1993). *A Single Person Housing Need Survey* (Neath: Neath Homelessness Forum).

Hutson, S. (1994). *A Snapshot Survey of Single Homelessness in Swansea* (Swansea: Swansea Borough Council).

Hutson, S. (1995a). *The Experience of Education and Care*, a report for the Welsh Office (Swansea: University of Wales).

Hutson, S. (1995b). *Care-Leavers and Young Homeless People in Wales: The Exchange of Good Practice* (Cardiff: Welsh Office).

Hutson, S. (1997). *Supported Housing: The Experience of Care-Leavers* (London: Barnardos).

Hutson, S. and Jenkins, R. (1989). *Taking the Strain: Families, Unemployment and the Transition to Adulthood* (Milton Keynes: Open University Press).

Hutson, S. and Jones, S. (1997). *Rough Sleeping and Homelessness in Rhondda Cynon Taff* (Pontypridd: University of Glamorgan).

Hutson, S. and Jones, S. (forthcoming). 'Sleeping on the mountain: homelessness at the margins', in R. Byron and S. Black (eds.), *Local Enterprise on the North Atlantic Margin* (Aldershot: Ashgate).

Hutson, S. and Liddiard, M. (1991). *Young and Homeless in Wales: Government Policies, Insecure Accommodation and Agency Support* (Swansea: University of Wales).

Hutson, S. and Liddiard, M. (1994). *Youth Homelessness: The Construction of a Social Issue* (London: Macmillan).

Hutson, S. and Liddiard, M. (1997). 'Youth homelessness: marginalising the marginalised', in H. Jones (ed.), *Towards a Classless Society?* (London: Routledge).

Hutson, S. and Liddiard, M. (forthcoming). 'Youth homelessness: the media career of a social issue', in S. Allan, B. Adam and C. Carter (eds.), *Environmental Risks and the Media* (London: Routledge).

Hutson, S., Sutton, M. and Thomas, J. (1995). *The Housing and Support Needs of Young Homeless People in Merthyr Tydfil*, Occasional Paper, 28 (Swansea: University of Wales).

Jones, G. (1995). *Family Support for Young People* (London: Family Policy Centre and Joseph Rowntree).

Jones, G. and Wallace, C. (1992). *Youth, Family and Citizenship* (Buckingham: Open University Press).

Leonard, D. (1980). *Sex and Generation: A Study of Courtship and Weddings* (London: Tavistock Publications).

Liddiard, M. (1998). 'Housing policies', in H. Jones and S. Macgregor (eds.), *Social Issues and Party Politics* (London: Routledge).

Murphy, D. (1998). *Of No Benefit: The Effects of the Single Room Rent* (Swansea: Shelter Cymru).

Randall, G. and Brown, S. (1993). *The Rough Sleepers Initiative: An Evaluation* (London: HMSO).

Roberts, K. (1997). 'Youth training', in H. Jones (ed.), *Towards a Classless Society?* (London: Routledge).

Strathdee, R. (1992). *No Way Back: Homeless Sixteen and Seventeen Year Olds in the 90s* (London: Centrepoint Soho).

Tai Cymru (1991). *Report of the Working Party on Single Homelessness* (Cardiff: Tai Cymru).

11 Child Welfare in Wales

MATTHEW COLTON

Introduction

We can learn much about a society from the provision that it makes for its weakest members: what it values and cherishes, what it disdains and chooses to disregard. Children who require support, protection and care from social welfare agencies are among our most vulnerable members. As such, the quality of the services that we provide to meet their needs represents an important barometer of our collective conscience.

This chapter will attempt to evaluate social welfare provision for children and young people in Wales, beginning with a concise account of the aims, principles and key provisions of the Children Act 1989. Three vital elements of the child welfare system are then examined sequentially: family support services; protective services for children at risk of abuse and neglect; and care for children 'looked after' by local authorities, which will include discussion of the abuse of children in residential child-care settings. The chapter is informed by the findings of recent research on child welfare undertaken in Wales.

It is important to acknowledge at the outset that the account that follows is by no means exhaustive. Even if the space allowed were considerably less constrained, a large degree of selectivity would be required in such a broad field. An effort has, however, been made to avoid the arbitrary choice of material. The topics covered are of central concern to all those with an interest in the welfare of our most vulnerable children.

The Children Act 1989

Wales has the same child-care legislation as England, whereas Scotland and Northern Ireland have their own child-care law. The Children Act 1989 is widely seen as the most important piece of child-care law passed by Parliament this century. The overarching aims of the Act were to make the law concerning children easier to understand and use, more consistent but also more flexible, and more child-centred.

The 1989 Act 'rests on the belief that children are best looked after within the family with both parents playing a full part and without resort to legal proceedings' (Department of Health 1989a, 1). That belief is partly reflected in the concept of parental responsibility, which replaced the notion of 'parental rights' and was intended to emphasize the obligations of parents towards their children. Parents are only given rights through exercising responsibility. Parental responsibility can be shared, thus allowing the inclusion of absent parents, such as unmarried fathers, and other close relatives.

The Act also acknowledges that parents may need support in fulfilling their responsibilities. Therefore, previously restricted notions of prevention were supplanted by 'family support' and local authorities were given a new duty to facilitate the upbringing of children by their parents. Moreover, the Act promotes partnership between parents and local authorities. Local authorities must work on the basis of negotiation and voluntary agreements. Where this fails and children are removed, parents must be kept fully informed and can only be denied access to their children in exceptional circumstances.

The child's welfare is paramount and must be considered in the context of his or her physical, emotional and educational needs, age, gender, background and the capacity of care-givers adequately to perform their task. Also, when resort is made to the legal process delay must be avoided: emergency protection orders must be of short duration and courts must work to timetables to prevent children suffering the adverse consequences of delay. In addition, no order should be made unless it is considered preferable to no order at all. Finally, the child's voice must be heard: children's wishes and feelings must be taken into account when decisions are made.

The Act seeks a balance between children and parents, the state and families, courts and local authorities. Where power is unequal, the Act attempts to safeguard the weak. Thus, the needs of children are placed first because of their dependence and vulnerability, but parents and other significant adults are accorded increased respect and consideration (Packman and Jordan 1991).

Specific reference is made in the Act to race, culture, language and religion as factors that must be considered in relation to the welfare of children. The Act conferred a new duty on local authorities to take account of the different racial groups to which children in need belong when providing day care or accommodation. The Department of Health (1989b) publication, *The Care of Children, Principles and Practice in Regulations and Guidance*, emphasizes the special issues that arise for black children and young people and those from ethnic minority groups. It states that such children need to develop a positive self-image which includes their cultural and ethnic origins, and that this must be taken into account by services planners and care-givers.

It should be noted that the law on the adoption of children was little affected by the 1989 Act. More recent legislation in Wales and England has addressed youth justice (Criminal Justice Acts 1991 and 1993) and Education (Education Act 1993). Nevertheless, the Children Act 1989 represents the main legal context of social welfare provision for children in Wales. The Act deals with most areas of child welfare, including family support, child protection and the care of children looked after by local authorities. These three key topics will now be examined in turn.

Family Support

Under section 17 of the Children Act 1989 children are in need if they require local authority services to achieve or maintain a reasonable standard of health or development, or they need local authority services to prevent significant or further impairment of their health and development, or they are disabled. This definition is wide enough, potentially, to embrace all children who could be helped by the provision of services. However, it is clear that the 1989 Act does not subscribe to a universal welfare system for all.

Rather, it instructs social services to define 'in need' according to local needs and to limit services to the most vulnerable.

Although local authorities have wide discretion to determine the range and level of services, the Act includes specific powers and duties which give some indication of the purposes for which family support services should be provided. These are: preventing ill treatment and neglect; reducing the need to bring care or related proceedings; reducing delinquency and criminal proceedings against children; minimizing the effects of disability on children with disabilities; and promoting family reunification and contact.

Colton *et al.* (1995a and 1995b) carried out a comprehensive evaluative study of services for children in need in Wales under the 1989 Act. This research, which was funded by the Welsh Office, showed that social services managers in all (the then eight) local authorities wanted to give more emphasis to preventative work but in practice concentrated resources on children at risk of abuse and neglect. The level of services available to support families, including services for children with disabilities, was judged by both managers and social workers to be generally inadequate.

Colton *et al.* (1995a and 1995b) also examined partnership between families and social work agencies. Most parents interviewed did feel that they had participated in decision-making, and two-thirds felt that social services had helped them in bringing up their children. Parents particularly appreciated the provision of emotional support. However, the partnership element most lacking between agencies and families was the sharing of information. Only 29 per cent of the children interviewed felt that their social workers had told them things they needed to know, and only 13 per cent of parents felt that they knew enough about the kinds of services available to help them (from other agencies as well as social services).

Statham (1997) carried out a study of day care services for children in Wales. Whilst Welsh-language issues were being addressed by day-care providers, little attention was given to equal opportunities issues and the need to help children develop positive attitudes in relation to cultural and racial diversity; indeed, many day carers in Statham's study saw such issues as irrelevant to their role.

Colton *et al.* (1995a and 1995b) found that half of (the then eight) social services departments lacked written policies on Welsh language and culture, and had no plans to introduce such policies because managers felt them to be unnecessary in view of the small proportion of Welsh-speakers in each of the areas concerned. Similar, equally unsatisfactory, explanations were given where written policies were lacking in relation to religious needs and the needs of black and ethnic minority communities. Overall, it was evident that much more effort and commitment would be required to ensure that service provision adequately reflected the linguistic, racial, cultural and religious diversity in Wales.

At the time of Colton et al.'s (1995a and 1995b) research, local authority social services departments did appear to be striking an appropriate balance between offering specialist services to children with disabilities and giving them access to general programmes and facilities. However, the identification of children in specific categories of disability was problematic, largely because of poor liaison between social services, health and education authorities. The registration of children with disabilities was another area of difficulty. Some parents were reluctant to register their children because they perceived that inclusion in the register would carry a stigma and lead to little benefit. The requirement that registers be complete means that effective and ethical ways must be sought to persuade reluctant parents to register their children.

It is interesting to note, therefore, that contrary to an important aim of the Children Act, more recent research undertaken by Colton and colleagues as part of an international study shows that stigma continues to be part and parcel of the experience of using child welfare services in Wales (Colton et al. 1997).

This partly reflects the current organization of service delivery in Wales, which is often incompatible with the concept of family support contained in Part III of the 1989 Act. Family support services should be decentralized on a local neighbourhood basis, and family centres should play a central role in the delivery of services. Under the 1989 Act family centres are one of a range of family support services local authorities are required to provide 'as appropriate' in their area, and are formally recognized as a major component of preventive provision to meet need (Colton et al. 1995a and 1995b).

However, perhaps more than any other factor, social exclusion threatens the practical achievement of effective family support services. High levels of child poverty, unemployment, inadequate housing and poor health and educational provision significantly increase the pressure on vulnerable families. The successful implementation of Part III of the Children Act in Wales necessitates that social exclusion is placed at the heart of the policy, practice and research agenda. Quite simply, there is no substitute for government action to tackle this problem (Colton *et al.* 1995a and 1995b).

Child Protection

One of the most important technical definitions of child abuse deriving from legislation is 'significant harm'. Section 31 of the Children Act 1989 defines harm thus:

> 'harm' means ill-treatment or the impairment of health or development;
> 'development' means physical, intellectual, emotional, social or behavioural development;
> 'health' means physical or mental health;
> and 'ill-treatment' includes sexual abuse and forms of 'ill-treatment' which are not physical.

Department of Health guidance on inter-agency working in respect of child abuse adopts four defined categories of abuse, which inform professionals making decisions about whether to place a child's name on the child protection register. The categories are: neglect, physical injury, sexual abuse and emotional abuse (Home Office *et al.* 1991). At 31 March 1996, 1,649 children in Wales were on child protection registers. Some 26 per cent were recorded in the neglect (only) category, 34 per cent under physical abuse (only), 14 per cent under sexual abuse (only) and 18 per cent under emotional abuse. Physical abuse was involved in 41 per cent of registered cases and sexual abuse in 18 per cent of such cases (Welsh Office 1997). Around the same period, approximately 40,000 children were on child protection registers in the UK as a whole (National Commission of Inquiry into the Prevention of Child Abuse, 1996).

However, the figures on child protection registers cannot be taken as estimates of the true extent of abuse. For example, the taboo nature of sexual abuse impedes discovery and deters reporting. Moreover, the report of the National Commission of Inquiry into the Prevention of Child Abuse (1996, 4) notes that 'child protection agencies tend to work to narrow legal and technical definitions of abuse, partly because of fears of widening the net for formal intervention or actions and partly because of the need to allocate scarce resources'.

A substantial body of evidence on child protection and child abuse has been established in recent years. This indicates that local authorities are initiating child protection procedures on the basis of injuries to children and are failing fully to consider the child's wider situation. Vital family support services that could be provided under Part III of the Children Act 1989 are often overlooked, with social workers instead focusing on a bureaucratic response to identified injuries. Large numbers of children are inappropriately drawn into the child protection system. Yet when it is clear that protective measures are unnecessary, the needs of such children for services are often left unmet (Department of Health, 1995).

Jackson et al. (1994) were commissioned by the Welsh Office to evaluate the effectiveness of (the then eight) Area Child Protection Committees (ACPCs) as organs for the transmission of official child protection policy to the local level. The study found that those aspects of official policy concerned with the identification and investigation of suspected abuse, and with the operation of case conferences and registration, were generally effectively dealt with by the ACPC structure. Inter-agency collaboration associated with this work was also impressive. However, those aspects of child protection policy relating to prevention and treatment were less effectively attended to. This imbalance was mirrored in the varying levels of involvement by different agencies in the activities of the ACPC. Many members of ACPCs regretted this and would have liked to have been more actively involved in these aspects of policy, but felt that a clearer lead from government was needed to enable this to happen. The researchers echo many others in calling for greater integration of child protection and other child welfare services. Child abuse tragedies have been influential in shaping child welfare legislation, policy and practice throughout the post-war period. ACPCs currently have responsibility for conducting reviews of such cases in accordance with Part 8 of *Working Together Under the Children Act* 1989 (Home Office et al. 1991). Colton et al. (1996) were commissioned to carry out an independent analysis of twenty-one Part 8 Review reports submitted to the Welsh Office since 1991. Considerable variation was found in the quality, structure and content of the Review reports. The researchers conclude that a more systematic approach to the review of child abuse tragedies is required. These findings are supported by a recently published government report, which acknowledges that Part 8 review reports are currently of 'variable quality and thoroughness' (Department of Health 1998).

Because of their restricted terms of reference, Part 8 Reviews focus on procedural issues. Consequently, they fail to address the causes of child abuse fatalities. This means that there is a lack of precisely the sort of information that might help to prevent such tragedies. In general, the reports examined by Colton *et al.* (1996) provide an inadequate description of what agencies did, with incomplete consideration of what could have been done better, irrespective of whether or not those actions were seen to play a role in the fatality. There was also a conspicuous lack of information regarding the implementation and monitoring of recommendations put forward as a result of the Review process. Finally, it is obvious that an independent input into the review process is required to ensure that objectivity is maintained.

Looking After Children

Under the Children Act 1989 the term 'looked after' denotes all children subject to a care order or who are provided with accommodation on a voluntary basis for more than twenty-four hours. The number of children in public care has steadily decreased since the 1970s. On 31 March 1994 roughly 3,000 children were 'looked after' by local authorities in Wales, compared with 49,000 in England. Some 55 per cent of these youngsters were male and 44 per cent female; 24 per cent had been 'looked after' for under a year and 10 per cent for over ten years; over half (1,979) were aged ten or over (NCH 1996). About two-thirds of children 'looked after' in Wales are placed with foster carers, with a little under 20 per cent placed in residential homes (NCH 1996).

Over the past ten years the public care system has repeatedly been shown to have failed to protect youngsters living in children's homes from sexual abuse by paedophiles operating alone or as part of semi-organized 'rings'. For example, major child abuse inquiries have been undertaken involving clusters of children's homes in north Wales. In June 1996 the former Secretary of State for Wales established a public inquiry chaired by Sir Ronald Waterhouse. Full hearings ran from January 1997 until the middle of March 1998. The tribunal took evidence from local authority employees, witnesses alleging abuse, witnesses against whom allegations were made, the police and the Welsh Office. In addition, written submissions of evidence were received. The Chair of the Tribunal was expected to submit his Report to the Secretary of State in the Autumn of 1998. At the time of writing it appears that large numbers of children were sexually abused while in care in north Wales. Most of the victims are now young adults, and it is anticipated that large awards will be made by the Criminal Injuries Compensation Board.

Of course, the cost in humans terms is incalculable. Child sexual abuse can have far-reaching adverse consequences for victims, and has been linked with short- and long-term emotional and behavioural problems (Colton and Vanstone 1996). Some twelve suicides of former residents in children's homes in north Wales have been linked to the abuse they suffered as children in care (NCH 1996).

Sir William Utting recently prepared a report for the Department of Health based on a review established in 1996 in response to ongoing disclosure of abuse suffered by children living away from home (Utting 1997). Sir William's main criticisms about the quality of care for such children include: inappropriate residential care placements; poor standards of health and education in residential care; inadequate regulation of foster carers; no inspection of residential maintained special schools; children in prison sharing accommodation with adult offenders; and inadequate regulation with regard to the recruitment of staff working with children.

Extensive research undertaken in the 1980s showed that the child-care system was failing badly when judged against the outcomes for children and young people. All aspects of their development were found to be more problematic than those of children cared for by their own families or adopted at a young age (Department of Health 1991). In response to such findings, the (then) Department of Health and Social Security set up an independent working party to consider the question of outcomes in child-care (Parker *et al.* 1991). This resulted in the production of the 'Looking After Children' (LAC) materials which are designed to improve the parenting experience of children looked after by local authorities and other agencies.

In the light of further research and development work, the original LAC materials were recently revised (Ward 1995). These materials are now being adopted by local authorities throughout Wales with the encouragement of the Welsh Office and the Central Council for Education and Training in Social Work/Cymru. The materials constitute an integrated package that can help social workers and care-givers set an agenda for work with children and young people, and ensure that these plans are acted upon.

A study undertaken by Thomas and O'Kane (1996) on children's participation in decision-making indicates that the LAC materials can also help to ensure that the child's voice is heard. The study was funded by the Nuffield Foundation and was carried out in 1996 and 1997 in seven local authorities in Wales and the English borders. It was found that where the LAC materials were in use, 63 per cent of children were invited to attend the whole of their review meeting, compared with only 38 per cent of children for whom the materials were not being used.

Conclusion

The child welfare scene in the 1990s has been dominated by a number of major concerns. These include the struggle effectively to implement Part III of the Children Act 1989. Although support for vulnerable families lies at the very core of the Act, it is clear that much work remains to be done in order to establish an effective system of family support in Wales. Progress has been impeded by a number of factors. The pressures on vulnerable families have significantly increased over the last two decades. For example, the extent of child poverty increased threefold, and poor families in Wales were among the very hardest hit in the United Kingdom (Colton *et al.* 1995a, 1995b). In a context of increasing social distress, the Children Act 1989 substantially enlarged local authorities' duties towards children in need and their families. Unfortunately, a corresponding increase in resources was not forthcoming.

An effective family support system necessitates a comprehensive approach embracing primary, secondary and tertiary prevention.

In relation to the first of these, there can be no substitute for action by central government to tackle social exclusion. Government measures are also required to ensure that social welfare personnel possess the attitudes, skills and resources to enable them to fulfil their duties at the second and third levels of prevention. The organization, structure and delivery of services must be conducive to the full implementation of Part III of the Children Act. Policy and practice must operationalize the provisions contained in the legislation, and reflect the linguistic, cultural and ethnic diversity of Wales. In addition, a more appropriate balance has to be sought between prevention and child protection. Currently, local authorities in Wales, as in England, give priority to protecting children at risk. Insufficient resources are devoted to the kind of preventive work with families that would avert the need for more serious and more costly interventions. The emphasis on protection owes much to the fact that local authorities have been obliged to prioritize against a background of severe resource constraint, coupled with relentless, and often unfair, criticism in relation to child abuse tragedies. Unfortunately, while local authorities have understandably given priority to child protection, it seems that the usefulness of this work is open to doubt. Studies show that large numbers of children in need are inappropriately drawn into the child protection system, and even then do not receive the services they require.

At the time of writing, however, it is provision for children placed away from home that gives rise to greatest concern. The most disturbing recent occurrence in the field of child welfare in Wales and, indeed, other parts of the United Kingdom, has been the revelation of a deplorable catalogue of child abuse, including sexual abuse in residential homes. Much of this abuse appears to have been perpetrated by so-called 'care-givers' who have betrayed positions of trust, responsibility and respect. Appallingly, it appears that rather than being afforded additional care and protection, youngsters removed from their families – supposedly in their 'best interests' – are frequently exposed to even greater risk.

This shameful state of affairs can only serve to further fuel long-standing unease about the quality of the public care system. Sadly, it also inevitably detracts from the commitment and achievements of other child welfare workers. Notwithstanding the challenges highlighted in this account, it should not be overlooked that much important and successful work is accomplished. Invariably, the vast majority of child welfare practitioners and administrators in Wales strive diligently and honourably, in extremely testing circumstances, to provide high standards of service for children, young people and their families. Decisive and urgent action is required to improve the public care system. Thus, the government's recent announcement that it is to establish an expert team to raise the quality of care for children 'looked after' by local authorities is welcome. This programme has been trailed as the first in a series of measures to improve standards of children's services (Brindle and Gentleman 1998).

Ensuring a better deal for vulnerable children also requires increased emphasis on children's rights. The much vaunted Children Act 1989 does seem to take children's rights more seriously than previous legislation, and provides new opportunities for advancing the wishes, autonomy and independent actions of children and young people. However, the Act does this in a very qualified way. A broader, more creative, approach is required. As a useful first step, therefore, local authorities in Wales should ensure that their services fully adhere to the 1989 United Nations Convention on the Rights of the Child. This recognizes that children are holders of a specific body of rights, which include the traditional areas of prevention, protection and provision but also of participation.

We are moving toward a new system of devolved government in Wales, with the prospect of greater autonomy in social affairs and increased scope for enhancing provision for children in need and their families. To achieve this, it is essential that policy and practice are supported by research. Despite the fact that this chapter has endeavoured to draw on studies specifically carried out in Wales, in truth, comparatively little research is actually undertaken in Wales. Much of the information that informs service provision in Wales is drawn second-hand from research conducted in England. It is a considerable disadvantage that Wales is currently the only country in the United Kingdom that does not have a single government-funded research centre that is wholly, or in substantial part, dedicated to the study of child welfare.

This conspicuous shortcoming will have to be rectified if devolution is to contribute to the development of an integrated and coherent system of child welfare in Wales. Such a system would be characterized by the provision of proactive, preventive, help for vulnerable children and their families; highly competent, and intelligently targeted, protection for children at risk of abuse and neglect; and skilled, imaginative, child-centred care and after-care for children placed away from home. Many countries, great and small, in Europe and beyond would envy such a system.

References

Brindle, D. and Gentleman, A. (1998). 'Top social services team aims to improve child-care', *Guardian* (22 September).

Colton, M., Drury, C. and Williams, M. (1995a). *Children in Need* (Aldershot: Avebury).

Colton, M., Drury, C. and Williams, M. (1995b). *Staying Together: Supporting Families Under the Children Act 1989* (Aldershot: Arena).

Colton, M., Roberts, S. and Sanders, R. (1996). *An Analysis of Area Child Protection Committee Reviews on Child Deaths and Other Cases of Public Concern in Wales: A Report for the Welsh Office* (Swansea: University of Wales, Swansea).

Colton, M. and Vanstone, M. (1996). *Betrayal of Trust: Sexual Abuse by Men Who Work with Children* (London: Free Association Books).

Colton, M., Casas, F., Drakeford, M., Roberts, S., Scholte, E. and Williams, M. (1997). *Stigma and Social Welfare: An International Comparative Study* (Aldershot: Avebury).

Department of Health (1989a). *An Introduction to the Children Act 1989* (London: HMSO).

Department of Health (1989b). *The Care of Children, Principles and Practice in Regulations and Guidance* (London: HMSO).

Department of Health (1991). *Patterns and Outcomes in Child Placement: Messages from Current Research and their Implications* (London: HMSO).

Department of Health (1995). *Child Protection: Messages from Research* (London: HMSO).

Department of Health (1998). *Working Together to Safeguard Children: New Proposals for Inter-agency Co-operation: Consultation Paper* (Leeds: Department of Health).

Jackson, S., Sanders, R. and Thomas, N. (1994). *Protecting Children in Wales: The Role and Effectiveness of Area Child Protection Committees* (Swansea: University of Wales, Swansea).

National Commission of Inquiry into the Prevention of Child Abuse (1996). *Childhood Matters* (London: HMSO).

NCH – Action for Children (1997). *Factfile 96/97* (London: NCH – Action for Children).

Packman, J. and Jordan, B. (1991). 'The Children Act: looking forward, looking back', *British Journal of Social Work*, 21, 4.

Parker, R., Ward, H., Jackson, S., Aldgate, J. and Wedge, P. (eds.) (1991). *Looking After Children: Assessing Outcomes in Child-care* (London: HMSO).

Statham, J. (1997). *Day Care Services for Children Under Eight: An Evaluation of the Implementation of the Children Act in Wales* (London: Thomas Coram Research Unit, University of London).

Thomas, N. and O'Kane, C. (1996). 'Children's participation in plans and reviews', paper presented to National Children's Bureau conference, Plans Reviews: Getting it Right for Young People, London, October.

Utting, W. (1997). *People Like Us: The Report of the Review of the Safeguards for Children Living Away from Home* (London: HMSO).

Ward, H. (1995). *Looking After Children: Research into Practice* (London: HMSO).

Welsh Office (1997). *Child Protection Register: Statistics for Wales 1997* (Cardiff: Welsh Office).

12 Health and Health Delivery in Wales

MARCUS LONGLEY and MORTON WARNER

There has been a common misconception in many developed countries in modern times that the health of a nation is produced solely by its health services – in the case of Wales, the National Health Service. Nothing could be further from the truth! Wales, as the birthplace of Aneurin Bevan, the founder of the NHS, might be forgiven for this error, but as this chapter will reveal the *social* determinants of ill health are extremely varied and so, too, are the policies and services that respond to health problems.

Two major strands will be examined. The first involves a look at a small amount of historical data about the changing health problems of people in Wales and concludes with a more detailed look at the results of the Welsh Health Survey of 1996 – the emphasis throughout is on medical and social epidemiology. The second focuses on the political responses over time, but particularly since 1989, with the development of a health strategy for Wales, and the supply-side items – programmes, manpower, facilities and education and training – which now exist in the NHS, local authorities and the voluntary and private sectors.

Throughout recent decades, 'health' has become a very political commodity; and the chapter ends on a more speculative note with a consideration of the potential future impact of recent events – the arrival of a Welsh Assembly. Will it, as a body, be closer to the people of Wales and their communities, and tackle the broad agenda associated with the social determinants of health?

The Purpose of the NHS

For most of its existence, the NHS has not been troubled by the question: what is its purpose? For most people the answer was obvious: to help people get better when they fall ill, and to a lesser extent to help them stay well. But the question becomes a little more difficult when one asks: how can its success be measured? Most commonly, the performance of the NHS is measured in terms of what it does – for example, how many people are treated, how long they had to wait. The assumption is that the more treatments carried out – and the less time people have to wait for treatment – the better. But is this necessarily the case? What do such measurements of activity really convey? After all, the fact that more operations were carried out last year than the year before, could indicate successful treatment, or failure to prevent people becoming ill in the first place.

There are therefore several important questions to answer before we can be sure about the purpose of the health service. They include:

- What is 'health'?
- What causes ill health?
- What can the NHS realistically expect to do about improving health?

What is health?

Perhaps the most famous definition of health is that developed by the World Health Organization, the international body which brings together most countries in the world to improve the health of the population. Their definition states: 'health is a state of complete physical, mental and social well-being, rather than just the absence of disease' (World Health Organization 1978). But is 'health' – defined in such a way – ever really achieveable? Can anyone ever expect to attain such a degree of happiness? Many people do not believe so. However, the definition is useful because it does emphasize that health is more than just the absence of disease – and therefore the business of the NHS should be about enabling people to attain their full potential, in this broader sense.

What causes 'ill health'?

A vast array of factors, many of them interrelated, can contribute to ill health (see Figure 12.1). Everyone has a set of innate

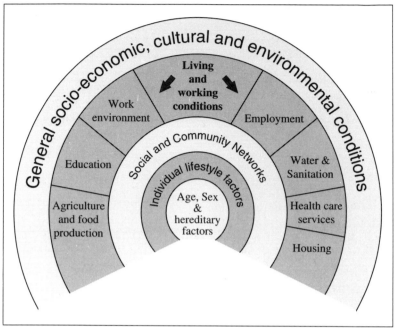

Figure 12.1. *The main determinants of health.*

characteristics, about which they can do little, but which will have an influence on their health throughout their lives. Particularly important here are inheritance, sex and age. Individual lifestyle factors – such as smoking, exercise and diet – are also important. They are, in part, a product of personal choice, but are also influenced more subtly by the social and community networks in which we live and work. These, in turn, are influenced by the various aspects labelled in the diagram as 'living and working conditions' – the material counterpart to the networks. Important areas here include education, working environment, whether one is employed or not – with health care services merely being one factor amongst many. All of these influences are set in the context of general socio-economic, cultural and environmental conditions.

Patterns of ill health have changed significantly over time, and historically, the influence of health-care services has been small (McKeown 1979). The death rate per 1,000 population has declined dramatically in England and Wales during the last 150 years. In 1841, when reliable records began, the standardized death rate for

Table 12.1. Reduction of mortality, 1848/54 to 1971, England and Wales

	Percentage of reduction
Conditions attributable to micro-organisms:	74
Air borne diseases	40
Water and food borne diseases	21
Other conditions	13
Conditions not attributable to micro-organisms	26
All diseases	100

Source: McKeown (1979).

males was approximately 23 per 1,000 population; the comparable figure in 1971 was approximately eight. The majority of this improvement resulted from the control of infectious diseases (see Table 12.1), where the contribution of health services was small in comparison with measures to improve sanitation and general living conditions.

Any attempt to improve people's health must therefore take account of all of the wider determinants of health. The health service on its own is important, but relatively impotent when pitched against all of the other factors.

What can the NHS realistically expect to do about improving health?
The NHS carries out four broad functions:

1. It tries to promote good health, and prevent ill health. This is done by providing services directly to individual patients – such as immunization against various infectious diseases, or ante-natal care for pregnant women – and also by promoting 'health messages', such as health promotion activities in schools and anti-smoking campaigns.

2. It diagnoses specific illnesses or conditions. There is a vast – and expanding – array of tests, ranging from blood tests, to x-rays and tests of physical functioning, all of which help clinical staff to decide what is causing ill health.

3. It treats illness. This can range from emergency procedures and 'one-off' treatments, to lifelong care for people with conditions such as diabetes which can be controlled but not cured.

4. It provides rehabilitation and long-term care. Typically, this is for patients recovering from illness, or for whom there is no

effective treatment but a need for care and the alleviation of suffering.

Each of these makes an important contribution to improving health. But when viewed against the total burden of disease, it is clear that more could also be done. Part of the evidence for this lies in Figure 12.1, which identifies all of the other factors which contribute to society's ill health. In addition to its direct role in providing health services, the NHS increasingly works with the other sectors – employers, environmental agencies, agriculture – to encourage them to do what they can to minimize the harm of their activities, and where possible actually to improve people's health. Health Promotion Wales at the national level, and local health promotion departments and others, all devote considerable energy to such activities, with tangible results.

The other reason for believing that more needs to be done comes from the evidence on inequalities in health (Black *et al.* 1988). There are astonishing differences in the life expectancy and level of illness of different sections within society. For example, the death rate per 100,000 population per year varies from 716 in relatively affluent Monmouthshire, to 936 in more deprived Merthyr Tydfil (Monaghan 1998). One standard measure of the state of health of the population – as opposed to the numbers of people dying – is the 'SF-36' questionnaire, which asks people to rate their own levels of health against a number of specific criteria. The recent Welsh Health Survey (Welsh Office 1996) used this approach, and the results also reveal considerable variation, ranging from a physical health summary score of 50.0 in Flintshire to 46.6 in Merthyr Tydfil (the higher the number the better the state of health).

So the NHS tries to do what it can – directly and with others – to prevent ill health and promote good health. But it devotes most of its energies to diagnosing, treating and caring for those already ill.

The Changing Organization of the NHS

The NHS is a large and complex organization, employing about 65,000 people in Wales, the main groups being doctors and dentists, nurses and midwives, administrative and clerical staff, and ambulance personnel. Some indication of its relative size is given by the much-quoted claim that the NHS is the second biggest organization in the world, after the Indian railway.

Until the establishment of the Welsh Assembly and Scottish Parliament, the NHS in the United Kingdom was organized into four geographical units, England, Scotland, Wales and Northern Ireland, each under a different minister within the UK Cabinet. Within Wales responsibility for the organization and management of the NHS rested with the Secretary of State. As a member of the British government he had a broad range of other responsibilities including education, roads, transport, housing, social services, agriculture and industry. The ministry of the Secretary of State was called the Welsh Office. The health service was managed, on behalf of the Secretary of State, by the Director of the Welsh Office Health Department. These arrangements have recently changed with the advent of the Assembly (see below).

Health-care delivery is administered through five health authorities. They purchase services for their resident populations from approximately fifteen NHS trusts and reimburse general practitioners, dentists, opticians and pharmacists, all of whom are independent practitioners. They are directly responsible now to the Welsh Assembly. Central control is achieved through a dual process of the Welsh Office regularly issuing guidance circulars and the holding of annual reviews with each authority or trust to monitor the overall performance.

In addition, there was a special health authority: the Health Promotion Authority for Wales (now incorporated within the Welsh Office), which as its name suggests actively campaigns to promote healthy living. Working both within the NHS and with other agencies the HPAW develops campaigns, such as Heartbeat Wales to reduce cardiovascular disease, and monitors and evaluates the trends over time.

Given this complexity, and the fact that the NHS is a highly sensitive political issue for all governments, it is perhaps not surprising that considerable energy and attention have been devoted over the years to reforming the organizational structure. In order to understand the current organization of the NHS in Wales, it is important to see how it has evolved since its inception in 1948.

The evolution of the current organization
The National Health Service was created in 1948, and was the

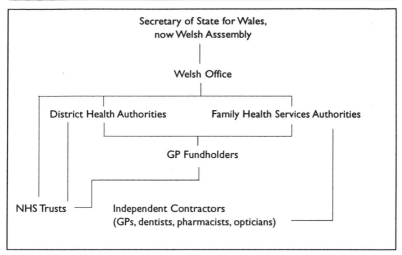

Figure 12.2. *NHS structure after the 1990 reforms, Wales.*

result of recommendations contained in the report on Social Insurance and Allied Services produced by Sir William Beveridge in 1942, building upon earlier provision. The recommendations made by Beveridge formed the basis for a post-war system of social welfare services (Webster 1998), and aimed to provide free health care to all citizens, through a system of public financing. It was based on the concept of equity, and sought to ensure that health services were readily accessible in all areas, and available on the basis of clinical need rather than a person's ability to pay. The concept has been sustained into the 1990s, and this is the only national health care system which is centrally financed and directed (Klein 1995).

There have been several reorganizations of the NHS during this period, however. The first of these came in the 1970s, when Keith Joseph, then Secretary of State for Health and Social Security, brought teaching hospitals and other elements of the service together under regional health authorities. Wales in effect constituted one regional health authority in its own right, although that responsibility was exercised on behalf of the Welsh Office and not the DHSS.

The managerial approach throughout the service following this reorganization emphasized the *collective* responsibility of doctors, nurses and administrators. Small teams drawn from these three disciplines made the key decisions about the direction and implementation of policy at the local and regional levels, with accountability to health authorities and the national government. Health authorities were composed of about sixteen members drawn in the main from local authorities and the voluntary sector.

The main exceptions to this pattern were the health-care professionals based in the community – general medical practitioners (GPs), general dental practitioners (dentists), pharmacists and opticians, often known collectively as the 'independent contractors'. None of these were employees of the NHS, a position which still obtains to this day. Instead, they are all self-employed, and their income from the NHS depends upon the provisions of their respective contracts, which are periodically renegotiated. This has historically given them considerable independence from the NHS. Any attempt to get GPs and the others to follow national strategy has therefore usually depended upon a complex mixture of (mainly financial) incentives and penalties.

During the 1980s, policy-makers concentrated on the introduction of a more 'managerialist' culture. This followed the review of NHS management conducted by a small team led by Roy Griffiths, of the Sainsbury supermarket chain (Griffiths 1983). Collective decision-making mechanisms were replaced by those of general management at all levels, with one person – usually from an administrative rather than a clinical background – taking responsibility for the organization under their control, although subject still to the overall responsibility of the health authority.

The next major reorganization was implemented by the National Health Service and Community Care Act 1990, together with a new Contract for General Practitioners. This was the biggest change to the NHS since its inception, and represented the Thatcher government's attempt to inject into the NHS something of the market philosophy which had guided their reforms of most of the rest of the public-sector services (see Figure 12.2).

The basic approach was predicated on the need to separate – within the NHS – the responsibility for deciding what services should be provided for a given population, from the responsibility for providing those services. Family Health Services Authorities (FHSAs) and District Health Authorities took the former role, and NHS Trusts and the independent contractors took the latter.

NHS trusts were operationally autonomous bodies, accountable directly to the Secretary of State, and typically consisted of one large hospital or a number of smaller hospitals and associated community services. They were managed by a group of ten board members, similar to the commercial model, with a chief executive (the direct descendant of the Griffiths-style general manager) and four executive directors (including a senior doctor and nurse), together with a part-time non-executive chair and four other non-executive directors with business and other experience. Health authorities had a similar membership.

GP fundholders were usually groups of five or more GPs who were given a budget with which to 'purchase' from NHS trusts certain elements of the health care for their practice populations. In addition, they continued to provide primary care for those patients themselves. The new contract required practices to extend the range of services offered to patients, publish a directory of services that they offered and an annual report on their practice (including the achievement of targets, list size and referrals). In addition, GPs were required to be available for patients for twenty-six hours per week, over five days, and to accept twenty-four-hour responsibility for patients.

Changing Health Policy

Most of the foregoing has been a description of how the NHS was reorganized in an attempt to ensure that it was better able to meet the objectives which the government set for it. The prime intention was to make the NHS more efficient, which was usually defined in terms of ensuring greater productivity. In other words, total budgets were constrained, and therefore in order to allow the service to treat more patients every year it had to be remodelled in ways which ensured that greater productivity.

But there were other developments – in which Wales took the lead – which focused on defining the core purpose of the NHS, and setting a strategic framework and specific targets to ensure that it lived up to this purpose. Two issues directly affected the way the NHS in Wales developed its health policy. First, health services for the future were to be delivered following an analysis of needs within districts; and, second, the purchaser and provider roles were

STRATEGIC INTENT

'to take the people of Wales into the 21st century
with a level of health on course to compare with
the best in Europe'

Figure 12.3.

Figure 12.4. *Strategic intent and direction for the NHS in Wales.*

separated, with contracts forming the basis of health service provision. For the NHS in Wales this meant that the three strategic concepts of health gain, people-centredness and resource effectiveness, the basis of their health policy, could be built into contracts and health gain given primacy.

In 1989 the NHS in Wales took as its starting-point the World Health Organization principles and committed itself to building them into the planning and functioning of the NHS in Wales. The result was a fundamental health policy document, *Strategic Intent and Direction for the NHS in Wales* (Welsh Office, Welsh Health Planning Forum, 1989a). Figures 12.3 and 12.4 illustrate both the strategic intent and strategic direction. The intent was designed to challenge the service, particularly its clinicians and managers. It is demanding but realistic in terms of the timescale for making progress. The direction explains how the intent can be secured through focusing on health gain, people-centredness and resource effectiveness. Health gain is the key to achieving the intent but the three themes are interdependent and must be pursued concurrently.

This strategic approach was driven forward in Wales for several years (Welsh Office, Welsh Health Planning Forum, 1989b), with promising signs of progress. However, interest began to wane as old pressures – financial constraints, waiting lists – continued to press in on politicians and managers, and a new political direction from the new Secretary of State, John Redwood, placed much greater emphasis on meeting the needs of the patient. This almost inevitably led the NHS to focus again on issues of organization, and the corresponding measures of success were once again the ability to increase productivity – numbers of patients treated – within constrained budgets.

The Future Health Policy Context

The advent of a Labour government in 1997 inaugurated a new period of rapid evolution in health policy. One common theme is the desire continually to raise the quality of all health services (Welsh Office 1998a). This is leading to the creation of national (England and Wales) bodies to identify and propagate best practice, and a framework – clinical governance –which will ensure that such practice is universally adopted. As part of this, more attention will be paid to the continuous development of all health-care professionals, and to appropriate procedures to ensure that their practice remains satisfactory. Increasingly, attention is also being paid to ensuring that all of the services received by patients are effectively co-ordinated to meet their particular needs.

The collective agenda is also being somewhat refocused, to give more effective emphasis to the improvement of the health of communities and ensuring equity of access to care (Welsh Office 1998b), as well as to the improvement of health services for individual patients. This development emphasizes the need for health care to work more closely with other agencies in local government and the community to meet local health needs.

There is a major restructuring of the arrangements for ensuring local influence over the direction of service developments, following the demise of GP fundholding. Local health groups have been established at the local level to bring together primary-care practitioners and others to develop local community, primary- and secondary-care services. Secondary-care providers now work more collaboratively with each other and with health authorities. Each of the major resources involved in delivering health care is being reviewed and provided with a new strategic direction. For example, the (still largely unrealized) potential of information technology is being addressed through a set of new strategic guidance; similarly, the complex demands of human resources in the NHS are receiving new attention.

The advent of the Welsh Assembly provides considerable potential for health policy in Wales to diverge from that of England and Scotland. Although the Assembly will have no powers to create or vary primary legislation, there is still much that can be achieved through the imaginative use of policy direction, combined with new secondary legislation and the ability to increase – or decrease – the proportion of the total Welsh budget allocated to health care.

Although the nature of the impact of devolution is largely a matter of speculation at present, two sorts of change are possible. The first will result from the fact that policy in Wales will for the first time be determined solely by people elected from Wales. This arguably will give them a greater sensitivity to the implications of policy change for their own electors, and there may as a result be a greater value placed on the availability of services locally. The second might reflect the different party-political affiliations of

Wales compared with the UK as a whole. In other words, the overwhelming support which the Welsh electorate gives to left-of-centre political parties will result in an Assembly similarly more committed to values such as equity on health than might be the case in the UK Parliament. The crucial question will be whether the new Assembly will break from the UK's previous obsession with measuring and altering the quantity of *health care* provided, and emphasize more the role of the NHS in improving people's *health*.

References

Black, D., Morris, J. N., Smith, C. and Townsend, P. (1988). 'The Black Report', in P. Townsend, N. Davidson and M. Whitehead (eds.), *Inequalities in Health* (London: Penguin).

Griffiths, R. (1983). *NHS Management Inquiry* (London: DHSS).

Home Office, Department of Health, Department of Education and Science and Welsh Office (1991). *Working Together under the Children Act 1989: A Guide to Arrangements for Inter-agency Co-operation for the Protection of Children from Abuse* (London: HMSO).

Klein, R. (1995). *The New Politics of the National Health Service*, 3rd edition (London: Longman).

McKeown, T. (1979). *The Role of Medicine*, 2nd edition (Oxford: Blackwell).

Monaghan, S. (1998). *An Atlas of Health Inequalities between Welsh Local Authorities* (Cardiff: Welsh Local Government Association).

Nettleton, S. (1995). *The Sociology of Health and Illness* (Cambridge: Polity Press).

Ranade, W. (1997). *A Future for the NHS? Health Care in the 1990s*, 2nd edition (London: Longman).

Timmins, N. (1996). *The Five Giants: A Biography of the Welfare State* (London: Fontana).

Webster, C. (1998). *The National Health Service: A Political History* (Oxford: Oxford University Press).

Welsh Office (1996). *Welsh Health Survey 1995* (Cardiff: Welsh Office).

Welsh Office (1998a). *Putting Patients First*, Cm. 3841 (Cardiff: Welsh Office).

Welsh Office (1998b). *Better Health, Better Wales*, Cm. 3922 (Cardiff: Welsh Office).

Welsh Office, Welsh Health Planning Forum (1989a). *Strategic Intent and Direction for the NHS in Wales* (Cardiff: Welsh Office).

Welsh Office, Welsh Health Planning Forum (1989b). *Local Strategies for Health* (Cardiff: Welsh Office).

World Health Organization (1978). *Alma Ata 1977, Primary Health Care* (Geneva: UNICEF).

13 Crime and Wales

ADRIAN BARTON, FIONA BROOKMAN and DAVID SMITH

Introduction

It is almost impossible to avoid talking about crime in our society. Television listings for virtually any day show that the major channels carry at least one programme that is crime based. Similarly, all of the major newspapers devote much of their space to reporting crime (often in the most lurid detail). The outcome of such extensive coverage has been to make crime and justice one of the most frequently discussed areas of social policy. This is, perhaps, less surprising when one realizes that in 1996 the largest police force within Wales (South Wales Police) had a rate of notifiable offences per 100,000 population as high as that of the Metropolitan Police and Merseyside Police forces (Central Statistical Office, 1997).

Our aim in this chapter is to give an overview of some of the processes and procedures involved in dealing with crime, rather than to attempt to provide a definitive answer to the 'crime' problem. We begin by examining the discretionary powers built into the criminal justice system; then consider how we measure the extent of criminal activity; discuss the problems posed by the 'dark figure' of hidden crime; and, finally, consider how the dark figure applies to one of the most visible crimes of all: homicide.

The Criminal Justice System

Criminal justice in Wales has been dominated by English law since the Tudor Union of Wales with England in 1536. Prior to that date Wales had a more ancient legal system in daily use, which comes down to us in manuscripts from the early thirteenth century, and is known as the law of Hywel Dda (Jenkins 1986). It is worth noting that the Welsh Office has almost no responsibility for criminal justice matters and that, even with the establishment of the National Assembly, the Home Office remains the central government department responsible for law and order within Wales. As a result, Wales (unlike Scotland and Northern Ireland) does not have a separate approach to crime and delinquency, making it impossible consistently to identify a distinctly Welsh dimension to the encompassing 'England and Wales' criminal justice system.[1]

Barclay (1995) describes the social arrangements for delivering justice as a 'system' which comprises several elements: police; Crown Prosecution Service; courts; probation and prisons. A further element is, of course, us – the public – and the roles we may play as victim, witness or offender. Many people do break the law (and are even prepared to admit to this), but significantly fewer people become 'criminals'. Central to this anomaly is the fact that becoming a 'criminal' is a complex process that involves a number of agencies.

While the criminal justice 'system' cannot be said to be fully articulated, the nature of the social arrangements for dealing with offenders permits us to demonstrate the process of criminalization in diagrammatic form (Figure 13.1). The amount of discretion surrounding the exercise of gatekeeping powers by each of the elements of the system is a central factor in understanding the complexity of that system, and we will now consider each of these elements in turn.

The public

Before any of the state agencies can deal with a crime it has to be reported, usually by the public. According to the findings of successive British Crime Surveys (BCS) the public are reluctant to report crime at all. For example, Taylor (1996) notes that the public reports 99 per cent of thefts of motor vehicles, whereas we report only 28 per cent of acts of vandalism. Therefore, the first area of discretion and gatekeeping lies with consistent under-reporting of crime by the public. The reasons most frequently given for failure to report victimization are: belief that the police would take no action; fear of the consequences of reporting; and that it is too much trouble.

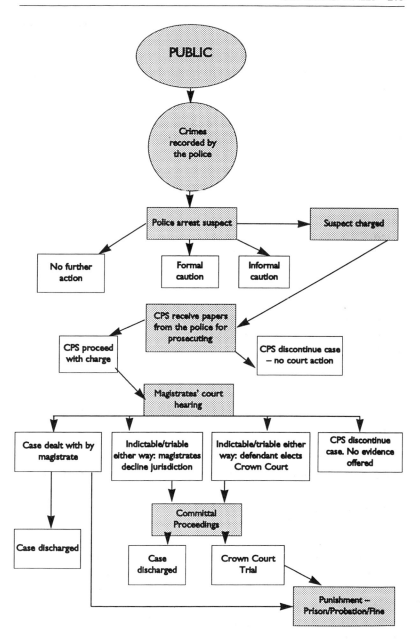

Figure 13.1. *The system for delivering criminal justice.*

The police

Wales contains four of the forty-three police forces in England and Wales, and these cover the geographical areas of Gwent, South Wales,[2] Dyfed–Powys and North Wales. In 1996 there were 6,523 police officers in Wales, of whom 783 (12 per cent) were female. The largest force is South Wales (2,913 police officers in 1996) and the smallest is Dyfed–Powys (998 officers).

In 1996, the proportion of notifiable offences recorded by the police which were cleared up was 50 per cent greater in Wales than England (37 per cent overall clear-up rate for Wales, as against 26 per cent overall clear-up for England). Only two of the forty-three police force areas of England and Wales achieved an overall clear-up rate greater than 50 per cent and both were forces in Wales (Dyfed–Powys and Gwent).

The police discover crime in several ways: by reports from victims or witnesses (as already mentioned above). They also discover crimes themselves. In 1995 less than 4 per cent of crimes recorded in Wales were attributable directly to police discovery. In the main, these tended to be 'victimless crimes', such as trading in illegal drugs, which are unlikely to be reported to the police either by seller or purchaser. In Wales 5,575 individuals were cautioned or found guilty of drug offences during 1995 of whom only 489 (9 per cent) were female.[3] The largest proportion of these offences was detected in South Wales (32 per cent), followed by North Wales (30 per cent), with Dyfed–Powys and Gwent having 20 per cent and 18 per cent respectively. Most of the drugs offences in Wales during 1995 involved the use of cannabis (86 per cent), irrespective of the gender of the offender. In the same year, offences involving the most serious Class A drugs (cocaine, dipipanone, heroin, methodone, LSD and ecstasy) represented use by less than 2 per cent of all known drugs offenders. The picture of drug use that this presents may fairly represent the reality but, since these are almost always offences discovered by the police themselves, it may also represent a picture of selective police attention focused onto cannabis use. We will return to the problem of interpreting crime data when we discuss the measurement of crime.

Regardless of how crime comes to their attention, the police have a number of options available to them – initially to decide whether the offence warrants investigation at all. If they decide to proceed with the case, police officers set about collecting information relating to the circumstances of the crime and details of probable suspects. If and when sufficient evidence has been collected to lead to the identification of a suspect, the police have considerable discretion in their choice of subsequent action:

- They can close the case by taking no further action.
- They can issue an informal caution, when the offender is warned to modify his or her conduct and no official record of the caution is made. These informal cautions have become the dominant method for disposing of minor offences, such as youths skateboarding on the pavement.
- They can decide to issue a formal caution, provided that the offender is prepared to admit guilt. Formal cautions are often made in order to remove the need for full collection of evidence. A senior officer cautions the offender and the caution is recorded and filed in the local criminal records office for three years. If the offender subsequently appears in court, any 'live' (unexpired) cautions may influence the severity of the sentence awarded by the court. Although a formal or an informal caution can be given to anyone, they are most often used in an attempt to divert young offenders from criminality without requiring their appearance at court. In Wales 10,813 individuals were issued with cautions during 1996, of whom 7,931 were male and 2,882 (27 per cent) were female.
- They can recommend prosecution. If and when the police believe that they have sufficient evidence, they pass the case on to the next part of the system: the Crown Prosecution Service (CPS).

The police act as gatekeepers for the rest of the system when they exercise their discretion in recording, investigating or discontinuing the processing of crime. The outcome is such that, of the 5 million crimes recorded by the police throughout England and Wales in 1996, only 576,000 (12 per cent) resulted in a charge or summons (Home Office 1998).

Clearly, the police possess a great deal of discretion and, it has been argued, the invisibility of police discretion can easily lead to situations where particular types of crime and particular types of suspect are dealt with in ways which may undermine the principles of justice and equity (Sanders 1994). However, it should also be noted that the courts have consistently upheld the constitutional independence of chief constables in exercising their discretion. Lord Denning put a final seal on the legal position when he proclaimed:

> I hold it to be the duty of . . . every chief constable to . . . decide whether or not suspected persons are to be prosecuted, and, if need be, bring the prosecution or see that it is brought; but in all these things he is not the servant of anyone, save of the law itself. No Minister of the Crown can tell him that he must or must not prosecute this man or that one. The responsibility for law enforcement lies on him. He is answerable to the law and to the law alone. (Lord Denning, *R. v. Commissioner of Police for the Metropolis, ex parte Blackburn*, 1968, 2 QB 118, p. 136)

The Crown Prosecution Service (CPS)

The CPS was established under the Prosecution of Offences Act 1985 and followed the recommendations made in the Phillips Commission Report of 1981. The centralization of criminal prosecution decision-making through the CPS, resulted from growing concern with the effects of police responsibility for both the investigation and prosecution of offenders (Davies *et al.* 1995). Once a charge has been made, the CPS checks the strength of police evidence against published criteria to establish if the evidence makes it likely that prosecution will be successful and then whether prosecution is in the public interest (CPS 1994). If the evidence is deemed insufficient, or a prosecution not in the public interest, the CPS lawyer can either discontinue the case or reduce the charge to a lesser offence.

The CPS discontinues an average 12 per cent of all cases, which is seen by many police officers as an implicit criticism of their work. For example, almost a quarter (24 per cent) of all cases received by the CPS in Wales during 1996 resulted in conditional or absolute discharge at court. This high proportion clearly calls into question the adequacy of the CPS decisions to prosecute these cases. Moreover, there are significant differences in the types of case discontinued: surprisingly, crimes of violence are more likely to be discontinued than are motoring offences (Home Office 1998a).

The CPS has also been accused (often unfairly) of causing unnecessary delay in bringing prosecutions to court. However, it is now clear that the CPS has been under-financed and under-staffed ever since it was first set up. Unfortunately, it is also clear that its attempts to improve the effectiveness and efficiency of the prosecution process have led to the most experienced lawyers becoming managers and the least experienced lawyers appearing in court (Home Office 1998a).

Dissatisfaction with the performance of the CPS has grown to such an extent as to require an independent and wide-ranging review of its work. The review has recently been published in the Glidewell Report (Home Office 1998a) which recommends that the CPS needs to:

- give much greater priority to more serious cases;
- create a new organization, structure and style of management;
- firmly establish its proper role in the criminal justice process.

However, the Glidewell Report clearly supports the fundamental principle that the investigation of crime should be distinctly separate from subsequent prosecution. There will not be a return to the pre-1986 situation in which police were responsible for both.

The courts

When the CPS has decided to prosecute, the case moves onto the courts. Three separate categories of offences and two distinct types of court exist. Offence types include:

- those which are triable only on indictment (serious cases such as murder, robbery and rape) which can only be tried at Crown Courts with a judge and jury;
- triable-either-way offences (cases such as assaults and 'take and drive away' of motor vehicles) for which a case can be heard either at a Magistrates Court or at Crown Court;
- summary offences, which are triable only at Magistrates Courts. These cases overwhelmingly relate to motoring offences.

There were 5,036,553 crimes recorded by the police throughout England and Wales in 1996, which include 246,246 in Wales alone.

Of these, 1,370,000 people were sentenced at Magistrates Courts in England and Wales combined (Home Office 1998b). In Wales during the same period, 90,017 people were found guilty at Magistrates Courts and a further 4,274 at Crown Courts.

In Magistrates Courts cases are heard either by 'lay' magistrates, who are unpaid members of the public without legal training or, less commonly, by stipendiary magistrates, who are paid professional lawyers with a number of years' experience. Both lay and stipendiary magistrates have the same powers but stipendiary magistrates sit alone, whereas lay magistrates usually sit in a panel of three and are advised on legal matters by a legally qualified clerk. In Magistrates Courts the magistrates determine guilt or innocence and also the sentence to be imposed on the guilty.

More serious offences, with greater possible punishments, are tried at the Crown Court. Crown Courts are usually presided over by a circuit judge recruited from the ranks of barristers and appointed by the Lord Chancellor. In Crown Courts guilt or innocence is decided by the jury: the judge's role is to ensure that proper procedures are followed during the trial and, in the event of a 'guilty' decision by the jury, to determine the sentence.

Juries consist of twelve people selected from the electoral register and living in the area where the trial is held. Jury service eligibility depends on a number of factors: age, residency in the UK, occupation, and, in some instances, not having a criminal record. Individuals may be exempted from serving on a jury if personal hardship will follow or if the potential juror is connected to the case.

Once the jury has established guilt, the judge awards a sentence. The sentence will depend on the seriousness of the offence and on the previous history of the offender and ranges from a non-custodial sentence (such as a fine or a community service order) to a custodial sentence. The decision to award a particular sentence for an offence may seem straightforward but is, in fact, subject to wide discretion and much of the judiciary's decision-making is of 'low visibility'. For example, Parker et al. (1989) show the extent to which newly appointed magistrates are influenced by the sentencing culture of their particular bench. The magistracy is relatively representative of the general population by gender (45 per cent are female), but only 2 per cent are from ethnic minority backgrounds (Davies et al. 1995). In terms of recruitment to the judiciary, Griffith (1991) notes that judges are predominantly white males from a public school/Oxbridge background.

Little is, or can be, known about how juries reach their decisions since they must deliberate in secret and are not accountable for their decisions. However, research into decision-making in 'mock' or 'shadow' juries suggests that jury decisions are often influenced by a range of extra-evidential considerations such as pre-trial publicity, personal sentiments and prejudices, and the physical appearance of witnesses and suspects (Stephenson 1992; Hollin 1997).

Punishment

It would appear that, in the eyes of many politicians and members of the public, sentences are broadly divided between 'hard' and 'soft' punishments. In recent times we have seen many calls for an increase in the use of the former at the expense of the latter. Often these calls have been politically inspired: as witness Michael Howard's assertion (when Home Secretary) that 'prison works' and Jack Straw's pledge (also when Home Secretary) to be 'tough on crime and tough on its causes'. The final part of this section examines the consequence of these 'tough' stances for the agencies that administer punishment and the offenders who receive it.

England and Wales currently have the highest prison populations in Europe, a phenomenon that can be attributed to the fact that magistrates and judges routinely choose the most severe form of punishment available to them – prison. Of the 4,379 people in Wales found guilty of offences at Crown Court, 2,757 were given immediate custodial sentences (63 per cent). Consequently, the prison population has risen to an all-time high of 62,000 people, which has not been matched by a corresponding increase in capacity. The resulting high level of overcrowding has created a situation in which many male, and all female, prisoners from Wales are sent to prisons in England. This often makes family visiting difficult and leads to tensions within families and also amongst staff and inmates.

However, perhaps the most dramatic effect of the current demand for 'toughness' at the punishment end of the justice system concerns proposed changes to non-custodial penalties and the probation service. This end of the punishment spectrum is often thought to be somewhat 'soft' on offenders and an area which, the Home Office suggests, needs to be perceived as more 'tough' because such a view is: 'completely out of line with . . . the expectation of the courts . . . (and) . . . the reality of the work which probation staff undertake' (Home Office 1998b; 2). Therefore, a recent government discussion paper suggests, it will be a valuable development to change the name of the probation service to reflect the move away from the traditional 'advise, assist and befriend' approach, to one which explicitly reflects the importance attached to supervision of punishment in the community. The new, more suitable titles, which have been suggested include 'Public Protection Agency' or 'Community Justice Enforcement Agency' (Home Office 1998b, 3).

The Crime and Disorder Act 1998 requires all local authorities to undertake crime audits of their areas. The first of these to have been successfully completed has taken place in Merthyr Tydfil under the auspices of Safer Merthyr Tydfil, together with South Wales Police, Groundwork Wales and Merthyr Tydfil Borough Council (King 1998). The development of crime audits represents a fundamental shift in crime control strategies towards a multi-agency approach to crime reduction. Safer Merthyr Tydfil may well provide the benchmark for such crime reduction strategies throughout Wales. The strategies being implemented there include the development of zero-tolerance initiatives in local areas; mentoring schemes for youths at risk; enhancement of physical residential security; and the effective use of closed-circuit television surveillance of the town centre and outlying areas. What distinguishes these initiatives from similar undertakings elsewhere is that they are unified into a coherent strategy for reducing crime, together with rigorous measurement of the effectiveness of the strategy (Smith 1998).

Measuring Crime

Crime is a social problem that causes concern and anguish amongst many groups in society. However, before policies can be developed to address the 'crime problem' government needs to gain a clear indication of the size of the task − in short, we need to measure how much crime is being committed. There are three ways in which this can be done and each measurement produces a different picture because each taps into different stages of the system displayed in Figure 13.1. This has, for example, led the Brantlinghams to conclude that 'criminal justice statistics distort the patterns in crime as they increase in procedural distance from the criminal event' (1984, 92).

The first method is to use official statistics. These provide us with a measure of all the crimes reported to and recorded by the police, for example, in 1994 there were 5.3 million offences recorded by the police in England and Wales. The second method for measuring crime is to ask people about their experiences of being victims. The most extensive of these kinds of survey is the Home Office British Crime Survey (BCS). Comparisons of victim surveys with official statistics always show a marked difference between the two sets of figures. For instance, 1996 figures show that the number of people who claimed to be victims of crime was about three times greater than the official figures. The final measuring instrument is the self-report study in which people are asked to give details of any crimes they have committed. Most of these types of study find that more than 90 per cent of those interviewed admit to breaking the law at some time or another.

It is clear is that there is a gap between the official crime figures and the number of actual crimes committed. This gap is known by criminologists as the 'dark figure' of hidden crime and will be discussed below.

The Dark Figure

As already indicated, the 'dark figure' of crime represents those crimes which have not been reported to or recorded by the police and, therefore, do not appear in the official statistics. Estimates of the amount of hidden crime vary across offence categories and, hence, the limitations of official statistics are more profound for some categories of crime than others. Shoplifting and criminal damage, for example, are likely to have a substantial dark figure and trafficking in controlled drugs and fraud offences are believed to contain the largest dark figure (Coleman and Moynihan 1996).

It is generally accepted that the police come to know about a very high proportion of homicides (Williams 1996) and because of this assumption researchers often neglect the existence and extent of the dark figure of homicide. What follows is a consideration of the ways in which a homicide may go unnoticed or undetected.

We will begin by clarifying the term homicide. Homicide refers to the killing of a human being, whether that killing is lawful (for example, during wartime) or unlawful. Unlawful homicide can be classified as murder, manslaughter or infanticide.[4] The major criteria under which these offences are distinguished essentially revolve around the issues of culpability or intention, which include some estimate of the degree of premeditation and the mental capacity of the defendant (Mitchell 1991). In the case of a murder conviction there needs to be evidence that the defendant actually intended unlawfully to kill or cause grievous bodily harm to another person (Card *et al.* 1995). Generally, any unlawful homicide not classified as murder falls within one of the two generic types of manslaughter: voluntary or involuntary. Voluntary manslaughter will be found where one person did intend to kill another, but circumstances may mitigate the gravity of the offence. For example, the accused may have been provoked or he or she may have had their judgement impaired by some abnormality (which is commonly referred to as 'diminished' responsibility). Conversely, involuntary manslaughter occurs where there is no clear intention and there are no mitigating circumstances. Here the jury must be satisfied that the defendant lacked sufficient foresight and awareness of the consequences of his or her actions. The killing must either have been committed recklessly or dangerously (for example, causing death by dangerous driving), or unintentionally.

Finally, the category of infanticide applies when a woman causes the death of her natural child who was under twelve months old while 'not having fully recovered from the effects of giving birth or by reason of the effect of lactation' (Infanticide Act 1938). Having briefly defined the various categories that comprise unlawful homicide we shall now examine the scope which exists for such crimes to remain hidden from official view.

Hidden Homicides

The question of how many homicides take place in a particular year may seem simple, but cannot be easily answered because several factors influence the official registration of a homicide.

First, we need the discovery of a body, which is, without doubt, the most common source of uncovering killings which have taken place in the open, on commercial premises at night and where attempts have been made to hide the body (Morris and Blom-Cooper 1964). But, we do not know how many killers manage to dispose of the bodies of their victims without trace. As Polk (1994, 10) has pointed out: 'Some killings are carefully planned and part of the plot may consist of disposing of the body in such a manner that its discovery is unlikely.' Occasionally the police may unexpectedly discover a body in the course of investigating other crimes. Sometimes such discoveries are made by people walking dogs or in the course of leisure activities as, for example, when four sub-aqua divers discovered skeletal remains wrapped in a series of bags and bin liners in Coniston Water in the Lake District during August 1997. In this case forensic examination revealed the remains to be that of a female schoolteacher who had vanished twenty-one years previously from her home fifteen miles away.

Secondly, a considerable number of people can be defined as 'missing persons'. The National Missing Persons Helpline (NMPH), established in 1992, suggests that there are about 250,000 people currently missing in Britain. Whilst many of these persons will have deliberately sought obscurity, it is possible that some of these may have become the victim of homicide. Further, there are undoubtedly persons 'missing' who are not registered as such, but who may have become the victims of homicide.

The tragic death of the teenager Karen Price in Cardiff in the late 1980s illustrates both the conversion of a previously defined 'missing person' into a homicide and the chance discovery of her body. Karen Price went missing from a community home in the south Wales Valleys in 1986 and was, eventually, recorded as a 'missing person'. In 1990 two builders discovered a body wrapped in a carpet and buried in the garden of the house which they were renovating. Forensic examination of the body clearly indicated that death was not accidental and also that a combination of post-mortem destruction and inevitable decomposition made identification very difficult. South Wales police undertook an extensive investigation to identify the body. This investigation included a successful attempt to reconstruct the appearance of the deceased from skeletal remains, using modelling clay to represent skin and underlying facial musculature. At the same time, investigation focused on identifying and questioning all of the previous occupants of the house. After much painstaking detective work, two men were convicted of involvement in the death of Karen.[5]

A further way in which a homicide may go undetected is related to the complexities that exist in establishing cause of death. In the case of a discovered body, it is not always possible to determine whether the death was unlawful. Apart from establishing cause of death, one of the key purposes of an autopsy is to establish the mode of death. Generally, four definitions of the mode of death are possible: natural, accidental, suicide or homicide (Geberth 1996), and distinguishing between the four categories is by no means a straightforward procedure. For example, apparent deaths by overdosing of legally prescribed medicine, or from 'natural causes', may sometimes turn out to be homicide victims. In the case of the nurse Beverley Allitt, found guilty in 1993 of murdering four children, it was a lengthy matter of contention to establish that the children had not, in fact, died of natural causes (White 1995).

Mortality statistics for 1996 indicate that Coroners Courts record 'open verdicts' on almost 2,000 people in England and Wales each year. Essentially these cases remain unresolved with respect to whether the fatal injuries sustained were accidentally or purposely inflicted, either by the victim or some other person. One can only speculate as to what proportion, if any, of these deaths could have been the result of unlawful killing. In short, difficulties involved in certifying cause of death mean that a number of homicides may go undetected each year. The combined effect of undiscovered bodies and incorrect diagnoses of death could indicate that the official statistics give a substantial underestimate of homicides.

Finally, there exist a number of 'killings' which occur each year throughout England and Wales, where perpetrators are known, but which do not appear as homicides in the official statistics. One such example concerns deaths on the roads. Around ten people are killed in road traffic accidents on Britain's roads every day[6] and the vast majority of drivers who cause deaths are charged with minor road traffic offences (Roadpeace 1997). Across the whole of Wales in 1996, 163 motorists were charged with causing death or bodily harm by dangerous driving. Forty-three (or 26 per cent) of these drivers were, despite the severity of the charge, dealt with only at the Magistrates Courts, which illustrates the leniency with which death and serious injury caused by motorists is treated. Had these deaths and injuries been caused other than by drivers, the cases would have been tried at Crown Court where the sentences could be much more severe. Roadpeace, which was set up to support the relatives of road traffic victims, notes that only around 10 per cent of drivers who kill on the roads are charged with causing death by dangerous driving and that the 'motor manslaughter' provision is so rarely used as to be effectively redundant. The important question which this raises, in the context of the present discussion, is what proportion of these fatal road accidents should really count as instances of homicide? It is particularly interesting that 'road rage' is now, as a result of media publicity, acknowledged as a serious crime warranting criminal prosecution, whereas the vastly greater problem (and deaths) caused by dangerous and negligent drivers remains largely ignored.

Criminal homicide is generally regarded as one of the most visible crimes in most countries and one that should, therefore, have a negligible dark figure. Yet, as this discussion has shown, there remains considerable scope for some (or many) homicides to remain hidden from official view each year.

Conclusion

Part of the reason for the existence of a 'dark figure' of hidden crime relates to the discretionary powers of the various criminal justice agencies. We have shown that these powers even include a high degree of discretion concerning the unlawful taking of a life, which most of us would consider the most serious crime. We can only assume, therefore, that other less serious offences are subject to even greater levels of discretion and larger 'dark figures' of hidden crime.

We noted at the beginning of this chapter that we would not attempt to provide a definitive answer to the 'crime problem'. Our discussion of the discretionary power of criminal justice agencies, together with our analysis of the extreme offence of homicide, should show why such a definitive answer does not exist. We know about the offences that are recorded and those offenders who are identified, but we cannot know about the offences which are not recorded and those offenders who are not identified. It is a huge leap of logic to assume that the people and offences constituting 'hidden crime' are similar to those people and offences which are not 'hidden' and about which we do know. Yet criminal justice policy is founded on information about known crime and criminals, so we should not be surprised that such policy has not solved the 'problem' of crime. Crime is a problem which appears to be endemic to social organization and we may as well, therefore, regard it as a normal and enduring feature of the social order (Durkheim 1895) of Wales and every other country.

Notes

1. Although it has been said that it is still legal to shoot any Welshman who crosses into England on a Friday. The Recognition of Borders Act (1772), deriving from the Act of Union, dealt with the growing influx of Welsh goods and trade to the Welsh border towns which passed through the weekend market. In Shrewsbury in 1776 seven Welshmen were killed, three by musket, three by sword and one was bludgeoned to death with his own crops. The Borders Act has never been repealed, but was resolved by subsequent English/Welsh taxation laws.
2. For further information on the history of the South Wales Police force in the twentieth century see the recent, exhaustive, study by the late David J. V. Jones (1996).
3. Statistics on crimes, offenders and disposals are derived from Government Statistical Service (1998) and from Welsh Office (1998). It should be noted that these data sources are constructed in such a way that a person appearing in court can be charged with more than one offence at the same time.
4. Paul Harrison (1995) describes sixteen 'cases of violent and untimely death across all areas of south Wales, from the eighteenth century to the very recent past.
5. R. v. Idris and another (1991).
6. Deaths from road accidents have substantially declined in Britain over the past fifteen years. For example, in Wales 187 people were killed in road accidents in 1993 compared with 338 in 1978 (Welsh Office, 1995).

References

Barclay, G. C. (1995). *The Criminal Justice System in England and Wales 1995* (London: Home Office).

Barclay, G. C., Tavares, C. and Prout, A. (1995). *Information on the Criminal Justice System in England and Wales* (London: Home Office Research and Statistics Department).

Brantlingham, P. and P. (1984). *Patterns in Crime* (New York: Macmillan).

Card, R., Cross, A. and Jones, A. (1995). *Criminal Law*, 13th edition (London: Butterworths).

Cavadino, M. and Dignan, J. (1992). *The Penal System: An Introduction* (London: Sage).

Central Statistical Office (1997). *Criminal Statistics, England and Wales 1996* (London: HMSO).

Coleman, C. and Moynihan, J. (1996). *Understanding Crime Data: Haunted by the Dark Figure* (Philadelphia: Open University Press).

CPS (1994). *The Code for Crown Prosecutors*, 3rd edition (London: Crown Prosecution Service; issued under section 10 of the Prosecution of Offenders Act 1985).

Davies, M., Croall, H. and Tyrer, J. (1995). *Criminal Justice: An Introduction to the Criminal Justice System in England and Wales* (London: Longman).

Durkheim, E. (1895). *The Rules of Sociological Method*, reprinted edition (New York: Free Press, 1964).

Geberth, V. J. (1996). *Practical Homicide Investigation: Tactics, Procedures and Forensic Techniques*, 3rd edition (New York: CRC Press).

Government Statistical Service (1998). *Criminal Statistics England and Wales, 1996* (London: HMSO).

Griffith, J. (1991). *The Politics of the Judiciary*, 4th edition (London: Fontana Press).

Harrison, P. (1995). *South Wales Murder Casebook* (Newbury: Countryside Books).

Havard, J. D. J. (1960). *The Detection of Secret Homicide: A Study of the Medico-Legal System of Investigation of Sudden and Unexplained Deaths* (London: Macmillan).

Hollin, C. R. (1997). *Psychology and Crime*, 2nd edition (London: Routledge).

Home Office (1995). *Information on the Criminal Justice System in England and Wales*, Digest 3 (London: Home Office Research and Statistics Department).

Home Office (1998a). *Glidewell Report* (London: HMSO).

Home Office (1998b). *Home Office Annual Report, 1998/1999* (London: HMSO).

Jenkins, D. (1986). *The Law of Hywel Dda* (Llandysul: Gomer Press).

Jones, D. J. V. (1996). *Crime and Policing in the Twentieth Century: The South Wales Experience* (Cardiff: University of Wales Press).

King, S. (1998). *Merthyr Tydfil Crime and Disorder Audit 1998* (Merthyr Tydfil: Borough Council).

Lewis, C. (1992). 'Crime statistics: their use and misuse', *Social Trends*, 22, 1–23.

McCormick-Watson, J. (1994). *Essential English Legal System* (London: Cavendish).

Mitchell, B. (1991). 'Distinguishing between murder and manslaughter', *New Law Journal*, 141, 935–37.

Morgan, R. and Newburn, T. (1997). *The Future of Policing* (Oxford: Oxford University Press).

Morris, T. and Blom-Cooper, L. (1964). *A Calendar of Murder: Criminal Homicide in England since 1957* (London: Michael Joseph).

Morrison, W. (1995). *Theoretical Criminology* (London: Cavendish Publishing).

Parker, H., Sumner, M. and Jarvis, G. (1989). *Unmasking the Magistrates: The 'Custody or Not' Decision in Sentencing Young Offenders* (Milton Keynes: Open University Press).

Polk, K. (1994). *When Men Kill: Scenarios of Masculine Violence* (Cambridge, Cambridge University Press).

Roadpeace (1997). *Newsletter*, 9 (Spring).

Sanders, A. (1994). 'From suspect to trial', in M. Maguire, R. Morgan and R. Reiner (eds.), *The Oxford Handbook of Criminology* (Oxford: Oxford University Press).

Smith, D. (1998). *Evaluating Zero Tolerance/Problem Oriented Policing in Dowlais, Aberfan and Merthyr Vale* (Merthyr Tydfil: Safer Merthyr Tydfil).

Stephenson, G. M. (1992). *The Psychology of Criminal Justice* (Oxford: Blackwell).

Taylor, P. (1996). *Criminology* (London: HLT Publications).

Von Hentig, H. (1938). 'Some problems regarding murder detection', *Journal of Criminal Law and Criminology*, 29, 108–18.

Welsh Office (1995). *Welsh Transport Statistics*, 11.

Welsh Office (1998). *Digest of Welsh Local Area Statistics 1998* (Cardiff: Welsh Office).

White, P. (1995). 'Homicide', in M. Walker (ed.), *Interpreting Crime Statistics* (Oxford: Clarendon Press).

Williams, J. (1995). *Bloody Valentine: A Killing in Cardiff* (London: Harper Collins).

Williams, K. (1996). *Textbook on Criminology* (London: Blackstone Press, 1996).

14   Education in Wales

GARETH REES and SARA DELAMONT

Introduction

Education has played a key role in shaping our conceptions about Welsh society. In the past, it has often been argued that the Welsh – more so than other sections of the British population – place a high value on educational achievement. In part, this was based on ideas about education as a means of improving occupational prospects. Whether based in fact or not, popular perceptions of the sons (and less frequently, the daughters) of miners or farm workers using educational success to move into middle-class occupations (stereo-typically as teachers or clergymen) have contributed significantly to notions of the Welsh social structure as being relatively open and meritocratic. Equally, educational achievement has been seen as being valued by the Welsh in its own right, as a mark of cultural attainment. Certainly, the links between education and literary, religious and wider cultural life (but, interestingly, not the scientific and technological spheres) have been commonly described as very close in Wales (for example, Central Advisory Council for Education, Wales, 1967).

Today, education continues to be seen as central to Welsh life, although in somewhat different terms from previously. Nowadays, the emphasis is very much on the value of education as a means of reviving the Welsh economy, following the collapse of employment in mining, steel and other manufacturing industries (Istance and Rees, 1994). Again, irrespective of the reality of the situation, improving education and training is widely viewed as the key vehicle for transforming Wales into a *modern* society, in which jobs

– and the spending patterns which they make possible – are based on high levels of skills and technological sophistication.

Given this importance of education to our ways of thinking about the Welsh social structure, it is perhaps rather surprising that systematic research into the workings of the Welsh education system has not been very well developed (certainly when compared with the situation in England or, indeed, Scotland). One important reason for this is that education in Wales has tended to be seen as indistinguishable from that in England. The now notorious entry in an earlier edition of the *Encyclopaedia Britannica*, 'For Wales, see England', accurately sums up the way in which the educational system in Wales has been analysed conventionally. Whilst the distinctiveness of education in Scotland and – if it is mentioned at all – Northern Ireland has been universally recognized, 'England and Wales' has been the routine unit of analysis. Therefore, it has often been impossible to disentangle the specifically Welsh evidence from materials published on 'England and Wales'. The famous Oxford study of education and social mobility provides a good example of this (Halsey *et al.* 1980).

Of course, education in Wales *does* reflect the general trends and developments which researchers have identified. However, these trends and developments frequently take specific forms in Wales and, therefore, we need to have specifically Welsh research to reflect this. In particular, policy-makers with responsibility for the Welsh education system need to have information and analysis which will enable them to develop strategies which are attuned to conditions in Wales. More so than in many other areas of social enquiry, the links between research and policy in education need to be tightly drawn.

In fact, it is intriguing that, over the past few decades, there has been an increasing devolution of control over education policy to Wales (an issue to which we return in the next section of the chapter) and this has been paralleled – at least to some extent – by a growth in research on the Welsh education system. Hence, although a great deal remains to be done, we are now in a much better position to explore the key features of education in Wales than we would have been even five years ago (Delamont and Rees 1997).

In what follows, therefore, we address some of these key features of the Welsh education system in terms of the evidence and analysis which is available to us. Certainly, we are very selective in what we cover. Our approach is broadly sociological and we do not attempt to include historical, political or economic research systematically. We are concerned primarily with schools in the maintained sector (and therefore say very little about independent (that is, private) schools). The very important aspects of education which take place after school are treated much more briefly. The chapter focuses upon three major themes. First, we examine the changing organization of the education system in Wales. Secondly, we discuss patterns of educational attainment in Wales. And finally, we analyse the relationships between education and the Welsh language and culture.

The Organization of the Welsh Education System

For most of the period since the Second World War, the organization of the education system in Wales has followed the pattern in England very closely. Although elements of distinctiveness – especially in respect of the Welsh language – had been officially recognized as long ago as the last decade of the nineteenth century, education policies in Wales originated in Westminster and Whitehall and the pattern of educational provision closely resembled that in England (certainly more so than that in Scotland or Northern Ireland) (for example, Jones 1997).

The post-1944 education system

As far as schools were concerned, this meant that provision for much of the post-war period was dominated by the 1944 Education Act. This introduced compulsory education, free of charge, for all pupils and raised the school-leaving age to fifteen. Previously, most children stayed at what were called elementary schools until they could leave at fourteen, and followed a restricted curriculum geared to equipping school-leavers for the manual jobs which were locally available or for domestic work. The 1944 Act introduced an examination at eleven, based on an intelligence test, plus English and maths papers, and this marked the end of primary schooling. Thereafter, pupils were allocated to one of three types of secondary school – grammar, technical or secondary modern – according to their performance in the '11-plus' examination.

In Wales, those with scores in the top 40 per cent or so went to grammar schools, while the bulk of the remainder went to secondary modern schools (in reality, there were very few technical schools) (Jones, 1990). The results were fixed so that equal proportions of boys and girls went to grammar schools (if the top 40 per cent had gone regardless of sex, two-thirds of the pupils in grammar schools would have been girls). Many grammar schools were single-sex. Overall, the proportion going to grammar schools in Wales was much higher than in England. Nevertheless, relatively few pupils stayed on at school after the minimum school-leaving age and only a tiny minority went to university.

Responsibility for the implementation of this new system was vested in the local authorities. It is striking that many local education authorities in Wales did not favour this tripartite system and wanted to have secondary schools which were multilateral (that is, catering for the large majority of pupils in the relevant age-group). As Jones (1990) shows, however, they had little scope to implement their wishes and were overruled by central government (in the shape of the Welsh Department of the Ministry of Education and the Central Advisory Council (Wales)). This itself illustrates the limitations of discretion within the Welsh education system at this time.

Comprehensive schools

The schools system ushered in by the 1944 Education Act remained relatively unchanged until the 1960s. In the primary sector, however, concerns were expressed about the consequences of school closures, especially in rural, predominantly Welsh-speaking areas, as populations declined (Nash, 1977). Moreover, controversy continued over the most appropriate organization of secondary schools. Critics of the tripartite system (in Wales and elsewhere) stressed that the '11-plus' discriminated against children from working-class backgrounds and thus led to an enormous waste of talent. Research by sociologists concerned with access to educational opportunities by children from different class backgrounds provided an important basis for these arguments (for example, Floud et al. 1956).

Hence, following the election of a Labour government in 1964, Welsh secondary schools were again subjected to a wholesale reorganization, as local education authorities were invited to abolish the '11-plus' examination and to introduce comprehensive schools, providing for almost all of the children from a given locality or catchment area. This time, however, the Welsh authorities were extremely receptive to the changes; as in Scotland (although not Northern Ireland and some parts of England), comprehensive systems were introduced across Wales as a whole (Benn and Chitty 1996).

Almost from their inception, the comprehensive schools attracted persistent criticisms from commentators who believed that they were responsible for lowering educational standards (as in the (in)famous Black Reports of the 1960s and 1970s: Wright 1977). These debates took a particular form in Wales, as we shall see in the next section. More recently, criticism has shifted towards the maintained schools generally, on the grounds that not only are adequate standards not being achieved, but also that school-leavers are not being prepared effectively to play a role in the economy (Ball 1990).

The Conservative transformation of schooling

These currents of thought crystallized during the 1980s, when a succession of Conservative governments brought about the wholesale transformation of the schools system. In particular, the influence of local education authorities was severely circumscribed, as schools were given increased control over their budgets (through the Local Management of Schools) as well as being offered the opportunity to opt out of local authority control altogether by becoming grant-maintained (funded more or less directly by central government). The 1988 Education Reform Act, moreover, allowed parents to express their preferences over the schools to be attended by their children and funded schools according to the number of pupils on their rolls. Schools were encouraged to compete for new pupils and thereby the planning and co-ordinating functions of the local education authorities were further undermined.

At the same time, a national curriculum and system of assessment was introduced for pupils in maintained schools up until the age of 16. For the first time, what pupils should learn and the levels of attainment they should achieve were prescribed centrally. The role of the local authorities was thus further weakened and the power of central government over the education system enormously strengthened (Ball 1990).

A Welsh education system?

Paradoxically, however, this period of intense centralization in the organization of the education system generally has been paralleled by the growth of a distinctive administrative structure for education in Wales. What we are referring to here is the striking – and, it has to be said, rather surprising – development of administrative devolution to Welsh educational institutions over recent years. Not only has the Welsh Office assumed responsibility for the whole of education policy (including training and economic development), but also there has been a proliferation of devolved institutions, which have taken over responsibility for the implementation of major areas of education policy within Wales. These include, for example, curriculum development and assessment within schools, initially through the Curriculum Council for Wales and, more recently, through the Curriculum and Assessment Authority for Wales. Similarly, further and higher education in Wales are now funded through the Welsh Funding Councils (which are separate, but have the same chief executive).

Clearly, it is quite another matter whether or not this administrative devolution is resulting in significantly different 'national' policies in Wales. However, it has been argued that many of the reforms instigated at the England and Wales level through the 1980s and 1990s – opting for grant-maintained status, City Technology Colleges, and so on – have exerted relatively little impact on the education system in Wales, thereby compounding historical peculiarities, such as the very small Welsh independent-schools sector (Reynolds 1990, 1995; Gorard 1996). In this way, therefore, a distinctive Welsh system comes to be defined in terms of a series of institutional 'gaps'. More positively, it has been suggested that the development of the National Curriculum in Wales has allowed the expression of a significant Welsh dimension, not only through according the Welsh language 'core' or 'foundation subject' status (thus requiring it to be taught in all schools to all pupils) but also through the shaping of distinctive curricula in history, geography, literature and so forth (Jones 1994; Jones and Lewis 1995; Daugherty 1995). Moreover, with the establishment of the National Assembly in 1999, it seems likely that there will be the scope for the further development of distinctive education policies for Wales.

Given this emergent pattern of 'separate development' in the Welsh educational system, it is not surprising that the debates over the *performance* of Welsh schools have intensified in recent years. This is not to suggest that concerns over the effectiveness of Welsh education are new (indeed, they can be traced back at least to the nineteenth century). However, the changes which have taken place in the organization of the education system in Wales – certainly since comprehensivization during the 1960s – have provided a new context for expressing them. Moreover, all educational issues have to be set against the deindustrialization of the Welsh (and British) economy over the past three decades, reflecting wider trends in the globalization of production and economic activity generally. The spectre of youth unemployment and the disappearance of many jobs traditionally done by young school-leavers have probably changed the patterns of education and training more than anything done *to* the education system by government or *in* education and training by its managers or practitioners.

Educational attainment and Welsh society

The performance of Welsh schools

As we have seen, then, particular concerns were expressed from the 1960s onwards that the introduction of comprehensive secondary schools was depressing levels of educational attainment. Given the actual evidence of the sharply rising attainment of both young men and women in terms of examination passes – in Wales as well as other parts of Britain – it has proved problematic to sustain this criticism in a simple form. This has led, for example, to the more recent emphasis by the critics on the purported decline in the standards required in the GCSE and A-level examinations themselves and the poor quality of some of the newly introduced, vocationally orientated qualifications such as the GNVQ (Ball 1990).

As Table 14.1 shows, the recent evidence from Wales confirms the general, long-term pattern of rising levels of attainment.[1]

Table 14.1. *Examination achievements (of pupils aged 15 at the beginning of the academic year): % gaining five or more A*–C grades at GCSE*

	1992/3	1993/4	1994/5	1995/6	1996/7
Total	37	39	41	42	44
Boys	32	35	36	37	39
Girls	42	44	46	47	49

However, the form which concerns over educational attainment have taken in Wales has been quite specific. Hence, a persistent theme – in this context as in so much else – has been that performance in Welsh schools has lagged behind that in English ones. Certainly, it is true that on indicators such as that used in Table 14.1, there is a significant gap between the two countries. In 1996/7, for example, the equivalent percentages for England of those gaining five or more GCSE passes at A*–C grades were 45.1 per cent in total, comprising 40.5 per cent of boys and 50.0 per cent of girls.

It is important to emphasize, however, that in other regards the Welsh education system is not so obviously disadvantaged. For instance, although children are not required to start school until they are five years old, in Wales over 90 per cent of three- and four-year-olds participate in education either full- or part-time. This compares with only 60 per cent in England. At the other end of the school career, whilst participation has increased significantly in both countries, more young people remain in full-time education after the minimum school-leaving age in Wales (see Table 14.2).

Table 14.2. *Participation in non-compulsory full-time education, 1996–1997 (%)*

	16	17	18
Wales	71	58	47
England	69	57	38

It is also the case that pupil–teacher ratios in Wales are somewhat better than those in England. In 1996/7, the ratio for primary schools in Wales was 22.6, compared with 23.7 in England; that for Welsh secondary schools was 16.2, whilst the English figure was 16.9. (It is worth pointing out that the figures for independent schools are 10.0 for Wales and 10.2 for England.) Similarly, in the past, expenditure per pupil in Welsh schools has been relatively high (Rees and Rees 1980). Even now, there is no evidence that the resourcing of the Welsh education system falls below the English level (Istance and Rees 1994).

What this emphasizes, however, is the complexity in interpreting data on the performance of schools. At first sight, it appears paradoxical that pupils towards the end of their school careers in Wales should perform less well than their English counterparts, when they tend to start school at an earlier age, enjoy better pupil–teacher ratios and are seemingly not significantly worse off in terms of resources. However, this takes no account of the influences on school performance of factors outside the education system itself; community, neighbourhood and family backgrounds exert an enormous impact on how pupils perform in schools. More specifically, starting school early may simply reflect the economic pressures on mothers to be employed and a relative poverty of adequate child-care provision, especially by employers in Wales (Rees 1999). Young people may stay on at school because the very limited alternatives discourage them from leaving (Rees et al. 1996). We can gain a better insight into the implications of these complex issues by looking in greater detail at some of the controversies over Welsh comprehensive schools.

'Schooled to fail'

Again, as we have already mentioned, the general debates about the effects of comprehensivization on educational attainment took a particular form in Wales. By the end of the 1970s, Welsh concern was focused not on the impacts on the higher levels of attainment, but rather about the failure of comprehensive schools to provide adequately for the needs of pupils of middle and lower ability. The latter were thought to be especially disadvantaged given the changes in employment opportunities which were occurring through deindustrialization. In part at least, this reflected the findings of academic research which showed that at least up until the end of the 1970s, Welsh schools produced *both* a high proportion of school-leavers who were relatively well qualified *and* a high proportion without formal qualifications at all (Rees and Rees 1980).

It was argued that this pattern of attainment reflected the retention of a 'grammar school ethos' within the comprehensives, with the academic attainment of abler pupils being prized at the expense of those of middle and lower ability. A high proportion of pupils, it was argued, were 'schooled to fail'. The origins of these arguments lay in the writings of academic educationists (Reynolds et al. 1987; Reynolds, 1990), but they were taken up powerfully by the Schools Inspectorate and teacher groups (Loosemore 1981). It is somewhat ironic, therefore, that these debates laid the foundations for what became a widespread indictment of the 'underperformance' of Welsh schools later in the 1980s and 1990s. In the hands of successive Conservative Secretaries of State for Wales during these years, this 'conventional wisdom' provided the basis not only for the introduction of targets for 'school improvement' some time in advance of England, but also fuelled stringent criticism of the teachers whose representative organizations had been instrumental in the original debates.

What is striking, however, is that by the 1990s, whilst the large proportion of unqualified school-leavers persisted, the performance of Welsh schools in respect of the top end of the distribution had also fallen behind that of other parts of the UK (Istance and Rees 1994). Table 14.3 gives an indication of the relative

Table 14.3. *Highest qualifications held by school-leavers of all ages in Wales, Scotland and England, 1995–1996 (% of age group)*

	Wales	Scotland	England
Women			
GCSE equivalent 5 or more A–C grades	47.6	59.7	49.4
1–4 A–C grades	24.7	26.5	26.5
1 or more D–G grades only	19.7	11.0	17.5
No graded results	8.9	2.8	6.6
2 or more A-level equivalents	30.2	33.4	32.4
Men			
GCSE equivalent 5 or more A–C grades	36.8	47.6	39.9
1–4 A–C grades	23.9	31.2	24.9
1 or more D–G grades only	26.7	16.8	26.3
No graded results	12.6	4.4	8.9
2 or more A-level equivalents	23.9	25.5	27.0

Source: Arnot *et al.* (1996).

performance in the constituent countries of Britain. Comparisons of this kind appeared to provide factual support for the thesis that schools in Wales were underperforming. However, appearances can be deceptive. As Gorard (1998a) has recently argued, if the effects of the social backgrounds of pupils in Welsh schools are taken into account (using statistical techniques), then the purported substandard performance of the Welsh schools (at least in comparison with English ones, which is what he examines) disappears. Indeed, he suggests that the results being achieved by schools in Wales are appreciably *higher* than what would be expected given the social and economic characteristics of their pupils.

The 'under-achievement' of boys

More recently still, concerns about pupils at the lower levels of attainment have become focused on the idea that the key factor here is that boys are failing to achieve their intellectual potential. In Wales (as elsewhere), considerable public attention has been directed at this purported problem of 'under-achieving boys'. It is widely held to have important implications for the limited employment opportunities of school-leavers, as well as other social problems (Rees *et al.* 1996).

Certainly, it is true that girls in Wales do perform better overall – although not in mathematics and sciences – than boys at all stages of schooling up to and including GCSE examinations (Salisbury 1996). However, once due account is taken of patterns of entry to examinations and, more importantly, the general improvement which has taken place in standards of educational attainment, then there is Welsh evidence to suggest that the gap in achievement between boys and girls is actually getting smaller (Gorard *et al.* 1998).

Moreover, it is at the very highest levels of attainment that boys are significantly under-represented (see Figure 14.1). Contrary to what might be inferred from the public debate, at lower levels of attainment, the gap between boys and girls is relatively small. The over-representation of boys at the middle levels of attainment may indicate that a proportion are achieving, for instance, C and D grades at GCSE, rather than the A or B grades of which they are capable. However, there is no well-founded evidence to support the idea that the differential between the attainment of boys and girls is a significant contributory factor to the problems of low school achievement and restricted employment opportunities amongst school-leavers in Wales (Gorard *et al.* 1998). Accordingly, as with more general notions of the poor performance of Welsh schools relative to those in England, considerable care needs to be taken in examining claims as to the nature and consequences of 'under-achievement' amongst boys in Welsh schools.

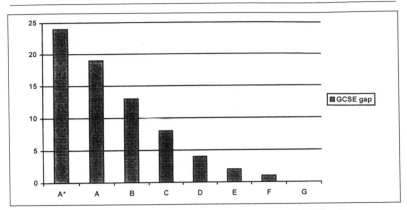

Figure 14.1. *Achievement gaps in favour of girls in 1997 – all GCSE subjects.*
Source: Gorard et al. (1998).

Policy on educational attainment

As we began to see earlier, these complexities in interpreting the patterns of educational attainment in Wales have not prevented the introduction of policies aimed at removing what has been understood as the 'under-performance' of Welsh schools (for one of the most recent examples, see Welsh Office 1997). Whilst there is clearly the need for further research to clarify these issues, a more productive relationship between educational research and the formulation of policy is also required.

Rather surprisingly, very similar conclusions apply to what is perhaps the best-known feature of the education system in Wales: bilingual education. We turn to this next.

Education and the Welsh Language

Welsh in schools

It has been the need for schools in Wales to make provision for the Welsh language that has been most widely recognized as distinguishing Welsh provision from that in England. For most of the post-1944 period, it was left to local education authorities to devise schemes for the teaching of Welsh which were appropriate to local linguistic patterns and wider social conditions (Jones 1997). What this meant in reality was the development of widely diverse practices, embodying different combinations of Welsh-medium teaching, learning Welsh as a second language and no Welsh at all. Since the 1988 Education Reform Act, however, Welsh – either as a medium of general instruction or as a second language – has become a compulsory part of the primary school curriculum and of the earlier stages of the secondary curriculum (with only a very limited number of exceptions).

Not surprisingly (especially to those directly involved in education in Wales), there have been substantial difficulties in actually implementing this programme, not least because of the shortage of teachers qualified to carry it out in the classroom. It has also become a highly charged political issue, as groups of parents campaign variously for the provision of Welsh-medium schools or against the imposition of Welsh in the curriculum. Nevertheless, Table 14.4 shows that Welsh does now play a very important role in schools in Wales. Clearly, Welsh remains less well established in the secondary schools. However, even here, there has been a dramatic growth: in 1980/81, for example, almost 50 per cent of secondary school pupils were recorded as receiving no Welsh of any kind.

Table 14.4. Welsh in primary and secondary schools (years 7–11), 1996–1997 (%)

	Primary	Secondary
Welsh-medium	17.2	12.6
Part of curriculum	2.6	
Second language	75.2	65.0
No Welsh	4.9	22.4

Welsh-medium schools

It is the growth of Welsh-medium schools, especially in those parts of Wales where English is the dominant language of everyday life, which has attracted most attention (Baker 1990). Not only has Welsh experience sometimes been used as a model for the development of bilingual education in other parts of the world, but also it has been the subject of systematic, broadly sociological research (see, for example, Khlief 1980; Delamont 1987).

Overwhelmingly, attention has been focused on Welsh-medium schools as vehicles for reproducing the language, with particular emphasis on the motivations underpinning parental choice, especially in those parts of the country where English is the predominant language and many parents choosing Welsh-medium schools for their children do not themselves speak Welsh (for example, Bush *et al*. 1981). Nevertheless, as yet, it still remains unclear whether school-leavers from the Welsh-medium schools will keep up their Welsh and actually generate the strengthening of the language to which most proponents of Welsh-medium education aspire. Experience from elsewhere suggests that it is unlikely that this will happen in the absence of opportunities to use the language in employment and other official spheres of adult life (Williams 1989).

A particular difficulty here is the extremely limited provision of Welsh-medium teaching outside schools. Although there has been an enormous growth of classes for adults who wish to learn Welsh (Morris forthcoming), further and higher education through the medium of Welsh is much more limited. With respect to the latter, whilst provision is made in some subjects in the constituent institutions of the University of Wales (especially at Aberystwyth and Bangor), its impact is inevitably limited. Indeed, more generally, the role of higher education in Wales is complicated by a pattern of participation which is unique amongst the countries of the UK. Simply put, about a half of Welsh university students go to universities in England; whilst about half of the students in Welsh universities are English (Rees and Istance 1997). Inevitably, therefore, the contribution of Welsh higher education to the Welsh language and culture more generally is equivocal.

Welsh-medium schools and educational attainment

Interestingly, more recently, arguments in support of Welsh-medium education have extended beyond considerations of the language itself. It has been argued that the Welsh-medium schools in the predominantly English-speaking south-east of Wales consistently achieve better examination results than their English-medium counterparts. Therefore, they offer important guidelines as to good practice, which could usefully be adopted to raise the standards of Welsh schools as a whole (Reynolds 1995; Reynolds *et al*. 1998)

Once again, however, there are considerable complexities in interpreting the performance of Welsh-medium schools adequately.

The issue of how far their superior results are explicable simply in terms of the social backgrounds of their pupils, rather than anything to do with the schools themselves is crucial. Reynolds *et al.* (1998) argue on the basis of a quite detailed analysis of four schools, 'matched' in terms of their intakes, that it is the 'school effects' which are more important. In sharp contrast, Gorard (1998b) uses a massively larger sample of schools in south Wales to argue that, once the social characteristics of school intakes were taken into account, there is no difference between the performances of Welsh- and English-medium schools.

Clearly, further research is required to establish why Welsh-medium schools tend to get better examination results. In this context, it is instructive that – as far as we know – *no* ethnographic work, based on detailed observation and interaction with staff and pupils in the schools, has been conducted in Welsh-medium schools, despite its importance in the development of educational research more generally. Hence, whether there are distinctive patterns of classroom interaction, pupil and teacher cultures, etc., remains unknown, and their impacts (on attainment amongst other things) are uncharted.

Conclusion

Much of the preceding discussion remains tentative. It maps out a *future* research agenda, as much as it identifies established features of the educational system in Wales. The changes which have taken place in the structure and organization of Welsh educational institutions during recent years highlight the need for a systematic exploration – a 'policy sociology' to use Ball's (1990) term – of the nature and origins of these institutional transformations themselves. Equally, however, the emergent distinctiveness of Welsh education policy further emphasizes the necessity for an analysis of the impacts on attainment patterns and opportunity structures, and on linguistic and cultural patterns, of the restructured Welsh educational system.

Moreover, the establishment of the National Assembly in 1999 raises at least the possibility of a further institutional sea-change in Welsh education policy, significantly extending democratic control. The prospect of greater scrutiny and debate that this offers only makes more pressing the task of developing a better analysis of education in Wales.

Note

1. Unless stated otherwise, all data are derived from the relevant volumes of *Statistics of Education in Wales*.

References

Arnot, M., David, M. and Weiner, G. (1996). *Educational Reform and Gender Equality in Schools* (Manchester: Equal Opportunities Commission).

Baker, C. (1990). 'The growth of bilingual education in the secondary schools of Wales', in W. Evans (ed.), *Perspectives on a Century of Secondary Education in Wales* (Aberystwyth: Centre for Educational Studies).

Ball, S. (1990). *Politics and Policy Making in Education: Explorations in Policy Sociology* (London: Routledge).

Benn, C. and Chitty, C. (1996). *Is Comprehensive Education Alive and Well or Struggling to Survive?* (London: David Fulton).

Bush, E., Atkinson, P. and Read, M. (1981). 'Addysg trwy gyfrwng y Gymraeg mewn ardal Seisnig: nodweddion ac ymagweddau'r rhieni', *Education for Development*, 6/3, 42–50.

Central Advisory Council for Education, Wales (1967). *Primary Education in Wales (The Gittins Report)* (London: HMSO).

Daugherty, R. (1995). *National Curriculum Assessment: A Review of Policy, 1987–1994* (London: Falmer).

Delamont, S. (1987). 'S4C and the grassroots', *Contemporary Wales*, 1, 53–72.

Delamont, S. and Rees, G. (1997). 'Understanding the Welsh education system: does Wales need a separate "policy sociology"?', *Working Paper 23* (Cardiff: School of Education, University of Wales).

Floud, J., Halsey, A. H. and Martin, F. M. (1956). *Social Class and Educational Opportunity* (London: Heinemann).

Gorard, S. (1996). 'Fee-paying schools in Britain – a peculiarly English phenomenon?', *Educational Review*, 48/1, 89–93.

Gorard, S. (1997). 'Paying for a "Little England" – school choice and the Welsh language', *Welsh Journal of Education*, 6/1, 19–32.

Gorard, S. (1998a). ' "Schooled to fail"? Revisiting the Welsh school-effect', *Journal of Education Policy*, 13/1.

Gorard, S. (1998b). 'Four errors . . . and a conspiracy? The effectiveness of schools in Wales', *Oxford Review of Education*, 24/4, 459–72.

Gorard, S., Salisbury, J., Rees, G. and Fitz, J. (1998). 'The comparative performance of boys and girls at school in Wales', *Report to ACCAC* (Cardiff: School of Education, University of Wales).

Halsey, A. H., Heath, A. F. and Ridge, J. M. (1980). *Origins and Destinations: Family, Class, and Education in Modern Britain* (Oxford: Clarendon Press).

Istance, D. and Rees, G. (1994). 'Education and training in Wales: problems and paradoxes revisited', *Contemporary Wales*, 7, 7–27.

Jones, B. and Lewis, I. (1995). 'A curriculum Cymreig', *Welsh Journal of Education*, 4/2, 22–35.

Jones, G. E. (1990). *Which Nation's Schools? Direction and Devolution in Welsh Education in the Twentieth Century* (Cardiff: University of Wales Press).

Jones, G. E. (1994). 'Which nation's curriculum? The case of Wales', *Curriculum Journal*, 5/1, 5–16.

Jones, G. E. (1997). *The Education of a Nation* (Cardiff: University of Wales Press).

Khleif, B. (1980). *Language, Ethnicity and Education in Wales* (The Hague: Mouton).

Loosemore, F. A. (1981). *Curriculum and Assessment in Wales: An Exploratory Study* (Cardiff: Schools Council for Wales).

Morris, S. (forthcoming). 'Welsh for adults: a policy for a bilingual Wales?', in R. Phillips, R. Daugherty and G. Rees (eds.), *Education Policy-Making in Wales: Explorations in Devolved Governance* (Cardiff: University of Wales Press).

Nash, R. (1977). *Schooling in Rural Societies* (London: Methuen).

Phillips, R. (1996). 'Education policy making in Wales: a research agenda', *Welsh Journal of Education*, 5/2, 26–42.

Rees, G. and Istance, D. (1997). 'Higher education in Wales: the (re-)emergence of a national system?', *Higher Education Quarterly* 51/1, 49–67.

Rees, G. and Rees, T. (1980). 'Educational inequality in Wales: some problems and paradoxes', in G. Rees and T. Rees (eds.), *Poverty and Social Inequality in Wales* (London: Croom Helm).

Rees, G., Williamson, H. and Istance, D. (1996). ' "Status Zero": a study of jobless school-leavers in south Wales', *Research Papers in Education*, 11/2, 219–35.

Rees, T. (1999). *Women and Work: Twenty Five Years of Gender Equality in Wales* (Cardiff: University of Wales Press).

Reynolds, D. (1990). 'The great Welsh education debate', *History of Education*, 19/3, 181–90.

Reynolds, D. (1995). 'Creating an educational system for Wales', *Welsh Journal of Education*, 4/2, 4–21.

Reynolds, D., Bellin, W. and ab Ieuan, R. (1998). *A Competitive Edge: Why Welsh Medium Schools Perform Better* (Cardiff: Institute of Welsh Affairs).

Reynolds, D. and Sullivan, M., with Murgatroyd, S. (1987). *The Comprehensive Experiment: A Comparison of the Selective and Non-selective System of School Organisation* (Lewes: Falmer Press).

Salisbury, J. (1996). *Educational Reforms and Gender Equality in Welsh Schools* (Manchester: EOC).

Welsh Office (1997). *Building Excellent Schools Together* (Cardiff: HMSO).

Williams, C. (1989). 'New domains of the Welsh language: education, planning and the law', *Contemporary Wales*, 3, 41–70.

Wright, N. (1977). *Progress in Education: A Review of Schooling in England and Wales* (London: Croom Helm).

15 Women in Wales

TERESA REES

Introduction

A notable year for women in Wales was 1975; the year in which the
Equal Pay Act and the Sex Discrimination Act came into force.
This legislation outlawed old practices of paying men and women
different rates for doing the same work, and refusing to give a
candidate a job because of their sex. It marked the end of the
'bright young man' and 'attractive Girl Friday' job adverts. It
followed on from the lifting of the last of the marriage bars in
1972, where women working in some parts of the public sector
were made to resign their posts if they got married. How has the
position of women changed in Wales since 1975? In this chapter we
explore the development of gender equality in Wales through the
1970s, the 1980s and the 1990s, and trace the evolution of ways of
thinking about gender relations and equal opportunities. Each of
these decades has been very different in terms of priorities, policies
and practice and in their effects on women's lives in Wales.

Equal Opportunities

Equality of opportunity is principally about social justice, but
there is always the link, stronger at some periods than others, with
labour-market needs: the 'business case' for equality. While
arguments for the latter can help to win ground, success gained can
be precarious if it is linked too strongly to economic imperatives
that come and go. There has been, then, a constantly shifting
balance over the last twenty-five years between the emphasis on

justice, citizens' rights and the principle of equality, and those business arguments of 'untapped potential' and 'wasted human resource' – the economics of equal opportunities (Humphries and Rubery 1995).

The industrial structure of Wales has changed dramatically over the last quarter-century. From the traditional domination of coal, steel and agriculture, much of the landscape is now characterized by reclaimed land and manufacturing plants owned by inward investors. The growth of the service sector – finance, insurance, tourism, leisure and the media – has generated a demand for workers with completely new skills. Big Pit in Blaenavon employs ex-miners as museum guides. The set-aside policy and collapse of agriculture has led to farmland being turned into leisure facilities such as golf courses. North Wales is increasingly known for its bed-and-breakfast accommodation, its studios and its production companies, rather than its slate quarries, its mine and its power station. Red-brick business parks and hotels now adorn the banks of the M4 in the south and the A55 in the north.

These tremendous upheavals in the industrial structure of Wales have had profound implications for the gender composition of the workforce. The decline in the traditional dominant industries has meant a net loss in men in the workforce, indeed, the proportion of men of working age in employment in Wales has shrunk to one of the lowest levels in the UK: in 1997, only 72 per cent of men of working age were in employment in Wales compared with 78 per cent in Britain (EOC 1998, 5). Poor health, early retirement and to a lesser extent more young people staying on in education accounts for this decline. Meanwhile, the expansion of the service sector has created jobs that have been taken by women. Hence, the proportion of women in employment, especially in part-time work, has grown from its low baseline rate almost to reach the level of the UK average. In 1997, 64 per cent of women of working age were in work in Wales, compared with 67 per cent in Britain as a whole (EOC 1998, 5).

The pay gap between men and women has reduced since the Equal Pay Act. In 1977, women working full-time earned 74 per cent of men's wages; in 1997 they received 83 per cent (EOC 1998, 5, original source New Earnings Survey 1997). This compares with 80 per cent in Britain as a whole: however, the reason the pay differential is smaller in Wales is that men's wages are lower. Girls are doing as well as, and in some subjects and levels better than, boys in school now (EOC 1998: 2). As many young women as men now stay on in post-compulsory education; they now constitute about half the student population. However, they are less likely to receive employer-sponsored training of more than three days, or be awarded a Modern Apprenticeship or to undertake vocational training courses in further education, and their jobs are less likely to be commensurate with their qualifications (Istance and Rees 1994). This issue is often overlooked in the general public concern about the under-achievement of boys in GCSEs and A-levels. Gender segregation is still a very strong feature of the Welsh labour force: 54 per cent of employed women are in occupational groups in which more than 60 per cent of workers are women (clerical and secretarial occupations; service jobs and sales workers), while 67 per cent of men are in occupational groups in which more than 60 per cent of workers are men (managers and administrators; professional, craft and related occupations; and plant and machine operatives) (EOC 1998). There are still very few women in senior management in Wales (Human Resources Group and Opinion Research Swansea 1999).

Shifts towards convergence in employment rates, pay and education are of course not all the result of equal opportunities policies, although these have undoubtedly had an impact. They are more a reflection of the patterns of industrial restructuring and changing nature of demand for jobs, especially for a flexible workforce prepared to work for relatively low wage rates in the service sector. Nevertheless, equal opportunities policies have had an increasingly important role to play in shaping the practices of the institutions that bear upon women's lives. How have the last three decades differed in their approaches? Has there been progress in understanding the complexity of equal opportunities? Have policies to foster equal opportunities been effective? And what are the prospects of gender equality in Wales for the future? This chapter begins to address some of these questions.

The 1970s: Equal Treatment

In the 1970s, the UK joined and then confirmed its membership of the European Community (hence the need to get in place a Sex Discrimination Act and Equal Pay Act to comply with European directives on equal treatment for men and women in jobs and training). The Equal Opportunities Commission (EOC) was set up in 1975, to monitor and advise on amendments to the law, to support individuals who wanted to bring cases to court and to foster equal opportunities between men and women. The EOC Office in Wales was opened in 1978. It was a decade, too, which saw the passing of the Race Relations Act and the setting up of the Commission for Racial Equality. The decade ended with a No vote for devolution and the beginning of eighteen years of Conservative government.

The model of equal opportunities operating in Wales in the 1970s, was, arguably, one of equal treatment. This was in part a consequence of the European legislation. The principle of equal treatment for men and women was enshrined in the 1957 Treaty of Rome setting up the European Economic Community (EEC). However, it was not until a series of directives were introduced in the 1970s that member states were obliged to ensure adherence to it through their own legislation. The EEC, and now the European Union (EU), has over the decades acted as a significant catalyst to the development of equal opportunities legislation in most of the member states, and certainly the UK (Rees 1998; Rossilli 1997).

The notion of equal treatment is rooted in eighteenth-century philosophy of the rights of citizens. The British philosopher Mary Wollstonecraft (1967 [1792]), sometimes writing under a male pseudonym, sought to extend Rousseau's treatise on the Rights of Man written in the context of the French Revolution to a vindication of the rights of woman. Equal treatment is clearly a sound social justice principle. The notion that women and men should work alongside each other and be paid different rates for the same work now seems outrageous to us but it was common practice up until the mid-1970s. Why?

The answer lies in the idea of a 'gender contract', that is, a deal and consequent division of labour between a breadwinner husband and a homemaker wife. It has been defined as a 'socio-cultural' consensus (Pfau-Effinger 1994, 1,359) which shapes the hegemonic ideology of countries, including notions of gender roles and relationships. The higher value assigned to male domains is built into the contract structurally (Pfau-Effinger 1994, 1,359). This gender contract underpinned the architecture of the post-war taxation systems and welfare state (Sainsbury 1994), it justified the use of marriage bars and it validated the concept of a family wage for men and supplementary wage (or pin money) for women, irrespective of their individual circumstances (Land 1980).

In reality, even in the 1970s, the model of a breadwinner husband, homemaker wife and two dependent children never described even the majority of households. There have always been working wives, child-free couples, gay couples, cohabiting extended families, the single, the widowed, the separated and the divorced, newly reconstituted families and, in Wales particularly, children being brought up by other relatives. In the mid-1990s, only a third of adults (many of these including working wives) live in households with dependent children: fewer than those living in 'other household types' (e.g. two non-pensioners or three or more adults with no dependent children) (Welsh Office 1998, 5). Nevertheless, this ideology of a particular form of family life dominated many of the systems, structures and institutions of post-war Britain and made unequal pay possible and even defensible. It ensured married women were not eligible for unemployment benefit, sick pay or pensions in their own right. It effectively excluded women from many areas of the labour market. It provided a reason for employers and for women themselves not to invest in their education and training. It made it almost impossible for women to earn an independent living. Even by 1994, divorced or separated women were the most dependent on rented accommodation (Welsh Office 1998, 8). Under the breadwinner/ homemaker gender contract, the 'choice' for women was to become dependent, to a greater or lesser extent, either on a man or on the state.

The 1970s, then, were about recognizing that some of the consequences of the breadwinner/homemaker gender contract were at odds with the principle of equal treatment for individuals. The legislation sought to address some of the more obvious manifestations of these consequences. Most of the work of the EOC during this period was in taking cases to court and clarifying the law. For example, one of the EOC's first cases stopped banks insisting on women being asked to provide a male guarantor when applying for credit. But there were other signs too that the breadwinner/ homemaker gender contract was not appropriate for everyone. It was in the 1970s that the Gay Liberation Movement was founded. In Wales, the first refuge for battered women was opened and Welsh Women's Aid was set up. The growth in the demand for places at the refuges was and is a stark reminder that family life is not a pleasant environment for everyone.

The 1980s: Positive Action

If the 1970s were the decade of equal treatment, the emphasis in the 1980s was on positive action. The decade began, however, with more European directives aimed at making the equal-treatment principle work by plugging the gaps: for example by extending the law to cover equal treatment for women among the self-employed or 'co-entrepreneurs', of whom there are many in Wales, women working on smallholdings or farms or in other family businesses. Ashton (1995) has documented the lifestyle of Welsh-speaking 'farmers' wives': up before dawn, feeding chickens, calves and children, driving tractors, doing the school run, ordering cattle feed, doing the evening milking, feeding the family and then settling down in the late evening with the farm accounts. None of these activities counted as work, and hence such women had no eligibility to sick pay, maternity leave or pension rights until the equal-treatment directives began to take effect.

In 1986, the UK, for a time the member state most frequently prosecuted by the European Commission on equality matters, was made to extend the Equal Pay Act to cover work of equal value. The segregation of women and men into different industries and occupations had meant there were relatively few women who could find a man as a 'comparator' with which to take a claim. It began to be recognized that the valuing of skills was influenced by gender. Breaking jobs down into their components and analysing them objectively revealed how pay rates had been linked to the gender of the majority of the job-holders, rather than the skill level of the job itself (Rees 1992).

Equal treatment is about treating men and women the same but the difficulty is, of course, that they are not the same. There are clear biological differences, but there are also socially constructed differences in relation to roles at home and work, underpinned by stereotyping and reinforced by the state and other institutions. While there are changes in the precise nature of gender segregation over time and space, the overall pattern of gender relations proves remarkably rigid (Walby 1997).

Factors which contribute to the reproduction of gender segregation in the labour market include young men and women 'choosing' gender appropriate subjects and careers. These 'choices' are made at a time in their lives when their personal and sexual identities are under close scrutiny and when pressures to conform are at their height (see Pilcher *et al.* 1988, for an account of occupational 'choices' among 500 south Wales schoolgirls). Men and women construct different patterns of participation in the labour market. Men have tended to stay in the labour market from leaving full-time education until they retire: pension schemes are built around this pattern of participation. Their long hours of work damage their health and efficiency, restrict their time with their families, and limit their opportunities to develop through other activities. Women tend to move in and out of paid work according to their stage in the life cycle and family demands; they alternate full- and part-time work, they sell their labour in accordance with their other commitments. This impairs their ability to accumulate experience of the world of work, and it damages their career prospects in a culture that values longevity of service and uninterrupted careers. Because of the way in which pensions are designed, it also consigns many of them to a life of poverty in old age. And lest we think that this describes only older women, a study by Juli Southall (1990, cited in Rees 1992) in 1990, of a group of sixteen-year-old south Wales girls leaving school, found that their aspirations and expectations were remarkably similar to the patterns of work and caring activities that had been followed by women who had left the same school fifteen years previously: to whit, a series of low-skilled, low-paid jobs interleaved with subsistence-level living while looking after their children full-time. For many working-class women, equal-treatment legislation has had little impact on the reality of their daily lives or indeed on their expectations for the future.

Equal treatment is limited in its effects. Differences between men and women in their subject and occupational choices and in their career patterns circumscribe the capacity of equal treatment. Neither equal access nor equal treatment necessarily leads to equal outcome. I am reminded of this by the cartoon (Figure 15.1). The shortcomings of equal treatment, this first model of equal opportunities, were recognized in the 1980s and led to the development of a second: positive action. This model recognizes

Figure 15.1. *Fair selection*

that there are differences between men and women and seeks to address the disadvantages experienced by women as a consequence of those differences.

Hence, in the 1980s, the EC co-funded a series of special measures designed to address the particular and different needs of women. Organizations, particularly in the voluntary sector, were able to use this opportunity to lever funding for projects designed to meet women's needs. The results include some notable projects in Wales: the award-winning South Glamorgan Women's Workshop, targeting disadvantaged women and equipping them for the labour market; the Dove Workshop in the Dulais Valley, hailed as a model project in Europe, drawing on the renewed confidence of women developed in the miners' support groups during the 1984/5 strike, and channelling it into access to education. There are other initiatives too in rural Wales, especially in Powys. These projects are designed to address the needs of disadvantaged women and provide them with the training and support necessary to help them to compete in the labour market.

Positive action measures start with the needs of women and design services to meet them, recognizing that existing systems, structures and organizations do not quite work for them. The popularity of such measures among women is extraordinary (Rees 1992). But they tend to be small initiatives, piecemeal projects, precariously funded, and to reach only a fraction of the population: they are, by definition, special.

During the 1980s, a growing number of organizations developed in Wales to express women's voices: for example, the Women's Advisory Council of the Wales TUC; the Wales Assembly of Women, which advises the Women's National Commission in the Cabinet Office on the views of women in Wales; and Honno, the women's press, which publishes Welsh women writers. Red Flannel Films, the women's film co-operative, premiered *Mam* in 1988 in Treorchy's Parc and Dare Hall: this film contested the relevance of the stereotype image of the Welsh 'mam', drawing on biographies of women involved in a wide range of activities, showing the diversity of their identities and experiences. In the 1980s, too, women walked from Wales to Greenham Common to set up peace camps.

Positive action recognizes difference, creates spaces and allows other voices to be heard. But it can only ever be limited in its effects. It also carries a health warning. In order to enable women better to fit in to a male world, compromises are sometimes made. In the late 1980s I evaluated some positive-action training courses for women in middle management to groom them for senior management. The curriculum included: 'how to develop a killer instinct, how to deal with the office Romeo, how to make yourself heard in meetings, how to dress appropriately (dark suits, no dangly earrings)' – in other words, how to become an honorary male (Rees 1992). The issue here is that the model of management practices is passed off as being gender-neutral. It is the responsibility of women to fit in – and to 'travel light' domestically. For many organizations, equal opportunities are considered to have been achieved if a few women can fit in with the status quo. Marshall's research (1995) focuses on high-flying corporate women who 'drop out' with stress-related health problems. It is not the work that causes the stress but the masculinist work culture. Some positive-action measures collude with the status quo and help some women to fit in better – by becoming more like men. It is important to recognize the androcentricity of organizations and their hierarchies and structures (Smith 1987) when seeking to explain patterns of gender segregation, rather than to operate with a deficit model of women.

The 1990s: Mainstreaming Equality

The 1990s brought a new agenda and a new approach to equality, one grounded in making the most of differences rather than simply accommodating them. Other equality dimensions began to get better recognition in law, for example in the Disability Act and the Welsh Language Act. Disability Wales developed a higher profile and the Commission for Racial Equality opened an office in Wales.

The complexity of gender equality was better recognized. It was realized, for example, that although some progress had been made for women in the labour market, no apparent change had been witnessed in the home. While their partners returned to paid work in increasing numbers, rather than contributing more to the housework, child-care and care of the elderly, men worked longer and longer hours. The EC is seeking to address this through the Parental Leave Directive, which makes it financially attractive for men to spend more time at home with their children.

The inter-relationship between gender and other identities in Wales was explored in a collection of essays published in 1994 called *Our Sisters' Land: The Changing Identities of Women in Wales* (Aaron et al. 1994). Here, Elizabeth Muir, the first woman on the Confederation of British Industry in Wales, described the paradox of being a Welsh woman member of the business fraternity. Angharad Tomos wrote of being imprisoned for burning down a second home in the same week as she was awarded a Chair at the National Eisteddfod. Roni Crwydren described the experience of being a lesbian Welsh-speaker, inhabiting two, seemingly incompatible, worlds. Enid Morgan wrote of the contradiction between her vocation as a churchwoman, and her anger at (then) being excluded from ordination by the Church in Wales. Charlotte Williams (1997, 30), whose mother was a white, north Walian, Welsh-speaker and whose father was a black Guyanese, has written since about how both her Welshness and her black identity have been challenged as being mutually exclusive.

The differences among women and among men began to emerge more visibly in the 1990s. Multiple identities are difficult to address in legislation or in policy. Many countries, including Northern Ireland, have dispensed with single-issue equality agencies and merged them into one. Would this benefit the new kids on the equality block, such as the disabled? Would they be advantaged by association with the older more established agencies such as the EOC and the Commission for Racial Equality? Would employers welcome negotiating with just one agency in seeking to ensure they comply with the legislation and develop good equal opportunities policies? But at the same time, how much do these equality dimensions have in common? Are policies that are appropriate for one equally suitable for the others?

Let us take the example of monitoring. Gender monitoring is relatively easy to do and is an essential element of gender-equality policies and plans. It facilitates transparency, the setting of goals and review of progress. But monitoring is a more complex issue for ethnic origin, it is difficult to apply to disability and it is potentially intrusive and unwelcome for sexual orientation: indeed, Stonewall, the gay and lesbian lobby group, advise against it.

In the case of gender, however, the political arithmetic exercises that statistical monitoring allows are extremely powerful in pointing up the impact of gender on the allocation of positions in the workplace (see EOC 1998; Welsh Office 1998). If we look at figures for Wales in the 1990s, we find that women now constitute nearly half the workforce, an increase from a third twenty-five years ago. However, the vast majority remain clustered in a narrow range of industries and occupations and precious few have percolated through to senior posts even by the late 1990s.

Such figures show us that it is not all progress. Local government reorganization in 1996 resulted in a reduction in both the number of women chief officers and women councillors in Wales. Indeed, rather than women moving into male-dominated sectors or into top jobs in Wales, they have lost ground to men entering tradition-ally female sectors. Less than half the primary school heads are women and only 12 per cent of secondary school heads. Looked at another way, of all male primary teachers, over half are now heads or deputy heads, compared with 18 per cent of women. Similarly, nearly 10 per cent of all male secondary school teachers are heads or deputies, compared with 2.5 per cent of women (Rees 1999).

For women working part-time, and especially women in blue-collar jobs, it is very hard to see any progress at all in the last twenty-five years. Although employment rights have improved for some, pay rates for many remain at or below the minimum wage. For some, terms and conditions have deteriorated into what Will Hutton (1995) describes as a 'nil hours' contract, where the employee has to guarantee to be available but no hours of work are necessarily offered: the new flexible form of employment. Part-time work is equated with lack of commitment and yet, because the UK has a longer working week than any other EU member state, some part-time workers do roughly the same number of hours as people considered to be working full-time elsewhere.

Although there have been some changes over the last twenty-five years, gender still remains the major organizing principle of the labour market in Wales, more so than in the rest of Britain. There has been some progress for some women, especially in those professions that demand qualifications for entry (Crompton 1990). But even here, women tend to be segregated within the professions, and any speciality that attracts women seems automatically not to be valued, such as public-health medicine, family law, public-sector accountancy (Rees 1992). In those areas of work where the entry requirements are less specified, such as senior management in the private sector, fewer women have been accepted apart from those whose place on the board is earned through a background in personnel or, more recently, accounting. Networking is crucial in recruitment to such positions, but this is difficult for women who are excluded from freemasonry and from some of the business clubs and golf clubs in Wales where such networking takes place. Male networks have been identified by business women in Britain as the single most important barrier to their success (and therefore to the contribution they can make to the economy) (Coe 1992).

The rigidity of gender as an organizing principle in the labour market represents a considerable waste in the context of a global economy where levels of technological sophistication are converging and it is the smart use of human resources that gives an economy a competitive edge. The European Commission, concerned about the competitiveness of the Single Market, is beginning to respond to the complexity of equal opportunities and the confusion of individuals' multiple identities in proposing policies to the member states. Hence, the 1997 Amsterdam Treaty, which comes into effect in 1999, extends the principle of equal treatment to all citizens on the basis of ethnic origin and race, religious belief, sexual orientation, disability and age. It also incorporates a strengthened legal basis for positive-action measures for equal treatment of men and women. Finally, it confirms a commitment to pursuing a third model: mainstreaming equality. This approach is more complicated, more ambitious and more of a long-term strategic approach designed to complement the effects of equal treatment and positive action: it is not a substitute for them. But what is mainstreaming?

Essentially mainstreaming invites us to recognize that existing systems and structures are not gender-neutral in their effects. We should analyse how organizational infrastructure and methods of working impact upon different sections of the population differently. It means essentially integrating equal opportunities into all organizations and their policies, programmes and actions. This should not extend simply to recruitment, selection, promotion and training procedures which are internal to an organization, but to how the business of the organization is conducted; the external delivery of goods and services – be it education, media, transport, finance or whatever. Mainstreaming is a highly complex approach, as befits the multi-faceted nature of equal opportunities. In my view, combined with the first two models, mainstreaming has the capacity to make a profound difference not just to women but to all disadvantaged groups (see Rees 1998).

The key element of mainstreaming is recognizing that existing systems and structures are not gender-neutral. The recent introduction by the armed forces of gender-neutral physical tests is a welcome example of an institution seeking to address this. Up until then, in marching for example, the male stride was taken as the norm. Only very tall women could manage it comfortably. Other, perfectly fit, women failed mixed selection tests because marching to the male stride led to pelvic inflammation, and occasionally, to dislocation of the hip! Similarly, job evaluation exercises continue to assist in reducing the pay gap, the use of independent assessment centres have led to more women being promoted, and those occupations and professions where applicants have to present qualifications to enter are more likely to recruit women than those which do not (Crompton 1990).

The European Union Council of Ministers adopted a Communication on integrating equal opportunities into all EU policies, programmes and actions in 1996 (CEC 1996). Equality of opportunity is now a significant element in the reform of the Structural Funds, upon which Wales is so dependent for resources for training, job creation and infrastructure. Local authorities, training and enterprise councils, employers, trade unions, enterprise agencies, further and higher education institutions and so on will all now have to show how they are integrating equal opportunities into their projects if they wish to continue to receive EU funding. Equality of opportunity is being taken seriously, largely because the economic case for equality is currently in the ascendancy.

Mainstreaming as an approach to equal opportunities is endorsed by the UK government, indeed a Cabinet subcommittee on mainstreaming has been set up and all legislation is being gender-audited. Mainstreaming is in line with the Labour Party's politics and policies of 'inclusion'. It has been the main strategic approach of the EOC for many years. Rather than seeking to assist women to fit into square holes, this model of equal opportunities works on making the holes themselves more adaptable. It seeks, at least in my interpretation, to recognize and lay bare the male-centredness of supposedly neutral organizations and redesign them to accommodate difference. It means a dramatic rethink.

Conclusion

Equal treatment in the law is a vital ingredient of equality policies, but it is limited in its effects. Positive-action projects develop good practice but are temporary and piecemeal. If we are to reduce the effect that gender has on determining occupational life-chances, we need a more strategic approach to complement equal treatment and positive action.

Women in many parts of the world are taking an active part in encouraging governments to put mainstreaming on the agenda. In 1995, the Fourth United Nations World Conference on Women in Beijing constructed a Platform of Action for delegates to take back to their countries with mainstreaming equality as one of the ten items on an agenda for action. In Wales, the EOC co-ordinated a coalition of women's organizations to take this forward, including older established bodies such as the Women's Institutes and Merched y Wawr, the 1980s organizations such as the Wales Assembly of Women, Welsh Women's Aid and the Euro Network of Women and 1990s groups such as Mewn Cymru, the black and ethnic minority women's network.

The National Assembly for Wales is a key target for the work of the coalition. It provides a unique opportunity to do things differently, to embed equality into procedures and practices, as well as into policy delivery. The Welsh Assembly looks set to introduce family-friendly ways of organizing itself. But it could go much further and integrate equality into the business procedures, reporting mechanisms and, crucially, the ways of thinking and doing of the Assembly, and through its influence, all the organizations in Wales for which it will have responsibility. This would start to unpick the effects of the gender contract and the disadvantages it spells for women. If this opportunity is seized, the position of women in Wales may well be very different in twenty-five years' time.

References

Aaron, J., Rees, T., Betts. S. and Vincentelli. M. (eds.) (1994). *Our Sisters' Land: The Changing Identities of Women in Wales* (Cardiff: University of Wales Press).

Ashton, S. (1994). 'The farmer needs a wife: farm women in Wales', in J. Aaron, T. Rees, S. Betts and M. Vincentelli (eds.), *Our Sisters' Land: The Changing Identities of Women in Wales* (Cardiff: University of Wales Press).

Blackaby, D., Charles, N., Davies, C., Murphy, P., O'Leary, N. and Ransome, P. (1999). *Women in Senior Management in Wales* (Manchester: Equal Opportunities Commission).

Coe, T. (1992). *The Key to the Men's Club: Opening Doors to Women in Management* (London: Institute of Management).

Commission of the European Communities (1996). *Incorporating Equal Opportunities for Women and Men into all Community Policies and Activities*, Communication from the Commission COM(96) 67 (final) (Luxembourg: Office for Official Publications of the European Communities).

Crompton, R. (1990). 'Credentials and careers', in G. Payne and P. Abbott (eds.), *The Social Mobility of Women* (Basingstoke: Falmer Press).

Crwydren, R. (1994). 'Welsh lesbian feminist: a contradiction in terms?', in J. Aaron, T. Rees, S. Betts and M. Vincentelli (eds.), *Our Sisters' Land: The Changing Identities of Women in Wales*.

EOC (1998). *Facts about Women and Men in Great Britain 1998* (Manchester: Equal Opportunities Commission).

Hutton, W. (1995). *The State We're in* (London: Jonathan Cape).

Humphries, J. and Rubery, J. (eds.) (1995). *The Economics of Equal Opportunities* (Manchester: Equal Opportunities Commission).

Istance, D. and Rees, T. (1994). *Women in Post-Compulsory Education and Training in Wales,* Discussion Paper No. 8 (Manchester: Equal Opportunities Commission).

Land, H. (1980). 'The family wage', *Feminist Review*, 6, 55–77.

Marshall, J. (1995). *Women Managers Moving on: Exploring Career and Life Choices* (London: Routledge).

Morgan, E. (1994). 'Religion ana identity', in J. Aaron, T. Rees, S. Betts and M. Vincentelli (eds.), *Our Sisters' Land: The Changing Identities of Women in Wales.*

Muir, E. (1994). 'The highest honour', in J. Aaron, T. Rees, S. Betts and M. Vincentelli (eds.), *Our Sisters' Land: The Changing Identities of Women in Wales.*

Pfau-Effinger, B. (1994). 'The gender contract and part-time work by women: Finland and Germany compared', *Environment and Planning A*, 26 1,355–76.

Pilcher, J., Delamont, S., Powell, G. and Rees, T. (1988). 'Women's training roadshows and the manipulation of schoolgirls' career choices', *British Journal of Education and Work*, 2/2, 61–6.

Rees, T. (1992). *Women and the Labour Market* (London: Routledge).

Rees, T. (1998). *Mainstreaming Equality in the European Union* (London: Routledge).

Rees, T. (1999). *Women and Work: Twenty-Five Years of Gender Equality in Wales* (Cardiff: University of Wales Press).

Rossilli, M. (1997). 'The European Community's policy on the equality of women: from the Treaty of Rome to the present', *European Journal of Women's Studies*, 4/1, 63–82.

Sainsbury, D. (ed) (1994). *Gendering Welfare States* (London: Sage).

Southall, J. (1990). 'Girls, women and occupational choice', unpublished M.Sc. Econ. Women's Studies Dissertation (University of Wales, Cardiff).

Smith, D. (1987). *The Everyday World as Problematic* (Milton Keynes: Open University Press).

Tomos, A. (1994). 'A Welsh lady', in J. Aaron, T. Rees, S. Betts and M. Vincentelli (eds.), *Our Sisters' Land: The Changing Identities of Women in Wales.*

Walby, S. (1997). *Gender Transformations* (London: Routledge).

Welsh Office (1998). *Women: A Statistical Focus on Wales* (Cardiff: Government Statistical Service).

Williams, C. (1997). 'Colour in the pictures: a Welsh Guyanese childhood', *Planet: The Welsh Internationalist*, 125, 25–30.

Wollstonecraft, M. (1967). *A Vindication of the Rights of Woman* (New York: W. W. Norton, first published 1792).

16 'Race' and Racism: What's Special about Wales?

CHARLOTTE WILLIAMS

Introduction

The Welsh have traditionally regarded themselves as a welcoming and tolerant people viewing with contempt the narrow xenophobia and overt racism of much of English nationalism. Popular images of Wales abound as a country where a mêlée of cultures has settled harmoniously in a type of colour-blind co-operation. In the film *The Proud Valley* there is a vision of the Welsh miners free from any prejudice opening the arms of camaraderie to Paul Robeson in their joint struggles against oppression. More recently a BBC soap opera *Tiger Bay* sought to capture an image of Cardiff as a diverse yet well integrated city. The idea of tolerance as a national characteristic is not exclusive to Wales. The Danes and the Swedes have long prided themselves on their open-mindedness and tolerance in the face of racial and cultural differences. What is increasingly clear is that these culturally sustained notions have a significant bearing on the treatment of 'race'[1] and racism within such societies. It is now acknowledged that there can be neither a generalized theory of racism nor a generalizable set of solutions to the problems of racism. Similarly the *idea* of 'race' will change within a given context and across time. Thus the pursuit of universal explanations has given way to an exploration of the specificities of distinct locales. It has become important to understand the way in which key variables in the social structural arrangements of a society such as class, cultural and other social groupings produce particularized racialized relations. These relationships are also in part determined by aspects of the historical development of particular societies. It is pertinent to ask, therefore, *what is it that is special about Wales in relation to an understanding of 'race' and racism?*

Wales provides an interesting research territory in this respect for a number of reasons. First, the nature and distribution of the black and ethnic minority population of Wales presents some idiosyncratic features. By far the majority of the literature on black and ethnic minorities has been focused on populations of immigrant peoples of relatively recent arrival, such as peoples from the Caribbean and the Indian subcontinent who came to post-war Britain in response to a demand for their labour. This is not the case for Wales, with a significant proportion of its black and ethnic minority population being indigenous to Wales, many families having residence over generations. Secondly, much of the available literature has targeted urban areas with sizeable ethnic minority populations. Relatively little attention has been paid to the effects of rurality, isolation and dispersal, either in respect of the experiences of the minority population or the attitudes of the dominant majority. Thirdly, the idea of tolerance and the strong sense of empathy with oppressed peoples as an expression of the Welsh national character deserves closer inspection. Is it indeed possible to speak of a tolerant/intolerant people as though these were permanent qualities? Finally, 'race' has not entered the political agenda of Wales in the ways in which it has marked English politics. It has not been defined as a problem of Wales and, therefore, there exists a noticeable silence around the issue within the nation. Within Wales there is an obvious neglect or at best complacency about the issue of 'race' and racism that has important implications.

Ethnic Minorities in Wales

The term 'ethnic minority' is not the preserve of peoples of colour. Ethnicity and 'race' are often seen as synonymous but ethnicity is a term that embraces factors such as the language and culture of a people, their sense of common identity, their religion, territory or any combination of these factors. Similarly 'race' is a complex term which has been used with biological connotation to determine groups by perceived physical characteristics (not always skin colour) and more latterly to determine groups on the basis of cultural attributes. The Welsh are an ethnic group that includes people of colour and people of mixed ethnicity. The 1991 Census provided the first comprehensive picture of ethnic minorities in Wales including as it did an 'ethnic question' which produced details of 'non-white groups' and peoples with minority ethnicities such as the Irish, Polish and so on. The term 'ethnic minorities' in this chapter refers to the 'non-white groups' delineated under the census categories 'Black' groups, 'Asian' groups and 'Chinese and Others'. Whilst these categories are in many ways unsatisfactory, they are the single most reliable picture we currently have of the ethnic populations of Great Britain.

In a population of just over 2.8 million, the ethnic minority population of Wales is 41,600. They make up 1.5 per cent of the population of Wales. This compares with Scotland which has a population double that of Wales and where the ethnic minority population of 62,600 forms 1.3 per cent of the total population. Wales is divided up into twenty-two local authority areas and each authority has a minority ethnic population, some quite substantial. For example, the old county of South Glamorgan (now the county boroughs of Cardiff and the Vale of Glamorgan) was ranked eleventh in a list of counties in Great Britain with the largest populations of ethnic minorities with these groups forming 4.8 per cent of the county's population.

For many historical reasons the spatial distribution of the ethnic minority population of Wales is quite unique, with over half of this population living in or proximate to Cardiff. This geographic dispersal reflects a particular historical settlement pattern within the country. Cardiff, a once fast-growing port city, attracted many African seamen at the turn of the century, who subsequently settled in the area attracted by its mild climate. Wales is accordingly home to one of the oldest black communities in Great Britain, surpassed only by Liverpool and Bristol. Fryer (1984) dates the earliest community of black people in Wales at 1870 but notes a much longer history of individual black settlement right across Wales, most notably ex-slaves.

Wales did not experience the post-war immigration waves of ethnic minority groups as is the case elsewhere in Britain, most probably because of the lack of employment opportunities. Hence, with the exception of Newport and Swansea, no substantive settlements of ethnic minority communities has occurred outside

Table 16.1. *Ethnic minorities in the unitary authorities of Wales*

	1991 population (000s)	Ethnic minorities (%)	Actual nos.
Ynys Môn	69.1	0.5	359
Gwynedd	113.3	1.0	1088
Conwy	106.3	0.7	775
Denbighshire	90.6	0.6	573
Flintshire	141.3	0.5	713
Wrexham	121.3	0.8	917
Powys	119.0	0.6	694
Ceredigion	63.1	1.3	809
Pembrokeshire	112.1	0.6	658
Carmarthenshire	168.4	0.6	919
Swansea	223.2	1.6	3467
Neath Port Talbot	138.2	0.7	1019
Bridgend	128.2	0.9	1130
Vale of Glamorgan	117.9	1.3	1564
Cardiff	285.4	6.0	17228
Rhondda Cynon Taff	232.3	0.8	1873
Merthyr Tydfil	59.3	0.8	442
Caerphilly	169.6	0.7	1159
Blaenau Gwent	72.6	0.5	374
Torfaen	90.5	0.7	627
Monmouthshire	78.9	0.7	539
Newport	133.3	3.5	4624
Total Wales	**2835.073**	**1.5**	**41551**

Source: Welsh Office Estimates.

Cardiff. Looking across Wales to the less densely populated areas, the picture is one of relatively small populations of ethnic minorities, with some concentrations in districts containing large educational establishments such as Arfon and Ceredigion. However, there is no county borough in Wales with an ethnic minority population of fewer than 359 people. Those with the lowest percentages are Ynys Môn, Flintshire, Blaenau Gwent and Camarthenshire, all with recorded non-white populations of 0.5 per cent.

Within the broad category 'ethnic minority population' there is some considerable diversity. All the census category 'non-white' groups are represented in Wales. The largest grouping 'Chinese and Others' make up 39.8 per cent of the total ethnic minority population. This compares with 20.8 per cent in England (Owen 1992–5). This group includes the category 'Other-Other', or people

of mixed descent, which is a very significant factor of the demography of ethnic minorities in Wales. The 'Other-Other' group is
the largest single ethnic group in Wales which, along with Merseyside in national statistics, reflects the high incidence of persons of
mixed ethnic origin in the areas of long settlement such as Cardiff
and Liverpool (Owen 1992–5). This higher than national average,
therefore, confirms both long settlement and intermarriage and
indicates a population socialized in and indigenous to the area.
The category 'South Asian' makes up the second largest grouping
within Wales. This group includes peoples from the Indian
subcontinent, Pakistan and Bangladesh. 'Black' groups account for
9,500 of the population of Wales and include Africans, such as the
Somali community of Cardiff, Afro-Caribbeans and those who are
identified as 'Black Other'.

It is increasingly acknowledged, however, that these census
categories are a rather poor indicator of people's ethnic origin.
There has been criticism of the ethnic classifications, confusing as
they do racial, national and ethnic factors. For example, whilst
'white' and 'black' are questionably racial categories based on skin
colour, 'Indian', 'Pakistani' and 'Bangladeshi' are legal nationalities,
'Chinese' is a nationality, an ethnic descriptor and a linguistic group.
The category 'Other-Other' has proved particularly unsatisfactory
in the context of Wales as a signifier of mixed Welsh descent. People
of mixed black and Welsh descent may identify wholly as Welsh in
terms of their ethnicity and therefore may not readily find
appropriate classifications within the categories offered.

In terms of the age and gender structure of the total ethnic
minority population of Wales there is approximately a fifty-fifty
split of children to adults and about a fifty-fifty split of men to
women, although the gender ratio (the number of men to every one
hundred women) indicates that in 1991 Wales displayed relatively
higher ratios of males to females compared with Britain as a
whole. The ethnic minority population of Wales is relatively
young, the median age being 24.6 as compared with the median age
of 36.5 in the entire population of Great Britain. There is just a
tiny proportion of this population in Wales in the retirement age
bracket (3.9 per cent). The overall picture is one of a relatively
youthful and healthy ethnic minority population.

This demographic profile highlights several factors pertinent to
an understanding of 'race' and racism in Wales. The level of

intermarriage/mixed cohabitation and the long settlement of particular minority groups should not be overlooked. Small's (1991) study of Liverpool, which manifests a similar pattern, notes the significance of such factors in the shaping of racialized relations and the importance of noting the changing black experience as such populations now include a significant minority indigenous to the culture of the community and whose identity is shaped in relation to place. The idea of 'black Welsh' is not new, but there is some way to go in developing an understanding of the meanings this terminology carries for the individual and in popular conceptualizations. In the case of Liverpool, Small (1991) rather disappointingly documents an entrenched antipathy to black people of mixed origins and a virulent racial hostility despite length of residence, legal changes and changes in personal experiences. Thus the indigenous nature of a community cannot guarantee racial harmony.

The particular geographical dispersal of the ethnic population of Wales raises the associated issues of territoriality and accessibility. The particular spatial distribution mitigates against the formation of a coherent black community of Wales. It has been noted, in this vein, how spatial concentration of ethnic minority groups increases access to political power and the potential for networks and resistance to racism (Anwar 1986). Arguably, the distribution of the black and ethnic minority populations of Wales has a limiting effect on the opportunity for the articulation of a black community voice. Even Cardiff, which represents the strongest territorial foothold in Wales for such minorities, has not proved to be a strong locus of black and ethnic minority political power. Popular perceptions confirm a strongly held geographical picture of what is essentially seen to be the 'white' Wales and what might be a 'black' Wales. To those in the north of Wales, south Wales from Newtown onward is identified as multi-racial. From the point of view of the Valleys, 'white' Wales includes Swansea and Bridgend and stops at Cardiff city limits. For some in Taff Ely, Cardiff is also seen as very white. The issue of 'race' and concern about racism therefore comes to be seen as having a specific geographical locale within the nation; most usually being seen as a south Wales issue.

Accessibility is also a key factor related to spatial concentrations. That is, access to resources such as public facilities, services and employment opportunities and even protected markets can be safeguarded by the presence of significant numbers. In Wales it is often the case that the perception of small numbers of people from black and ethnic minority backgrounds leads to considerable neglect and 'colour-blind' policies.

Historical Development of 'Racialized Relations' in Wales

Since the last century cultural diversity has been part and parcel of Welsh society. Evans (1991) documents that the 1911 Census showed substantial foreign minorities located within Wales. Much of the locus of this diversity was in south Wales 'which attracted incomers at a rate only surpassed within the Western world by the United States' (Evans 1991, 6). At that time Cardiff came second only to London in the league tables of cities with the highest proportions of those foreign-born, with Swansea coming fourth. By far the majority were Europeans, Italians, Russian Jews, Spaniards, but a significant group of these, some 700, were Africans and West Indians, in the main seamen. This population had risen to 3,000 by April 1919 (Fryer 1984). In contrast to the cosmopolitan cities of Cardiff, Newport and Swansea, rural Wales was relatively homogeneous, predominating in the table of counties for the whole of Britain with the highest proportion of native-born residents. This historical legacy in the spatial distribution of black ethnic minorities has been sustained despite post-war immigration to Britain. There are now several documents reporting on the plight of these black seamen in south Wales, indicating racialized relations in job opportunities and settlement patterns, local prejudice and of course the infamous racial riots of 1919 (Fryer 1984; Robinson 1984; Holmes 1991; Evans 1991). Whilst the historians have largely located the trigger for the riots in conflict over economic resources, most specifically jobs, there is plenty of evidence to suggest widespread prejudice against black people, fear of miscegenation, discrimination and racial hostility (Fryer 1984).

Cardiff does not, however, tell the whole story of race relations in Wales. Two other broad factors indicate something of the Welsh consciousness of 'race' and racism, namely religion and industry. Other aspects of Welsh industrial development indicate a strong connection with the slave trade. In north Wales Richard Pennant of Flint, the first Baron Penrhyn, inherited the largest sugar estate in Jamaica and devoted his plantation profits to the development of the Penrhyn slate quarries, built roads and constructed the Port Penrhyn harbour near Bangor in 1790. In the south, Anthony Bacon secured a contract to provide 'seasoned, able and working negroes' (Fryer 1984, 466) to the governments of several Caribbean islands and with the proceeds of this trade bought 4,000 acres of virgin mineral land near to Merthyr Tydfil where he developed the iron and coal mining, amassing a considerable fortune. Thomas Harris, a Bristol slave merchant, is also known to have invested in the country in 1768, buying an interest in the Dowlais ironworks (Fryer 1984). Coupled with these accounts go a smattering of personal stories or reportage of individual slaves in households in Wales. Wales, therefore, is disassociated neither from imperialism nor from the wider racist ideologies that drove the slave trade and later racisms in Britain.

Perhaps an equally powerful factor in the formulations of attitudes of the Welsh to black people comes from an examination of missionary activity and missionary writings (see, for example, William Hughes 1887; Ann Evans 1818; Margaret Jones 1883). In the Gwyn Jones Annual Lecture 1997, Jane Aaron provides a powerful account of the plethora of missionary activity from Wales to every corner of the Empire and the feast of accounts these travels brought to villages in Wales: 'The imperial fields of the Lord were these villagers' romance, the missionaries their knights in shining armour, and each black convert a pearl that would shine forever in their heavenly crown' (Aaron 1997, 41). Aaron locates this missionary activity not only as part of the imperialist project, but as significant to Wales's concept of itself as holding something of the moral high ground in its distancing from the rabid, exploitative imperialism of the English. She also very pertinently comments:

> I cannot be the only person over forty brought up in a small town in north and west Wales whose first introduction to racial difference came with those wistful Sunday school hymns which sang of faraway children with coloured skins and nobody to speak to them of God. (Aaron 1997, 46)

These historical formulations of the nature of the black community and Wales's relationship to black people are instructive in understanding contemporary attitudes to 'race' and racism in Wales.

The Idea of Tolerance

The strong anti-imperialist sentiment expressed in Wales partly accounts for Wales's imagining of itself as a tolerant nation. Yet the idea of tolerance has several, interlinked strands, the oldest of which is probably the *gwerin* – an almost untranslatable term which refers to a type of community built on mutual understanding, harmony and tolerance amongst a highly cultured, moral and upright people. The *gwerin* is a historical concept but remains central to ideas of the Welsh national character as hospitable, open-minded and essentially internationalist in outlook. The *gwerin*, it is argued, transcends class divisions and by inference has the potential to transcend divisions of 'race' as it is based on the ideas of shared culture. Many of the imaginings of the Welsh rural community are based on the notion of the *gwerin* community, where reciprocity, integration and harmony are the cornerstones of community. This idyll is deeply embedded in the national consciousness. The *gwerin* is, however, problematic. It is based on the idea of cultural homogeneity, clinging to an imagining of sameness and embracing a view of culture as fixed and static rather than fluid and ever changing. Further, it reflects a type of ethnic absolutism that cannot be sustained; that is, a notion of *Welshness* that is rigid, and relates to highly specified attributes that are somehow seen to be immutable. It could be argued that in many areas of Wales the idea of tolerance has not been significantly tested and that racial and ethnic prejudice exist latently in the absence of any visible target population.

The empirical evidence that does exist fails to support this widespread and culturally sustained myth. Evans's (1991) examination of the treatment of immigrants in Wales over a period of 150 years finds two parallel accounts: one appealing to the harmony of the *gwerin* and the other a hard document of intolerance, racial animosity and overt violence in the face of multiculturalism. Wales has on its record books a substantial number of violent ethnic conflicts: anti-Irish outbreaks as early as the 1800s, anti-Jewish and anti-Chinese riots in 1911, anti-Italian animosities and the Cardiff racial rioting of 1919. Nor does the contemporary picture give cause for complacency. In 1995 South Wales Police recorded the third highest number of reported racially motivated incidents in Great Britain, being second only to Manchester in terms of rate of increase. Despite a decrease in the figures since 1996 to around 350 per year, the rates remain uncomfortably high. In 1994 Mohan Kullah, a Gwent shopkeeper, was murdered in a racist attack. One headline, in line with popular nostalgic conceptions of Wales read: 'Race attacks challenge idyll of welcome in the Welsh Valleys' (*Guardian*, 3 December 1994). 'Valleys racism' has become a matter of increasing concern in Wales. In rural areas individuals and families may be isolated in almost wholly white communities and readily become the target of outbursts of racial animosity and xenophobia (Evans 1995). Rural racism is often, however, more hidden than its urban counterpart as victims are reluctant to come forward to the reporting agencies for fear of further victimization. Consequently the low figures recorded by police authorities like North Wales and Dyfed–Powys may well belie a more invidious picture. Many rural areas of Wales have become target areas for recruitment of members to fascist organizations such as the British Nationalist Party (BNP) and Combat 18. The *Western Mail* has reported on efforts to recruit farmers in Wales (7 May 1998). The actions of police authorities themselves have made news in their treatment of racial minorities, with disquiet over the police treatment of the Butetown Two (*South Wales Echo*, 4 August 1998) and the high rates of Stop and Search arrests of black people in Dyfed–Powys (*Guardian*, 27 July 1998). A national survey of twenty-eight police authorities in England and Wales found Dyfed–Powys to have the fourth highest rate for Stop and Search (118 per 1,000) and the sixth highest rate for arrests of black people (206 per 1,000).There is little evidence therefore of the nation being particularly tolerant, either historically or in contemporary Wales.

A further clue to the tenacity of the idea of tolerance in the public consciousness comes from an understanding of the treatment of the majority of Welsh themselves. As a society that has itself been marginalized historically, it is argued that Wales has produced a different understanding and articulation of racial superiority and inferiority. For many in Wales the experience of oppression is salient and this, it is suggested, provides a focus for the understanding of the oppression of others. The concept of 'internal colonialism', first put forward by Michael Hechter (1975), suggests Wales as a society that has been and continues to be the object of English oppression. Hechter has argued that the Celtic Fringe nations were subject to a process of annexation and imperialism in which these different cultural and ethnic groups were deliberately held in a state of economic backwardness with élites from the core culture dominating these internal colonies by controlling key positions within these societies. Hechter's work has been the subject of extensive criticism on several counts (Adamson 1991), not least because of its assumption of a one-way exploitative relationship between England and Wales. What has held more currency, however, is the notion of 'cultural imperialism' which is widely adopted within Wales and very specifically applied to the oppression of Welsh-language speakers (Jones 1974). The language of 'race' is frequently deployed to draw parallels between the oppression of the Welsh and that of black people: for example, Meibion Glyndŵr's popularized expression 'white settlers' in reference to English in-migration. It is not uncommon to hear the expression 'I'm not white, I'm Welsh', which reflects both a distancing from the forces of English imperialism and the articulation of the solidarity this sense of oppression produces. The common enemy of black people and of Welsh people is seen to be the English and in this common oppression there is the potential for empathy, tolerance and solidarity. The logic of this position is that racism is a problem of the English, which leads to a widespread distancing from the responsibility of examining racism within Welsh society.

Yet another sub-theme of the tolerance idea relates to the proletarian solidarity of the mining communities of Wales and the sense of class solidarity won through industrial strife. This is the image presented in the film *The Proud Valley*. Again this is an ambivalent positioning, with history attesting both to strong animosity in the mining communities when threatened by economic migrants and incidences of camaraderie.

These parallels might be empirically unwarranted but the belief in the idea of tolerance does hold important implications. This conflation of minority experiences serves to mask important differences in terms of the historical articulation of the oppression and its contemporary manifestations. We cannot assume that an experience of oppression will automatically lead to such empathy and tolerance. There are many examples of oppressed groups becoming oppressors as political, social and economic climates change. Beyond the level of jibes and stereotypes (Williams 1994) it is fair to say that the Welsh diaspora has not incurred any significant ethnic discrimination.

Further, the claim of tolerance leads to a complacency around issues of race and racism within the nation, powerfully protected by ideas of 'there's no problem here' or a type of racial amnesia that is not productive in terms of recognizing and addressing prejudice, discrimination and inequalities. Finally the claims of tolerance and mutuality are countered by the often overt hostility along the English/Welsh divide and to outsider status as and when it is perceived as a threat to Welsh language and culture.

The Politics of 'Race' and the Politics of Wales

The silencing of 'race' in Wales is not simply the product of the tolerance thesis. Other factors have conspired to produce a situation in Wales where the most ready response to the question 'What is to be done about Welsh racism?' is 'What racism?' 'Race' has not been forced onto the political agenda in Wales in the ways in which it has in England. The geographical distribution of ethnic minority groups and their relative lack of participation in democratic structures in Wales may be one reason. It is clear that the black and ethnic minority populations of Wales do not command a powerful voice as some groups do in England. Nor have they been perceived as a significant internal threat to the nation in the way in which post-war immigration was interpreted in England. There has been no governmental responsibility for addressing these issues or taking them forward within Wales. The Welsh Office has had no statutory brief for ensuring attention to these issues through, for example, systematic monitoring. Until 1995 there was no Commission for Racial Equality (CRE) office operating with a Wales-specific brief and the four Race Equality Councils operated with a localized mandate. No co-ordinated bureaucratic structure existed, therefore, to bring these issues onto a public agenda. Arguably this absence of formalized bodies may have been a symptom and not a cause of the country's malaise.

In Wales, language entered the political discourse in the 1960s with the rise of the Welsh Language Movement and the first Plaid Cymru MP. This was about the same time as 'race' entered the English political agenda and ethnic minority communities were defined as an internal threat to the nation. It can be argued that language politics has served to neutralize the racialization of politics in Wales in the same ways in which the 'National Question' in Scotland shaped the Scottish political agenda (Miles and Dunlop 1986). Similarly in the politics of everyday life the axis of insider/outsider status is more usually defined as Welsh/English than as black/white as in England, reflecting the significant threat to political investments the marker 'English' carries. 'Race' has not been seen as a significant threat to national identity in Wales as it has in England. Welsh xenophobia is more readily applied to the English. All these factors have contributed to a depoliticizing of 'race' in Wales.

Language politics and 'race' have not proved to be cosy bedfellows in the way in which the tolerance arguments would suggest. These key lines of division form an intersection that is at times complementary and at times conflictual. The most notable debates have been around language ring-fencing of jobs and the potential discriminatory effect this might have on other minorities. With this concern in mind the Welsh Language Board and the CRE signed an accord in 1997 which seeks to safeguard against the potential for indirect or unfair discrimination. Other concerns have been focused on the emergence of a new cultural élite within Wales or a 'Welsh class' (Fevre *et al.* 1999) and the potential of this new power grouping to command an advantaged, inaccessible and exclusive community of interest. It is certainly the case that proficiency in the Welsh language commands no small amount of social prestige and economic opportunity in the new linguistically conscious Wales. One can but speculate on the impact of this development on ethnic minority groups in Wales (*Western Mail*, 13 November 1997).

The New Wales

Only a handful of studies provide any insight into the position of black and ethnic minorities in contemporary Wales and many are small-scale localized studies, largely unpublished and focusing on the needs of specific groups (Jaquest 1993; Shah 1993; South Glamorgan 1994; Jamall 1995; Barauh 1997) and gaps in service provision (Coulton and Drury 1994; Robinson 1997). Research aimed at addressing racial discrimination carried out under a local authority initiative in Torfaen County Borough found service delivery largely ignorant of the needs of these communities and failing to carry out the necessary ethnic monitoring (Williams 1998). Disadvantage in terms of job opportunities continues unabated amongst certain minority groups. In 1994 a report by the Equal Opportunities Commission showed male unemployment rates in Cardiff amongst the group 'Black Other' running at 35 per cent and 'Black-Caribbean' at 28 per cent, compared with the white male unemployment rate of 11 per cent. Amongst women from ethnic minority backgrounds the rate is 13.1 per cent, double the rate for white women, 6.6 per cent, with figures rising particularly for women from Pakistani and Bangladeshi backgrounds. Despite a strong phalanx of legislation now requiring authorities to address the needs of minority communities and redress discrimination, the overall picture suggests patterns of disadvantage and discrimination to match those of the black and ethnic minority experience in Britain as a whole. Whether it be employment, housing, education and health or relations with the criminal justice system, the evidence that exists suggests continuing racial disadvantage and a culture of apathy in Welsh public agencies.

The paucity of research extends to studies of black or mixed identity within Wales. There has been very little academic debate addressing the issue of inclusiveness or exclusivity in relation to constructions of Welsh nationhood (Denny et al. 1991; Williams 1998). At the same time, popularized representations are shifting and a political rhetoric of inclusiveness is emerging. In the lead-up to the devolution vote, the BBC *Video Nation* series featured a black young Welsh-speaking woman arguing for home rule. Plaid Cymru has launched a manifesto which boldly states: 'Plaid Cymru stands and fights for every single person in Wales whatever their background, their birthplace, the colour of their skin, their religious belief or the language they speak – be it English or Welsh' (1998, 1).

The success of the devolution vote and the establishment of an Assembly in Wales clearly marks out an opportunity to redress some of the old ills within the nation. A common perception is that once national liberation has been secured democracy will automatically proceed. Inequalities within a nation are often laid at the door of the external oppressor. Such an assumption may be misplaced. The widespread complacency about issues of 'race' and racism within the nation, protected by the often heard slogan 'there is no problem here', will continue to produce the silencing of an open debate on the issues and arrest the development of real commitment to address racism within Wales. Wales now has an opportunity to shift from a national imagining of itself as a tolerant nation to establishing itself as a truly multicultural society.

Note

1. The term 'race' is put in quotation marks throughout this chapter in reference to the debate on the social construction of 'race', as opposed to references that carry a biological connotation.

References

Aaron, J. (1997). 'Slaughter and salvation', *New Welsh Review*, 38, 36–46.

Adamson, D. (1991). *Class, Ideology and the Nation: A Theory of Welsh Nationalism* (Cardiff: University of Wales Press).

Anwar, M. (1986). *Race and Politics* (London: Tavistock).

Barauh, M. (1997). *Making Voices Heard: Access to Services by Black and Ethnic Minority Women*, Mewn Cymru (Cardiff: Equal Opportunities Commission).

Coulton, M. and Drury, C. (1994). 'Policies on ethnic, linguistic and religious needs in Wales under the Children Act 1989', *Social Work and Social Services Review*, 5/1, 47–63.

Denny, D., Borland, J. and Fevre, R. (1991). 'Racism, nationalism and conflict in Wales', *Contemporary Wales*, 4, 150–165.

EOC (1994). *Black and Ethnic Minority Women and Men in Britain* (Manchester: Equal Opportunities Commission).

Evans, A. (1818). *Llythyr Ann Evans* (Bala: R. Saunderson).

Evans, N. (1991). 'Immigrants and minorities in Wales 1840–1990: a comparative perspective', *Llafur*, 4/5, 5–26.

Evans, S. (1995). 'What's to be done about Welsh racism', *Planet*, 110, 114–16.

Fevre, R., Denny, D. and Borland, J. (1999). 'Nation, community and conflict: housing policy and immigration in north Wales', in R. Fevre and A. Thompson (eds.), *Nation, Identity and Social Theory: Perspectives from Wales* (Cardiff: University of Wales Press).

Fryer, P. (1984). *Staying Power: The History of Black People in Britain* (London: Pluto Press).

Guardian (1994). 'Race attacks challenge idyll of welcome in Welsh Valleys' (3 December).

Guardian (1998). 'Police stop blacks eight times more than whites' (27 July).

Hechter, M. (1975). *Internal Colonialism: The Celtic Fringe in British National Development 1536–1966* (London: Routledge & Kegan Paul).

Holmes, C. (1991). *Immigrants, Refugees and Minorities in Britain* (London: Faber & Faber).

Hughes, W. (1887). *The Dark Continent and the Way Out* (Colwyn Bay).

Jamall, A. (1995). 'An assessment of the health and social care needs of black and ethnic minority groups in West Glamorgan', unpublished M.Sc. thesis (University College of Medicine, Wales, Department of Health Education and Health Promotion).

Jaquest, P. (1993). 'Needs survey of ethnic minority adults in West Glamorgan', unpublished report (Swansea: West Glamorgan Race Equality Council).

Jones, Bobi (1974). 'The roots of Welsh inferiority', *Planet*, 22, 53–72.

Jones, M. (1883). *Morocco a'r Hyn a Welais Yno* (Wrexham: Hughes and Son).

Miles, R. and Dunlop, A. (1986). 'The racialisation of politics in Britain: why Scotland is different', *Patterns of Prejudice*, 20/1, 23–32.

Owen, D. (1992–5). *Census Statistical Papers* Nos. 1–10 (Warwick: University of Warwick, Centre for Ethnic Relations).

Plaid Cymru (1998). *The Best for Wales: Plaid Cymru's Programme for the New Millennium* (Cardiff: Plaid Cymru).

Robinson, V. (1984). 'Racial antipathy in south Wales and its social and demographic correlates', *New Community*, 12/1.

Robinson, V. (1997). *Refugees in Wales: An Invisible Minority* (Swansea: University of Wales, Swansea).

Shah, L. (1993). 'An assessment of the health and social care needs of black and ethnic minority populations in South Glamorgan', unpublished M.Sc. thesis (University College of Medicine, Wales, Department of Applied Public Health).

Small, S. (1991). 'Racialised relations in Liverpool: a contemporary anomaly', *New Community*, 17 (4), 511–37.

South Glamorgan Race Equality Council and South Glamorgan Social Services Department (1994). *The Goal Project: Towards a Good old Age*. Annual Report 1994/5 (Cardiff: SGREC).

Western Mail (1998). 'Racist groups target Wales for new recruits' (7 May).

Western Mail (1997). 'Language Act could cause new racism' (13 November).

Williams, C. (1998). *European Year Against Racism: The Torfaen Report* (Torfaen: Torfaen County Borough Council).

Williams, C. (1999). 'Passports to Wales? Race, nation and identity', in R. Fevre and A. Thompson (eds.), *Nation, Identity and Social Theory: Perspectives from Wales* (Cardiff: University of Wales Press).

Williams, K. (1994). 'And even the Welsh?', *Planet*, 104, 16–19.

17 Politics in Wales: A New Era?

ALYS THOMAS

Introduction

Since the wafer-thin majority in favour of the Welsh Assembly in the referendum in September 1997 one question may never be asked again: namely, does 'Welsh politics' exist? This question has certainly provided a significant subtext to the important studies on political history, territorial politics and government and electoral politics in Wales. The starting-point for these studies has often been the question, 'Is Wales different?' An affirmative reply begs further questions: 'In what way is Wales different?' and 'Why is Wales different?' These questions represent the vital link between the institutional developments and policy evolution which have occurred in a Welsh context, and the abstract themes of nation, culture and identity which have produced conflict yet at the same time acted as a political catalyst.

History, Politics and Identity

The history of Wales as a coherent political entity has been ambiguous. Those figures revered in pre-modern history, such as Owain Glyndŵr, might have harboured ambitions regarding a unified territory, but any unity achieved proved transitory. It took the Tudors with their modernizing and centralizing impulses to impose administrative order on Wales through the Act of Union in 1536. Up until the early nineteenth century, Wales, to outside visitors, remained an inaccessible wilderness isolated by geography, language and culture, but the industrial revolution brought demographic change and dynamism to society and divided Wales between the English-speaking industrial and Welsh-speaking rural areas. By the late nineteenth century the establishment of national institutions, such as the University of Wales and the National Library, provided a starting-point for later political institution-building and also represented a nascent national consciousness. During the twentieth century Wales developed a territorial administration and became a recognizable political entity (Jones 1988, 49).

Welsh identity, however, remains elusive. In the early 1980s Balsom's 'Three Wales' model identified Y Fro Gymraeg, Welsh Wales and British Wales, which revealed a fragmented identity reflected in voting patterns (Balsom 1985). From 1922 onwards Labour dominated Welsh politics, but the triumph of Plaid Cymru in a by-election at Carmarthen in 1966 highlighted the emerging coherence of the nationalist dimension to Welsh politics. There can be little doubt that the interest manifested by the Labour leader-ship in creating devolved assemblies for Wales and Scotland was partly a device to counteract nationalist forces. The Labour move-ment was sharply divided over the 1974–9 Labour government's devolution proposals for Wales. Local authorities were largely opposed, there was evidence of cultural cleavage between Welsh-speakers and non-Welsh-speakers, and mutual suspicion between north and south Wales. When the proposals for Wales were so comprehensively rejected in the referendum,[1] the received wisdom was that London-based, centralized government had drastically misread grassroots opinion in Wales. Thus devolution for Wales was deemed to be dead and buried on the overwhelming say-so of the Welsh electorate.

Government and Administration of Wales 1964–1997

In 1964 the Wilson government created a Secretary of State for Wales post with Cabinet status, and Jim Griffiths became the first incumbent. There has been a certain amount of dispute about the extent to which the creation of the Welsh Office was an exercise in rationalizing administration and recognition of distinct Welsh sentiment (Randall 1972), and the perception that it represented an *ad hoc* concession which offered the minimum powers necessary to satisfy demands. At the outset its powers were limited, including those inherited from the Department of Housing and Local Government, the Department of Transport and some related to regional economic planning. Responsibilities over health were acquired in 1969, and primary and secondary education in 1970. In 1975 industry functions were added, along with agriculture and further and higher education in 1978. The powers granted to the Welsh Office allowed 'ample opportunity for further symbolic gestures by periodic transfer of functions', and it could also be anticipated that future Secretaries of State would strive for increased powers and greater political clout in terms of spending capacity and in the Cabinet (Thomas 1987, 145).

The Secretary of State

Of significant importance in the development of the Welsh Office has been the approach of the individual occupants of the office of Secretary of State. Jim Griffiths was a veteran politician in the twilight of his career. George Thomas's occupancy saw a Labour Secretary of State in direct confrontation with nationalists and linguistic activists at the end of the 1960s, when the Investiture of the Prince of Wales at Caernarfon attracted protests. Thomas himself felt that his antipathy towards devolution led Harold Wilson first to appoint him as Secretary of State in 1968 to 'slow down the bandwagon', and then to replace him with John Morris when Labour regained power (Thomas 1985). Morris's own tenure was taken up with steering the devolution legislation through Parliament, although the Welsh Development Agency, Development Board for Rural Wales and Land Authority for Wales were also established during this period.

In 1979 Nicholas Edwards became Secretary of State, occupying the post until 1987. His period in office was dominated by the impact of industrial restructuring. From 1987 until 1997 there followed a series of incumbents who sat for English seats. This was not a new phenomenon, as Peter Thomas, Secretary of State between 1970 and 1974, had sat for an English seat. Peter Walker's appointment by Mrs Thatcher was widely interpreted as a deliberate humiliation that she fully expected him to reject. In his memoirs, however, Walker reported that he only agreed to accept the position if he was given a 'free hand', which the Prime Minister conceded (Walker 1991). This was apparently reflected in the broadly interventionist approach to economic development initiatives which was emulated by his successors, David Hunt and William Hague, although the bone-dry John Redwood provided an exception to the rule. The constant during most Conservative incumbency was Wyn Roberts, who served as Junior Minister and Minister of State between 1979 and 1994 and who was certainly influential in areas such as Welsh-language policy and the inclusion of Welsh in the National Curriculum (Wigley 1993). John Major was reported to have put the question 'Does Wyn think it is important?', when confronted with Welsh issues (Williams 1998, 49). By the end of the Conservative administration Secretaries of State were being described as viceroys whose role was no longer to represent Wales in the Cabinet but to represent the Cabinet in Wales (Osmond 1995).

A distinct policy process?

Evidence for a distinct Welsh political context may be found in the presence of policy actors such as Welsh-based pressure groups. Political parties acknowledge the Welsh context in terms of their administration and production of Welsh manifestos at election time. The real question, however, is about the distinctiveness of policy in Wales. The parties (with the exception of Plaid Cymru), pressure groups and the Welsh Office may present a Welsh face but it has been a question of dispute as to how far policy in Wales has been distinct. Institutional distinctiveness has not necessarily led to distinctiveness in terms of policy (Griffiths, 1995).

Successive Secretaries of State strove to reconcile their position as a member of a Conservative administration, with overseeing a territory which voted for the opposition and which made claims to cultural distinctiveness. One way in which incumbents could have squared this circle was through exploitation of the discretionary powers available to the Secretary of State in terms of deciding spending priorities and use of secondary legislation. The Secretary of State had 'absolute discretion' within the block rules of the Barnett formula but 'the real issue is whether a Secretary of State has the powers to exercise that statute' (Thain and Wright 1995, 320–1) and, moreover, whether he had the will to exercise such powers. It should not be forgotten that the Secretary of State was bound by the principle of Cabinet responsibility.

It remains questionable whether recent Secretaries of State have chosen to exercise discretion in policy-making. The Welsh Office itself described most of its policies as 'refined to meet particular Welsh needs but . . . broadly similar to those in England', notable exceptions being Welsh-language policy and the Valleys Initiative (House of Commons Welsh Affairs Committee 1993). Nevertheless, Walker and Hunt made much of their interventionist, 'wet' Conservative credentials. Hunt argued that Wales did not need its own assembly because it had the Welsh Office (House of Commons Debates 1991). Griffiths (1995) tested the extent of Welsh divergence in terms of economic and urban regeneration policy and found that the Welsh experience did not significantly diverge from that of England and noted that, wherever possible, the private sector was encouraged to take a leading role. If attention is focused away from particular events and personalities (Griffiths rightly points out that much of the 'hype' about policy exceptionalism came from the mouths of the Secretaries of State themselves), and more towards the structure of government in Wales, there is little evidence to support policy exceptionalism. Paradoxically, there is evidence that John Redwood was more proactive in flexing his discretionary muscles. His political adviser, Hywel Williams, claims that a speech critical of health policy, which enraged Health Secretary Virginia Bottomley, 'was not a random event but an exercise in hype and a raid on Bottomley's fiefdom' (Williams 1998, 54–5). Redwood, something of a 'policy wonk', used his incumbency in Wales to make speeches across a broad sweep of policy areas and to test out ideas.

Studies of particular policy areas have thrown up some evidence of Welsh 'difference'. Sir Wyn Roberts claims that a distinctive Welsh education system was developing from the late 1980s (Roberts 1995, 3). This is supported by Farrell and Law who found that Welsh education was distinct from education in England, in that it had exceptional policies and that concurrent policies had a different impact (Farrell and Law 1998, 65). Trends in local government have become increasingly distinctive. Boyne *et al.* (1991) found important differences between English and Welsh local government, but many of these were of rather a negative character pertaining to issues of political culture related to one-party domination in many parts of Wales, and Madgwick *et al.*'s study of Cardiganshire politics revealed the persistence of the independent tradition in local government in rural Wales (1973). The process of local government reorganization in Wales was carried out separately from England, but ironically the fact that the process was different from England, where a Local Government Commission sat, meant that Wales received a uniform system of unitary local authorities which the government failed to secure for England (Thomas 1994).

The evolution of Welsh-language policy during the 1980s and 1990s under the Conservative administration developed in an *ad hoc* manner, moving from the voluntarism outlined by Nicholas Edwards in his 1981 Llanrwst speech, through Peter Walker's 'eight wise men' in the late 1980s and avowed reluctance to use the 'big stick of legislation', to the introduction of the Welsh Language Act in 1993 and the creation of a statutory language board. Conservative incumbents used Welsh-language policy as a means of political accommodation. Given the popular opposition to the impact of Thatcherite policies, steady decimation of Conservative support and the growing perception of a 'democratic deficit', supportive gestures in the direction of the language were seen as a means of making the Conservative government appear receptive to the national aspirations of the Welsh without making concessions in key policy areas (Thomas 1997).

The important question, however, as the reality of devolution approaches, will be how Welsh policy development will become more independent from Whitehall and the likely emergence of a more distinctive policy agenda. A comparison of a Welsh Office document with its Whitehall counterpart will often show evidence of 'topping and tailing' – basically the same document but with some Welsh references, an introduction from the Secretary of State and 'cymricized' cover. It may be predicted that this is likely to change.

Territorial Management in Parliament

Territorial management has been one of the 'accommodating strategies' employed by central government in response to demands from nationalist-orientated opinion in Wales and Scotland (Mitchell 1996, 32). Mechanisms for territorial management include the Welsh Grand Committee, which consists of all Welsh MPs, the Welsh Affairs Select Committee, which reflects party balance in the House of Commons, and Welsh questions.

Welsh Grand Committee business includes oral questions to ministers, ministerial statements and 'short debates'. It may also consider any public bill for the equivalent of a second reading debate, and any other matters relating exclusively to Wales which may be referred to it by the House of Commons. Since 1995 it has also had powers to call ministers for scrutiny.

Standing Order 86, which dates back to 1907, requires that all Welsh MPs should be entitled to sit on the committees established to scrutinize specific Welsh legislation. There has been very little legislation which has related to Wales alone, but recent years have seen the passage of the Welsh Language Bill (1993) and the Welsh Local Government Bill (1994). On both occasions Standing Order 86 was suspended by the Conservative government which asserted that the Parliament is that of the United Kingdom as a whole, and that as Welsh members are entitled to attend debates and vote on issues pertaining to England, English MPs should be entitled to do the same with regard to Wales. The opposition argued that Welsh MPs would always be a minority in Parliament and the entire *raison d'être* of procedures such as Standing Order 86 is to protect minority territorial interests in Parliament (Thomas 1995).

Welsh question time occurs once a month, when oral questions may be put to the Secretary of State and other Welsh Office ministers. There is also a Welsh Day set aside for debate on Welsh issues which is generally scheduled around 1 March. In early 1996 opposition MPs drew attention to the fact that English Conservative MPs were tabling questions during Welsh question time, with the result that Welsh members were prevented from a proper scrutiny of the Secretary of State. On 22 January 1996 six of the eleven questions put before William Hague were from English Conservatives (*Western Mail*, 23 January 1996).

Existing mechanisms for territorial management became strained under the Conservative administration, as a dwindling number of Welsh Conservative members meant that English MPs had to make up numbers on the Select Committee and people the green benches at Welsh questions. Mechanisms designed to accommodate minority territorial interests were actually highlighting their subordination to the will of the government and this contributed to the criticism of the perceived 'democratic deficit' in Wales under the Conservatives.

Table 17.1. *1997 general election results in Wales*

Party	% vote	MPs
Conservative	19.6	0
Labour	54.7	34
Liberal Democrat	12.4	2
Plaid Cymru	9.9	4
Referendum Party	2.4	0
Others	1.0	0
Turnout	73.6	40

The Political Parties, Elections and Welsh Identity

The 1997 general election saw the Conservatives lose all their seats in Wales (see Table 17.1), a feat achieved earlier in the century in the Liberal landslide of 1906. This represented the nadir of a progressive decline since the Conservative Party won fourteen of thirty-eight Welsh seats in the 1983 general election. Closer examination of electoral trends since 1970, however, reveals a stability which is not immediately obvious (Balsom 1998a, 13). The Conservatives in Wales have been casualties of the first-past-the-post electoral system. Certainly, the late 1980s and 1990s witnessed a decline in Conservative support but the party has retained its status as the second largest party in Wales behind Labour in general elections, consistently attracting between a quarter and a third of the votes. The combination of the Referendum Party presence and low turnout resulted in a decisive dip in the Conservative vote in 1997, which proved devastating to the remaining MPs and 'the loss of all seats exaggerates the real decline in support' (Balsom 1998a, 15). The massive swing to Labour nationally gave the party over 50 per cent of the vote for the first time since 1970, prompting gains in long-standing Conservative seats such as Clwyd West and Cardiff North.

The Conservative Party has historically been perceived as the 'English' party in Wales, in spite of initiatives as far back as the 1950s to amend this perception, such as creating a Minister of Welsh Affairs. The 'three Wales model', however, would place most seats held by the Conservatives over the years within 'British Wales'. That is, in those parts of Wales where fewer people identify themselves as Welsh rather than British or English. Despite Welsh packaging (a manifesto, a logo and so forth) it was difficult for the party to assert its Welshness when the apparent 'leader' of the Welsh party was an English MP, as was the case between 1987 and 1997. With the wipe-out of May 1997, however, and the creation of the National Assembly, the Conservatives in Wales appear to be taking serious stock. In autumn 1998 Rod Richards won a leadership contest held on the basis of 'one member, one vote' and during the campaign placed stress upon the need for the party to present a Welsh face to the electorate. Although the Conservatives had warned that Labour's plans for the Welsh Assembly could endanger the Union, it is difficult to escape the fact that the Welsh Conservatives seemed to be gearing up to the prospect with something approaching enthusiasm. As one Conservative noted: 'this prize is there for the Conservatives to win. However, the power of initiative will not rest with us for long unless we adopt a policy agenda tuned to the needs of Wales and establish a strong organisational structure' (Melding 1998, 23).

For the Labour Party the path towards the Assembly elections in May 1999 and the subsequent twelve months appeared straight-forward, with Ron Davies, the Secretary of State for Wales, having beaten off a challenge from Rhodri Morgan in a special leadership contest held in September 1998. Less than a month later, however, Ron Davies resigned from the government due to a self-confessed 'error of judgement' on Clapham Common, and for a remarkable fortnight the full glare of the metropolitan media was turned on Welsh politics. Events unfolded in rapid succession. Alun Michael, a Home Office minister, was appointed Secretary of State and immediately speculation began as to whether he would run for the leadership of the Assembly. Rhodri Morgan indicated that he would stand again. Within a week Michael announced that he would be seeking selection as a candidate for the Assembly and would wish to contest the leadership. The parameters for a bruising contest were put in place in which Michael was portrayed as the candidate who had been 'parachuted' into Wales against the grassroots favourite and 'off-message' Morgan. Michael could point out, with justifiable defensiveness, that his Welsh credentials were perfectly sound, and Morgan could point to an admirably loyal voting record in the Commons. Nevertheless, 'Blairite versus Maverick' is what the contest had become. This was partly to do with the press interest in what was perceived as the 'control freak' tendencies of the party leadership being exercised elsewhere in the UK, but the emergence of a group of leading Labour figures with the suggestion that Alun Michael should take the leadership as a 'unity' candidate, with Rhodri Morgan and another potential contender, Wayne David, as deputies, raised the political temperature even further. Morgan, sustaining the lead in various polls, was not responsive and eventually the Welsh Executive decided on an electoral college system and delayed the contest until February 1999. Alun Michael was in due course elected, gaining 52.68 per cent of the electoral-college vote to Rhodri Morgan's 47.32 per cent. However, the breakdown within the individual sections saw Alun Michael winning the unions and affiliated organizations section on 63.96 per cent of the vote and the MPs, MEPs and prospective National Assembly candidates section on 58.43 per cent. Rhodri Morgan won the constituency section with 64.35 per cent. Despite concerns voiced by sections of the party in the course of the campaign about the consultation procedures of individual unions within section two, Rhodri Morgan accepted the result but declared that 'I don't feel like a loser. A runner-up? Yes. A loser? Never' (*Western Mail*, 20 February 1999).

The episode was dramatic and remarkable because it seemed to underline how underprepared the Labour Party in Wales, as well as on a UK basis, was for the inevitable impact of having a devolved Assembly and fighting separate elections. This would have become increasingly clear once the Assembly was up and running, but Davies's abrupt departure from government accelerated the process. Blair had given early warning that he did not fully appreciate the implications of devolution for the organization of the Labour Party. In 1996, for example, he announced that Labour had no plans to vary taxation upwards, in the event of a Scottish Parliament being established. It did not seem to occur to him that potential MSPs and the Scottish Labour Party are increasingly likely to want to stand on their own manifesto. The Labour Party may have been able to exert some form of central vetting of candidates and manifesto in the run up to the first Scottish and Welsh elections, but it is unlikely to be sustainable beyond then.

The Labour Party has, with some justification, been able to describe itself as 'the party of the people of Wales', due to its overwhelming dominance from 1922 onwards. The party has been historically divided on the issue of Welsh devolution, with many Labour Party members nurturing a strong antipathy to nationalism and viewing a Welsh Assembly as a 'slippery slope' towards separatism. Many of these attitudes changed in the 1980s due to the reality of eighteen years in opposition, but also due to generational change. Given Labour's dominance of Welsh politics any devolution proposals would have to originate within the party, and after the third Conservative election victory in 1987 many Welsh Labour politicians felt the need to reassess the question of an elected Welsh body. A fourth victory in 1992 led one Welsh MP to comment, 'Wales has its nationalist party and so does Scotland. We can now see clearly that England does as well' (*Western Mail*, June 1992). The aftermath of Thatcherism impacted on the Labour Party in Wales in that the 'Welsh Wales' identity, focused on the pit or steelworks and rooted in Labour politics, suffered a crisis of confidence. After a century of asserting its modernity against a traditional Welsh-speaking, rural identity, it found itself labelled as equally anachronistic in the brave new Thatcherite world.

The first Assembly elections on 6 May 1999 delivered possibly the biggest shake-up the Labour Party in Wales had ever seen. Plaid Cymru, dogged in the past by its inability to break out of the traditional Welsh-speaking areas in general elections, succeeded in winning such totemic seats as the Rhondda and Islwyn and ended up with seventeen Assembly seats. The Liberal Democrats and the Conservatives both gained under AMS, winning five and ten seats respectively, despite seeing little change in their share of the vote since the 1997 general election. Labour emerged as the largest party with twenty-eight seats but failed to win the outright majority widely anticipated. Initial post-mortems revealed that many Labour voters in the heartlands had either stayed at home or voted for Plaid Cymru. Detailed analysis in the future will no doubt reveal the reasons for this. Part of the Plaid Cymru vote may have been a manifestation of a willingness to switch votes in 'second order' elections.[2] However, there were indicators of a stronger disenchantment with Labour which may have been related to the fallout from the leadership election. Low turnout was also a factor, the overall turnout for Wales a disappointing 46 per cent, but there were sharp variations between constituencies, with Plaid strongholds in the west seeing turnouts around the 60 per cent mark while some seats in the north-east saw percentage turnouts in the low thirties.

It may be anticipated that a distinctive party system will develop now that the National Assembly is in place. AMS, in denying Labour a majority and delivering seats to the smaller parties in Wales, has already presented a challenge to a monolithic political culture. However, the new voting system throws up some important challenges for the parties in terms of candidate selection and the question of how the Welsh electorate will continue to educate themselves about the system and experiment with such phenomena as 'ticket splitting' (Balsom 1998b, 21). Creative tensions will inevitably arise between parties in Wales and their central organizations and for the immediate future this appears to be a bigger challenge for the Labour Party in Wales, particularly as the administration in Wales will have to work with the other parties on an issue-by-issue basis if it is to govern effectively.

New Wales, New Politics?

The closeness of the referendum result[3] endorsing the Labour Party's devolution proposals (Welsh Office 1997) is of no little significance for the future of the Assembly, and Ron Davies was not slow in indicating the need for inclusivity and reconciliation. The creation of a National Assembly for Wales on the threshold of the twenty-first century holds the prospect of the birth of a new era for politics in Wales. A sixty-member Assembly will take over the tasks previously carried out by the Secretary of State and his ministers. Eighteen functions will be transferred from the Welsh Office to the Assembly, and decisions previously made about spending 'inside the Secretary of State's head' will be made by the National Assembly. A major task for the Assembly, therefore, will be deciding spending priorities. It will have at its disposal the block grant that falls within the responsibility of the Secretary of State for Wales under the terms of the Barnett formula.

Although Whitehall and Westminster will retain primary legislative powers with respect to Wales, the National Assembly has secondary legislative powers so that anything currently delegated to the Secretary of State under terms of primary legislation will be transferred. How far the Assembly will want to take advantage of this power is, at this stage, a matter of conjecture, but it can be predicted that the procedures for subordinate legislation will mean that the Assembly will take longer to enact secondary legislation than a Secretary of State. Welsh policy may, then, diverge from that of England simply due to the process itself.

Given that primary legislative powers remain at Westminster, an important issue is how the Welsh Office remains in the Whitehall/Westminster policy-making loop. The supposed solution to this problem is the negotiation of concordats between the Welsh Office and individual government departments. They have no legal basis, are not mentioned in the Act and were described by Ron Davies as 'ground rules for administrative co-operation and exchange of information' (House of Commons 1998). There are questions about how these will operate in practice. Concordats are a means of mediation between civil servants and are there to regulate administrative arrangements. If they fail it will become a political problem, requiring political resolution.

The cross-party National Assembly Advisory Committee (NAAG) was influential in persuading the government to support an amendment allowing for the Executive Committee to adopt a 'cabinet'-style organization (that is, appointed by the First Secretary) for the Assembly rather than the committee style proposed in the White Paper. It was hoped that the party balance in the Committee would provide an important 'check' on the Executive (NAAG 1998, para. 4.4). The National Assembly decided in its early days that the Committees would be made up of nine members, including the relevant Assembly Secretary and Chair. The party ratio in each Committee is four Labour, three Plaid Cymru and the Conservatives and Liberal Democrats with one apiece. The role envisaged for the committees would seem to combine elements of scrutiny and policy development through consultation with a 'wider Wales'. The fact that some committee chairmen, however, will be drawn from minority parties raises important questions about what sort of relationship will develop with the relevant Assembly Secretary, particularly in light of a minority Labour administration.

The advent of the National Assembly has produced high-minded expectations of a new inclusive politics, and the hope that the new institution will be free of the worst faults associated with Westminster and represent a break with the monolithic political culture of the past. Thus, it should be open and consensual, as well as representative of the Welsh population. These are aspirations expressed by many involved in the preparation process. The task for future students of Welsh politics will be to assess how far these aspirations have been fulfilled.

Conclusion

This chapter was written at a time when developments in Welsh politics lay on the cusp of far-reaching change. The opening paragraph noted that the recurrent questions posed by political scientists and political historians about Wales have been 'Is Wales different?' and 'Why is Wales different?' Developments in the twentieth century point to increased differentiation in politics, more often than not in response to a need to recognize Welsh identity in the conduct of political life. The elusive nature of Welsh identity, however, has meant that, more often than not, change has come about on an *ad hoc* basis as a response to the demands from different groups in Welsh society. The *petit oui* of the referendum result indicated the cautious approach of the people of Wales to the prospect of an Assembly. Nevertheless, that caution has brought with it difference. While much of the debate about devolution in Wales was conducted on the back of developments in Scotland, the upshot has been that Wales has emerged with a unique devolved settlement. The National Assembly will have important powers with regard to prioritizing spending and in terms of secondary legislation, but unlike Scotland it will not have primary legislative powers. This raises important questions about the future of intergovernmental relations between the National Assembly and Whitehall and Westminster. Further questions remain about how 'civil society' will develop in Wales once the Assembly is in place and how the political parties will adapt to the new level of government. The future is something of a blank page, but one thing is certain: political scientists will no longer be asking '*Is Wales different?*'

Notes

1. Results of the 1979 Referendum on devolution: Yes 20.3%, No 79.7%, turnout 58.8%.

2. In September 1998 an NOP/HTV poll put the Labour Party on 50% and Plaid Cymru on 24%.
3. Results of 1997 Referendum: Yes 50.3%, No 49.7%, turnout 50.3%.

References

Balsom, D. (1985). 'The three Wales model', in J. Osmond (ed.), *The National Question Again? Welsh Political Identity in the 1980s* (Llandysul: Gwasg Gomer).

Balsom, D. (1998a). 'The political year in Wales: a landslide and a close run thing', in D. Balsom (ed.), *The Wales Yearbook* (Cardiff: HTV).

Balsom, D. (1998b). 'The first elections', in J. Osmond (ed.), *The National Assembly Agenda* (Cardiff: Institute of Welsh Affairs).

Boyne, G. A., Griffiths, P., Lawton, A. and Law, J. (1991). *Local Government in Wales* (York: Joseph Rowntree Foundation).

Byrne, I. (1998). 'Voting for the Assembly', *Welsh Agenda: The Journal of the Institute of Welsh Affairs* (Winter), 17–19.

Farrell, C. M. and Law, J. (1998). 'Regional policy differences in the UK: education in Wales', *Public Policy and Administration*, 13/2, 54–67.

Griffiths, D. (1995). *Thatcherism and Territorial Politics* (Aldershot: Avebury).

House of Commons (1991). *Debates: Debate on Local Government Reorganisation in Wales* (Hansard, 17 July).

House of Commons (1998). *Written Answers: Reply to Question 32534* (Hansard, 2 February).

House of Commons Welsh Affairs Committee (1993). *The Work of the Welsh Office*, First Report, Minutes of Evidence, Memorandum WO8 (London: HMSO).

Jones, B. J. (1988). 'The development of Welsh territorial institutions: modernization theory re-visited', *Contemporary Wales*, 2, 47–61.

Madgwick, P. J., with Griffiths, N. and Walker, V. (1973). *The Politics of Rural Wales: A Study of Cardiganshire* (London: Hutchinson).

Melding, D. (1998). 'Choice between a new start or more misery', *Welsh Agenda: The Journal of the Institute of Welsh Affairs* (Winter), 22–3.

Mitchell, J. (1996). 'Conservatives and the changing meaning of Union', *Regional and Federal Studies*, 6/1, 30–44.

National Assembly Advisory Group (1998). *Recommendations on the National Assembly: Report to the Secretary of State* (Cardiff: HMSO).

Osmond, J. (1995). *Welsh Europeans* (Bridgend: Seren Books).

Randall, P. (1972). 'Wales in the structure of central government', *Public Administration*, 50, 352–72.

Roberts, W. (1995). *Fifteen Years at the Welsh Office*, Welsh Political Archive Lecture (Aberystwyth: National Library of Wales).

Thain, C. and Wright, M. (1995). *The Treasury and Whitehall: The Planning and Control of Public Expenditure 1976–1993* (Oxford: Clarendon Press).

Thomas, A. (1994). 'The myth of consensus: the Local Government Review in Wales', *Contemporary Wales*, 7, 47–60.

Thomas, A. (1995). 'Hardliners riding for a fall', *Parliamentary Brief*, 3/5, 59–60.

Thomas, A. (1997). 'Language policy and nationalism in Wales: a comparative analysis', *Nations and Nationalism*, 3/3, 323–44.

Thomas, G. (1985). *Mr Speaker: The Memoirs of Lord Tonypandy* (London: Harmondsworth).

Thomas, I. (1987). 'Giving direction to the Welsh Office', in R. Rose (ed.), *Functional Ministries* (Oxford: Clarendon Press).

Walker, P. (1991). *Staying Power* (London: Bloomsbury).

Welsh Office (1997). *A Voice for Wales: The Government's Proposals for a Welsh Assembly*, Cm. 3718, (Cardiff: HMSO).

Wigley, D. (1993). *Dal Ati*, Cyfrol 2, Cyfres Y Cewri 10 (Caernarfon: Gwasg Gwynedd).

Williams, H. (1998). *The Guilty Men* (London: Arium Press, 1998).

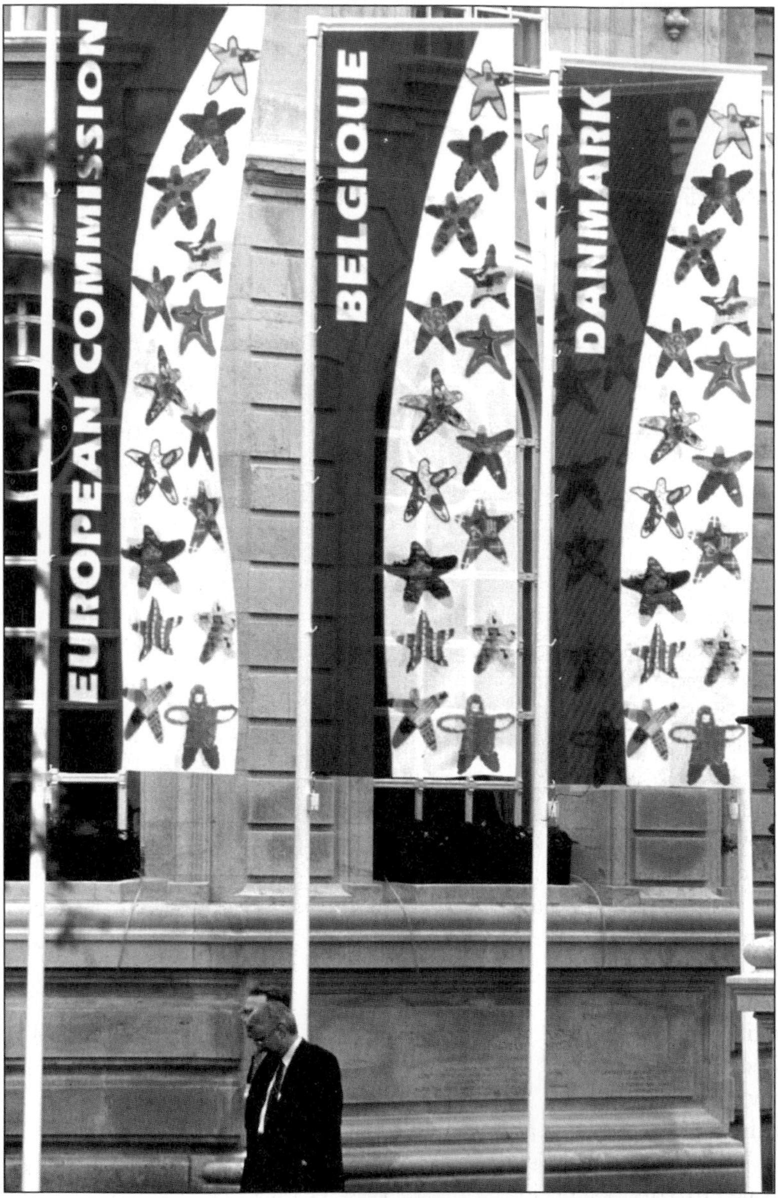
EUROPEAN COMMISSION
BELGIQUE
DANMARK

18 Wales in Europe

Introduction

Speaking at a meeting of the Cardiff Business Club in early 1990, Roy Jenkins (now Lord Jenkins of Hillhead) told his audience that the attitude of the government of the United Kingdom towards the European Union (EU)[1] could be likened to the individual who stands watching a train pulling out of the station, then jumps on at the very last minute only to complain that all the first-class seats are already taken. For Lord Jenkins, a former president of the European Commission, the consequence of the policy of the then Conservative administration was that the UK was 'in danger of missing out' (*South Wales Echo*, 13 February 1990) on having a constructive influence over developments unfolding at the level of the EU. The stance assumed by central government in relation to the EU casts a long shadow over the whole of the UK. In Wales, however, since the late 1980s, many of the main political parties and economic institutions have sought to portray Wales as having its own views on the question of membership of the EU. Formal representation of Welsh interests in the EU nevertheless continues to be directed through the government of the United Kingdom. The extent to which we will see a greater degree of flexibility in the existing arrangements is, however, an issue that will undoubtedly become the subject of growing discussion as we become more aware of the role the National Assembly will assume in relation to this area of policy-making.

This chapter offers an overview of some of the main issues at stake in this discussion. It begins by examining the mechanisms through which Welsh interests are represented within the various institutional forums that comprise the EU. The discussion moves on to examine the evolution of the changing attitudes in Wales towards the EU. The chapter concludes with a consideration of some of the issues that will be central to Wales's future relations with the EU.

Representing Wales in the EU

It is indicative of the growing strength of the pro-EU lobby in Wales that there have, on occasion, been clashes of opinion between central government and those parties who would like more manœuvrability when it comes to promoting Welsh interests in the EU, as separate from broader British concerns. One of the most significant of these clashes came in 1994, when John Redwood, then Conservative Secretary of State for Wales, challenged the Welsh Development Agency (WDA) over its use of the slogan 'Wales in Europe'. Reinforcing the formal position of central government, the Secretary of State reminded the WDA that as part of the United Kingdom Wales did not officially have a separate voice in the EU. Even with the establishment of the National Assembly in 1999, the principal mechanism through which Wales, as a constituent part of the UK, will be represented in the EU will be through the deeds of central government ministers. *A Voice for Wales* (1997), the government White Paper that outlined the blueprint for the National Assembly, argued that devolution would bring people in Wales a 'strong voice in Europe'. The present form of the political relations between Westminster and Cardiff ensures, however, that the voice of the government of the UK will remain the one that it is heard in the most powerful institutions in the EU. A report by the Constitution Unit starkly explains the ramifications of this situation, stating that Wales's membership of the UK is the factor which 'shapes all of the current relationships which Wales and Welsh institutions . . . maintain with the European Union' (1996, 103).

In the Council of Ministers, the chief legislative institution of the EU, Wales is represented by the appropriate central government minister. Thus, in matters of defence or general economic affairs, for example, Wales, like the rest of the UK, will be represented by the Secretary of State for Defence and the Chancellor of the

Exchequer, respectively. Circumstances in which the Secretary of State for Wales would act as the 'lead' representative of the government of the UK are rare. The Welsh Affairs Select Committee at Westminster (1995) reported that even where Secretaries of State for Wales had a right to attend sittings of the Council of Ministers, this was a privilege which had been under-utilized. As far as Wales is concerned, it seems unlikely that this mode of representation will change radically for the foreseeable future. In spite of comparisons made by the Wales Labour Party (1995), Plaid Cymru (Jones 1996) and the Institute of Welsh Affairs (Gray and Osmond 1997) among others, between Wales and the kind of autonomy that regional representatives exercise in Belgium or Germany, a similar role continues to remain firmly on the wish-list of regional representatives in the UK.

Representatives from Wales perform roles of varying degrees of importance in relation to some of the other institutions of the EU. Formal relations with the European Commission, the powerful executive body of the EU, are managed by the Welsh Office. Until the National Assembly is functioning, it will be through ministers and civil servants in the Welsh Office, particularly its European Affairs Division, that Welsh European business will be addressed. Presently it is through the Welsh Office that links are maintained with the Permanent Representation of the United Kingdom (UKREP) to the EU, the corps of UK civil servants responsible for monitoring the interests of the UK in relation to the European Commission. The Welsh Affairs Select Committee (1995) noted, however, that contact between the Welsh Office and the UKREP has been limited.

More direct involvement of Welsh politicians in the affairs of the EU rests with the five Welsh Members of the European Parliament. Although the MEPs cannot speak in a formal capacity for Wales, it would be short-sighted to maintain that the high profiles that a number of these politicians have within the European Parliament do not serve indirectly to promote the interests of the separate regions of Wales. Indeed, a study by Loughlin (1997) notes that policy actors in Wales viewed Welsh MEPs as being of greater importance for the development of the country than Welsh MPs at Westminster.

Welsh politicians are also members of the Committee of the Regions (COR), a body established under the 1992 Treaty of the

European Union. The COR acts as a forum for representatives of regional and local government to have an input in the policy-making process in the EU. The status of Welsh participation in the COR would undoubtedly be buttressed if in future the two members (and two alternate members) are representatives of a devolved government, rather than nominated representatives of local government. The COR is nevertheless the weakest institutional link in the policy-making process in the EU.

Elsewhere, representatives from Wales are involved in some of the growing number of 'Eurogroups' that operate across the EU. These networks bring together political representatives, often from local and regional government, who share common areas of interest, such as in the case of the Assembly of European Regions. The role of Welsh representatives in various 'Eurogroups' and in the COR are examples of how lobbying Welsh interests can be conducted beyond the purview of the UK government, but it is important to maintain a sense of perspective in this regard. These roles are undoubtedly of importance in improving general awareness throughout the EU of the situation in Wales, but for the immediate future central government will remain the most authoritative point of contact for those seeking to press their case in the EU (McAteer and Mitchell 1996).

Beyond these official channels of communication, there are a number of other conduits through which organizations based in Wales have developed contacts with EU institutions. The Wales European Centre (WEC), created in 1992 through the support of public- and private-sector organizations in Wales and managed by the WDA, is perhaps the most significant of these points of contact. Based in Brussels, the general remit of the WEC is to promote the interests of Welsh-based organizations, a role which it fulfils through providing information about the various EU programmes and facilitating contacts with organizations based in other EU member states. The WEC has done much to raise the public profile of Wales across the EU, and to keep organizations in Wales informed of developments in the EU. The WEC is formally restricted from lobbying on behalf of interested parties in Wales, although such a capacity is subject to a limited degree of flexibility (Welsh Affairs Select Committee 1995; Gray and Osmond 1997). Since 1995 the work of the WEC has been complemented by the Wales Commercial Centre (WCC), a WDA-funded agency that is responsible for helping Welsh companies in furthering business contacts in the EU (Wales European Centre 1995; Welsh Development Agency 1998). The WCC has, for example, been involved in promoting awareness of the business opportunities afforded by EU-sponsored programmes aiding the economic restructuring of Eastern Europe and a number of the states of the former Soviet Union (WDA, 1996).

The creation of the WEC and the WCC are examples of the efforts under way in Wales to promote the country in a way in which is not possible for central government to do, for practical and political reasons. Criticisms of central government, and of the Welsh Office in particular, have led to a growing number of organizations in Wales, supported by politicians of different hues, to push for a greater degree of autonomy in dealing with the EU. As the following sections will outline, the way in which Welsh interests will be represented in the EU in future has become an issue of considerable controversy.

Welsh Europeans? Changing Attitudes to the EU in Wales

Support for greater Welsh involvement in the affairs of the EU has increased in recent years, but enthusiasm for such a development has been growing in different forms for at least a decade (Jones 1997a). Such support was, however, in marked contrast to the 1970s and early 1980s, when the Labour Party was still diametrically opposed to UK membership of the EU and even within Plaid Cymru support for the idea of 'Wales in Europe' did not emerge until after the 1979 general election (Keating and Jones 1994). Nevertheless, by the latter half of the 1980s senior figures in politics and industry in Wales were espousing the benefits of European integration for Wales. In late 1988, for example, Dafydd Elis Thomas, then president of Plaid Cymru, told readers of the *Western Mail* that the 'New Year can be the opportunity when we think of ourselves more clearly as Welsh Europeans, ready for the challenges of that wider world, and their impact on the world of Wales' (*Western Mail*, 31 December 1988).

Plaid Cymru was not, and has not been, unique in seeking to promote greater awareness of the European dimensions of political and economic life in Wales. Each of the main political parties operating in Wales has underscored the importance of 'Wales in Europe', albeit to differing degrees (Osmond 1997). Among the business community, support for more Welsh influence over developments in the EU has also come from different quarters: from large organizations such as the Confederation of British Industry to those small and medium-sized companies involved in the links with the 'Four Motor' regions[2] (Cooke *et al.* 1997) and more recently those participating in the projects comprising the Regional Technology Plan (WDA 1997). The EU is not, of course, without its critics in Wales, but there has nevertheless been a growing acknowledgement in Wales of the necessity of more directly addressing developments in the EU.

With regard to the political culture in Wales, there are a number of factors that explain the changes in attitude towards the EU. One of the principal reasons why, since the late 1980s, organizations in Wales have increasingly looked outwards to the EU has been the availability of funding from a variety of EU programmes. Jim Hughes, of the WEC, has pointed out that such a view of the EU is a narrow one; nevertheless he adds that it is commonly perceived that the 'EU is about Loadsamoney' (1997, 21). As a report by the Institute of Welsh Affairs (Morgan and Price 1998) has argued, the impact of EU funding in Wales, especially the EU Structural Funds,[3] has been extremely valuable. As the authors of the report argue, 'the Structural Funds are much more than icing on the cake in Wales – in the West and the Valleys they constitute the cake itself' (1998, 22–3).

A second reason for the changing attitudes towards the EU in Wales is a growing recognition of the increasing importance of the EU in policy matters. Since the mid-1980s the EU has accrued growing legislative authority over a wide range of matters, most notably in the area of economic life. As Gray and Osmond suggest, because much of EU legislation in many key areas of economic life now takes precedence over laws passed in Westminster, 'the Welsh economy is more dependent on decisions made in Brussels than in London' (1997, 7). As governance in the EU has evolved, some observers have argued that the principle of 'subsidiarity' – which basically refers to decisions about which are the most appropriate tiers of government (the EU, national, regional or local government) for decision-making in particular areas of policy – should mean that more power should be devolved down to regional government, such as in Wales (Thomas 1997; Leicester 1998). More specifically, EU regional policy during this period has also served in Wales to stimulate discussion about the relations between central government, the regions and the EU (Bradbury and Mawson 1997).

A third major factor that contributed to the increasing support for more direct links between Wales and the EU was the experience of successive Conservative administrations between 1979 and 1997. For the Wales Labour Party this period brought to attention the need for a measure of devolved government in Wales in order to provide a check on central government. While the British Labour Party during the same period moved away from its opposition to membership of the EU towards a more pro-European stance, in Wales the Labour Party was advocating a Welsh Assembly that would increase Wales's participation in the EU (Wales Labour Party 1995). Although arguing for a greater degree of autonomy, Plaid Cymru similarly maintained that a separate voice for Wales would mean that the country would be able to step out of the shadow cast by central government in London. As it argued in *The Best for Wales*, a 'Powerhouse Parliament will put Wales at the heart of a new Europe of the Nations and historic Regions – no longer left on the furthest edge of the UK listening to the Euro-squabble of middle England' (1998, 2). It is this understanding, shared by the Welsh Labour Party, the Liberal Democrats and Plaid Cymru, that Welsh interests were marginalized throughout the period of Conservative government, that has galvanized cross-party support for devolution within the context of an evolving EU. Indeed, as some commentators have argued, it was developments within the EU that acted as the catalyst for the political metamorphosis in Wales (Jones 1997b).

Over the past decade or so, the above factors have underpinned the growth of a powerful lobby in Wales that has advocated more direct links with the EU. Wales has, in turn, benefited tremendously from these links. EU funding to various initiatives in Wales has played an important part in the economic restructuring of former industrial areas, as in the south Wales Valleys, and has supported the declining agricultural sector. In a period when central government funding for such programmes is becoming more difficult to obtain, funding from the EU is a welcome source of capital. Indeed, one commentator has remarked that, if Wales is 'unrecognisable from the industrial hulk drifting on to the rocks in the 1970s and 1980s', it is partly due to the 'not insignificant part played by the European Union in helping shape this economic miracle' (Humphries 1998, 1). As the matter of funding highlights, the EU is now a major political force and the changes that it has introduced have caused political ripples within each of the member states. In Wales organizations have been quick to recognize the significance of the EU, and have sought to make the most of the potential for forging new links with regions in different parts of the EU. The Regional Technology Plan, which Wales was initially one of only eight regions asked by the European Commission to design, is a good example of how organizations in Wales have availed themselves of the opportunities created by the EU.

The EU is, of course, moving into a very critical stage in its development, with the introduction of European Monetary Union and the approaching enlargement of its membership. Both of these developments hold important implications for organizations and people in Wales. With the establishment of the National Assembly, Wales, too, is entering into a new stage in its history. For policy-makers, industry and workers in Wales, it is these developments that are at the fore of discussions about how Wales should develop its future links with the EU.

Wales in Europe: The Next Decade

Developments over the next decade will indeed be decisive for Wales. As one writer has remarked: 'Wales is in a transitional period, seeking to break free from the legacy of its past and its label as a problem or unsuccessful region. Much has been achieved, but much remains to be done' (Alden, 1996). As the discussion above suggested, there has been a tremendous amount of activity in Wales over the last decade or so in terms of creating and consolidating networks of contacts within the EU. Whether or not this activity will bear significant fruit will, however, be greatly dependent on processes of change in the EU.

Nowhere is this more apparent than in relation to the allocation of the EU Structural Funds. Despite the speculation about the *potential* for Wales to blossom into one of the leading regional economies in the EU, as a number of studies have argued (Osmond 1995; Alden 1996; compare Lovering 1998, 1999), the present reality is that it is one of the weaker economic regions within the EU (Commission of the European Communities 1998). As a consequence, Wales has been a major recipient of funding from the EU. Between 1988 and 1993 Wales received nearly £300 million in EU grants (Commission of the European Communities 1998). During this period EU funding was directed towards aiding economic restructuring in industrial south Wales and east Clwyd as well as to rural west Wales. In the most recent round of the EU Structural Funds (1994–9) approximately £430 million in EU funding will have been dispersed throughout Wales as part of the Objective 2 and Objective 5b programmes, with most of the money this time being directed to industrial south Wales and rural Wales. Wales also benefited from its share of EU funding allocated to the UK in general (Morgan and Price 1998). All told, by 2000 Wales will have secured over £1 billion from the EU Structural Funds (Gray and Osmond 1997).

The next period of funding will be the last before the accession of some of the countries of Eastern Europe to the EU, and is therefore widely regarded as being the last opportunity for Wales to secure Objective 1[4] funding (Thomas 1998). Obtaining this funding could stimulate a quite considerable transformation in the economic fortunes of west Wales and the south Wales Valleys. Failure to secure Objective 1 status for this region of Wales would, a recent report (Morgan and Price 1998) has argued, have very negative consequences, including badly damaging the image of the EU in Wales. As the report darkly concluded, 'it scarcely seems possible that so much rides on a single decision but, in our view, the stakes are indeed that high' (1998, 28). Whether or not such dramatic predictions will be realized, a reduction in EU funding to Wales, either through the Structural Funds or the Common Agricultural Policy, would have serious implications for economic life in Wales. Hopes of a marked improvement, then, of social and economic conditions in Wales will be tied to future EU policy.

Many of these hopes in Wales rest with the successful growth of indigenous small and medium-sized enterprises (SMEs). In contrast to the campaign to ensure that Wales is officially designated one of the poorest regions of the EU, in a number of quarters the view has been expressed that Wales could emerge as one of the regional economic powerhouses of the EU. The hope is that Wales can emulate the success of other leading regional economies across the EU, such as Baden-Württemberg in Germany, through the growth of local SMEs specializing in innovative high technology manufacturing (Cooke et al. 1997). The potential for such growth will, research has suggested (Mackay and Audas 1998; Price and Morgan 1998), be tightly linked to the policies of the National Assembly and, once again, to those of the EU.

It has been a condition of the reforms to the EU Structural Funds that successful projects should increasingly be concerned with fostering the conditions for sustainable and innovative economic development. In this respect, the WDA, along with partner organizations in Austria, Italy and the Republic of Ireland, is involved in the 'Strategic Adaption to a Global Economy' programme. In addition, the WDA is also involved in the 'Intelligent Region' programme (again with development agencies in a number of other regions of the EU), an EU-funded initiative that sponsors collaboration between development agencies and university researchers with the objective of furthering economic growth. Organizations in Wales are also involved in a number of EU-funded programmes specifically designed to stimulate social and economic change via the use of new technologies. Of particular significance here are the Wales Regional Technology Plan and the 'Wales Information Society' programme, both of which are integral parts of parallel projects in selected regions across the EU. Making a success of these initiatives will depend on the collective efforts of the National Assembly, central government in London and the EU.

The National Assembly will not be a panacea for the social and economic ills of Wales. At least initially, it will be circumscribed by those limited amounts of powers that it has been accorded within the framework established by the Labour government. The manner in which the Assembly makes use of the powers at its disposal will nevertheless be crucially important. For a considerable time now it has been argued by some commentators that, if Wales was to have its own elected regional parliament or assembly, then this would be the catalyst for a marked improvement in the socio-economic conditions in the country (Osmond 1992; Cooke et al. 1997). The next couple of years will therefore be a testing time for the fledgling National Assembly. In this period it will be especially important that the Assembly establishes a strong European dimension to its activities, whether this be for the purpose of debating, and seeking to influence, the position of the government of the UK in advance of its participation in the business of the Council of Ministers, for fostering clearer links between the Assembly and the five Welsh MEPs or for examining EU legislation. Indeed, one report (Gray and Osmond 1997) has advocated the establishment of a committee comprising those who are, in various ways, involved in the representation of Welsh interests in the EU in order to maximize Welsh influence over decision-making processes in Brussels.

Some organizations have proposed more radical solutions to the problem of how Welsh interests might be best represented in the EU. Plaid Cymru (1995), for example, has advocated a Welsh Parliament with full legislative and executive powers of sovereignty, with Wales enjoying the same rights as those currently exercised by Westminster. The Welsh Liberal Democrats (1996) have also proposed ideas that are more radical than those introduced by the government, arguing for direct representation of the Assembly within the Council of Ministers. In practice, however, adding to the powers of the Assembly, and increasing Wales's influence in the EU, is more likely to be a slow, incremental process. For the immediate future it will be for the Assembly to demonstrate its ability, not least to the electorate in Wales. All of this will, as I have pointed out, take place against the backdrop of fundamental systemic changes in the EU. Under these conditions it is imperative that organizations in Wales, and in particular the Assembly, work to ensure that they maximize all the influence they can muster.

Conclusion

It will be some time before the full consequences of the changes through which we are currently living become apparent. The launch of the National Assembly in 1999 and the decision on the dispersal of the EU Structural Funds are the immediate concerns. This, though, will only be the beginning of the process. The extent to which the government is seen to represent 'British' interests in the EU will be under increasing scrutiny after 1999. As one commentator (Leicester 1998) has argued, defining 'the "national interest" that is to be defended in Brussels is already a complex task of balancing interests and departments. After devolution there will also be strong national and regional interests to be taken into account' (1998, 15). In this respect, the passing of legislation, in 1998, to create a Joint Ministerial Committee, which will bring together the British Prime Minister and the leading ministers from the different devolved institutions in the UK to discuss central government policy on matters that specifically pertain to the regions, may well have considerable implications as to how 'Britain' is represented in the EU. As Robbins has argued, so long as this kind of consensus politics exists, 'one might say that British European policy will become more truly British than it has been hitherto' (1998, 115).

For people throughout Wales these are changes that could, undoubtedly, bring with them a radical, ameliorative transformation in the socio-economic structure. In all of this, the influence of the EU looms large over the situation in Wales. For this reason, the success of organizations in Wales to press Welsh interests across the EU will be pivotal for ensuring that the changes that we are presently witnessing bring positive outcomes.

Notes

1. The term 'European Union' (EU) refers to the entity created by the 1992 Treaty of European Union, alternatively known as the Maastricht Treaty. Previously, the smaller, and less powerful, version of this entity was the 'European Economic Community' or the 'European Community' (1957–92). In its earliest incarnation, this alliance of European states was called the 'European Coal and Steel Community' (1952–7). Throughout this chapter I shall refer to this entity by its present title, the EU.
2. The term 'Four Motor Regions' refers to Baden-Württemberg (Germany), Catalonia (Spain), Rhône-Alps (France) and Lombardy (Italy).
3. The EU Structural Funds consist of the European Regional Development Fund, the European Social Fund, the European Agricultural Guidance and Guarantee Fund and the Financial Instrument for Fisheries. Together these funds support socially and economically disadvantaged regions across the EU. In general they are concerned with regenerating the economic infrastructure in selected regions, focusing in particular on innovative forms of economic growth, and developing skills among the workforce. Since the beginning of EU funding in the mid-1970s, the nature of the funds and the criteria by which regions are judged have undergone considerable change. Since the late 1980s, however, the Structural Funds have been divided into seven different objectives: 1. for the poorest regions of the EU; 2. for aiding regions seriously affected by industrial decline; 3. for tackling long-term unemployment and social exclusion; 4. for adaptation of workers to industrial change; 5a. for supporting the modernization of the fishing

industry; 5b. for assisting the restructuring of rural areas. 6. for assisting regions with extremely low population density. Objectives 1, 2, 5b and 6 are targeted at specific areas of the EU, while the remaining objectives are applicable to the whole of the EU. From 1999 these objectives will be reduced to three. Objective 1 will be for those regions still behind in development. Objective 2 will bring together initiatives previously funded under the Objective 2 and Objective 5b programmes, although the aim now is to develop a general plan for economic diversity. Objective 3 will house those projects which received funding from the old Objective 3 and Objective 4 programmes. The emphasis in future will be on an integrated approach to improving education, training and employment conditions.
4. Objective 1 status is reserved for those regions of the EU where the Gross Domestic Product represents 75%, or less, of the EU average. An Objective 1 region would, then, be one of the poorest regions in the EU.

References

Alden, J. (1996). 'The transfer from a problem to powerful region: the experience of Wales', in J. Alden and P. Boland (eds.), *Regional Development Strategies: A European Perspective* (London: Regional Studies Association/Jessica Kingsley).

Bradbury, J. and Mawson, J. (1997). 'Conclusion: the changing politics and governance of British regionalism', in J. Bradbury and J. Mawson (eds.), *British Regionalism and Devolution* (London: Jessica Kingsley).

Commission of the European Communities (1998). *The Wales–Europe Report 1998* (Cardiff: Commission of the European Communities).

Constitution Unit (1996). *An Assembly for Wales* (London: University College of London).

Cooke, P., Price, A. and Morgan, K. (1997). 'Regulating regional economies: Wales and Baden-Wurttemberg in transition', in M. Rhodes (ed.), *The Regions and the New Europe: Patterns in Core and Periphery Development* (Manchester: Manchester University Press).

Gray, J. and Osmond, J. (1997). *Wales in Europe: The Opportunity Presented by a Welsh Assembly* (Cardiff: Institute of Welsh Affairs).

Hughes, J. (1997). 'Changing Wales in an evolving Europe', *Agenda* (Summer 1997), 20–2.

Humphries, J. (1998). 'Towards a new future', *The Wales–Europe Report 1998* (Cardiff: Commission of the European Communities).

Jones, B. (1997a). 'Wales: a developing political economy', in M. Keating and J. Loughlin (eds.), *The Political Economy of Regionalism* (London: Frank Cass).

Jones, B. (1997b). 'Welsh politics and changing British and European contexts', in J. Bradbury and J. Mawson (eds.), *British Regionalism and Devolution* (London: Jessica Kingsley).

Jones, I. W. (1996). *Europe: The Challenge for Wales* (Tal-y-bont: Gwasg Taf Cyf).

Keating, M. and Jones, B. (1994). 'Nations, regions and Europe: the UK experience', in M. Keating and B. Jones (eds.), *Regions in the European Union* (Oxford: Clarendon Press).

Labour Party (1997). *A Voice for Wales* (London: HMSO).

Leicester, G. (1998). 'Devolution and Europe: Britain's double constitutional problem', *Regional and Federal Studies*, 8/1, 11–22.

Loughlin, J. (1997). *Wales in Europe: Welsh Regional Actors and European Integration*, Papers in Planning Research, 157 (Cardiff: Department of City and Regional Planning, Cardiff University).

Lovering, J. (1998). 'Celebrating globalization and misreading the Welsh economy: the "new regionalism" ', *Contemporary Wales*, 11, 12–60.

Lovering, J. (1999). 'Theory led by policy: the inadequacies of "the new regionalism" (illustrated from the case of Wales)', *International Journal of Urban and Regional Research*.

McAteer, M. and Mitchell, D. (1996). 'Peripheral lobbying! The territorial dimension of euro lobbying by Scottish and Welsh sub-central government', *Regional and Federal Studies*, 6/3, 1–27.

Mackay, R. and Audas, R. (1997). 'The economic impact of a Welsh Assembly', in R. MacKay, R. Audas, G. Holtman and B. Morgan, *The Economic Impact of a Welsh Assembly* (Cardiff: Institute of Welsh Affairs).

Morgan, K. and Price, A. (1998). *The Other Wales. The Case for Objective 1 Funding Post 1999* (Cardiff: Institute of Welsh Affairs).

Osmond, J. (1992). *The Democratic Challenge* (Llandysul: Gomer).

Osmond, J. (1995). *Welsh Europeans* (Cardiff: Seren Press).

Osmond, J. (1997). *The European Union and the Governance of Wales: A Background Paper* (Cardiff: Institute of Welsh Affairs).

Plaid Cymru (1995). *A Democratic Wales in a United Europe* (Cardiff: Plaid Cymru).

Plaid Cymru (1998). *The Best for Wales* (Cardiff: Plaid Cymru).

Pritchard, J. (1995) 'Prospects for Wales in Europe', *Welsh Economic Review*, 8/1, 46–55.

Robbins, K. (1998). 'Britain and Europe: devolution and foreign policy', *International Affairs*, 74/1, 105–18.

Thomas, A. (1997). 'Region, culture and function on the Celtic periphery: Wales, Cornwall and the EU', *Contemporary Wales*, 10, 7–31.

Thomas, S. (1998). 'The assembly's international role', in J. Osmond (ed.), *The National Assembly Agenda* (Cardiff: Institute of Welsh Affairs).

Wales European Centre (1998). *Wales in Europe* (Brussels: Wales European Centre).

Wales Labour Party (1995). *Wales and Europe* (Cardiff: Wales Labour Party).

Welsh Affairs Select Committee (1995). *Wales in Europe*, vol. 1. (London: HMSO).

Welsh Development Agency (1996). *Gateway Europe*, 20 (Summer).

Welsh Development Agency (1997). *Wales Regional Technology Plan: An Innovation and Technology Strategy for Wales* (Cardiff: Welsh Development Agency).

Welsh Development Agency (1998). *Wales Commercial Centre: Linking Welsh Business to Europe* (Cardiff: Welsh Development Agency).

Welsh Liberal Democrats (1996). *A Senedd for Wales: Beyond a Talking Shop* (Cardiff: Welsh Liberal Democrats).

Index